press

THE MINI ROUGH GUIDE TO

NEW YORK CITY

Forthcoming travel guides include

The Algarve • The Bahamas • Cambodia
Caribbean Islands • New York Restaurants

Forthcoming reference guides include

Chronicle: China (pocket history)
Online Travel • Weather

Rough Guides online

www.roughguides.com

Rough Guide Credits

Text editor: Richard Koss
Series editor: Mark Ellingham
Production: Helen Prior, Julia Bovis
Cartography: Melissa Baker

Publishing Information

This first edition published May 2002
by Rough Guides Ltd,
62–70 Shorts Gardens, London WC2H 9AH

Distributed by the Penguin Group:

Penguin Books Ltd, 80 Strand, London WC2R ORL.
Penguin Putnam, Inc. 375 Hudson Street, New York 10014, USA
Penguin Books Australia Ltd, 487 Maroondah Highway,
PO Box 257, Ringwood, Victoria 3134, Australia
Penguin Books Canada Ltd, 10 Alcorn Avenue,
Toronto, Ontario, Canada M4V 1E4
Penguin Books (NZ) Ltd,
182–190 Wairau Road, Auckland 10, New Zealand

Typeset in Bembo and Helvetica to an original design by Henry Iles.
Printed in Spain by GraphyCems.

© Martin Dunford and Jack Holland 2002
400pp, includes index
A catalogue record for this book is available from the British Library.

ISBN 1-85828-876-2

THE MINI ROUGH GUIDE TO

NEW YORK CITY

**by Martin Dunford
and Jack Holland**

with additional contributions by
Nicky Agate, Todd Obolsky,
and Nelson Taylor

ROUGH
GUIDES

We set out to do something different when the first Rough Guide was published in 1982. Mark Ellingham, just out of university, was traveling in Greece. He brought along the popular guides of the day, but found they were all lacking in some way. They were either strong on ruins and museums but went on for pages without mentioning a beach or taverna. Or they were so conscious of the need to save money that they lost sight of Greece's cultural and historical significance. Also, none of the books told him anything about Greece's contemporary life – its politics, its culture, its people, and how they lived.

So with no job in prospect, Mark decided to write his own guidebook, one which aimed to provide practical information that was second to none, detailing the best beaches and the hottest clubs and restaurants, while also giving hard-hitting accounts of every sight, both famous and obscure, and providing up-to-the-minute information on contemporary culture. It was a guide that encouraged independent travelers to find the best of Greece, and was a great success, getting shortlisted for the Thomas Cook travel guide award, and encouraging Mark, along with three friends, to expand the series.

The Rough Guide list grew rapidly and the letters flooded in, indicating a much broader readership than had been anticipated, but one which uniformly appreciated the Rough Guide mix of practical detail and humor, irreverence and enthusiasm. Things haven't changed. The same four friends who began the series are still the caretakers of the Rough Guide mission today: to provide the most reliable, up-to-date and entertaining information to independent-minded travelers of all ages, on all budgets.

We now publish more than 200 titles and have offices in London and New York. The travel guides are written and researched by a dedicated team of more than 100 authors, based in Britain, Europe, the USA, and Australia. We have also created a unique series of phrasebooks to accompany the travel series, along with an acclaimed series of music guides, and a best-selling pocket guide to the Internet and World Wide Web. We also publish comprehensive travel information on our website: www.roughguides.com

Help us update

We've gone to a lot of trouble to ensure that this Rough Guide is as up to date and accurate as possible. However, things do change and all suggestions, comments, and corrections are much appreciated – we'll send a copy of the next edition (or any other Rough Guide if you prefer) for the best letters.

Please mark letters **Rough Guide New York Update** and send to:

Rough Guides, 62–70 Shorts Gardens, London WC2H 9AH, or Rough Guides, 4th Floor, 345 Hudson St, New York, NY 10014.

Or send email to: mail@roughguides.co.uk
Online updates about this book can be found on
Rough Guides' website (see opposite)

Acknowledgments

Heartfelt thanks go to Melissa Baker for her mapmaking ingenuity, Nicky Agate for the judiciously compiled index and her dog-sitting skills, Russell Walton for his diligent proofreading, and Andrew Rosenberg, Jack Holland, and Martin Dunford for their astute guidance. Thanks also to Darren Colby and Theresa Swank, who together make New York feel so much like home.

Cover Credits

Front – Statue of Liberty © Robert Harding
Back (top) – telescope © Robert Harding
Back (lower) – taxi © Robert Harding

CONTENTS

Introduction

The most beguiling city in the world, New York is an adrenaline-charged, history-laden place that holds immense romantic appeal for visitors. Wandering the streets here, you'll cut between buildings that are icons to the modern age – and whether gazing at the flickering lights of the midtown skyscrapers as you speed across the Queensboro Bridge, experiencing the 4am half-life downtown, or just wasting the morning on the Staten Island ferry, you really would have to be made of stone not to be moved by it all. There's no place quite like it.

While the events of September 11, 2001, which demolished the World Trade Center, shook New York to its core, the populace responded resiliently under the composed aegis of then-Mayor Rudy Giuliani. Until the attacks, many New Yorkers loved to hate Giuliani, partly because they saw him as committed to making their city too much like everyone else's. To some extent he succeeded, and during the late Nineties New York seemed cleaner, safer, and more liveable, as the city took on a truly international allure and shook off the more notorious aspects to its reputation. However, the maverick quality of New York and its people still shines as brightly as it ever did. Even in the aftermath of the World Trade Center's collapse, New York remains a unique and fascinating city – and one you'll want to return to again and again.

You could spend weeks in New York and still barely scratch the surface, but there are some key attractions – and some pleasures – that you won't want to miss. There are the different **ethnic neighborhoods**, like lower Manhattan's Chinatown and the traditionally Jewish Lower East Side (not so much anymore); and the more artsy concentrations of SoHo, TriBeCa, and the East and West Villages. Of course, there is the celebrated **architecture** of corporate Manhattan, with the skyscrapers in downtown and midtown forming the most indelible images. There are the **museums**, not just the Metropolitan and MoMA, but countless other smaller collections that afford weeks of happy wandering. In between sights, you can **eat** just about anything, at any time, cooked in any style; you can **drink** in any kind of company; and sit through any number of obscure **movies**. The more established arts – **dance**, **theater**, **music** – are superbly catered for; and New York's **clubs** are as varied and exciting as you might expect. And for the avid consumer, the choice of **shops** is vast, almost numbingly exhaustive in this heartland of the great capitalist dream.

Some orientation and highlights

New York City comprises the central island of **Manhattan** along with four outer boroughs – **Brooklyn**, **Queens**, **the Bronx**, and **Staten Island**. Manhattan, to many, *is* New York – whatever your interests, it's here that you'll spend the most time and are likely to stay. New York is very much a city of **neighborhoods** and is best explored on foot – a fact reflected in the chapters of this guide, which are divided to reflect the best walking tours.

The guide starts at the southern tip of the island and

moves north: offshore, **the Statue of Liberty** and **Ellis Island** comprise the first section of New York (and America) that most nineteenth-century immigrants would have seen. The **Financial District** takes in the skyscrapers and historic buildings of Manhattan's southern reaches and was hardest hit by the destruction of perhaps its most famous landmarks, the Twin Towers of the World Trade Center. Just northeast is the area around **City Hall**, New York's well-appointed municipal center, which adjoins **TriBeCa**, known for its swanky restaurants, galleries, and nightlife. Moving east, **Chinatown** is Manhattan's most populous ethnic neighborhood, a vibrant locale that's great for food and shopping. Nearby, **Little Italy** bears few traces of the once-strong immigrant presence, while the **Lower East Side**, the city's traditional gateway neighborhood for new immigrants, is nowadays scattered with trendy bars and clubs. To the west, **SoHo** is one of the premier districts for galleries and the commercial art scene, not to mention designer shopping. Continuing north, the **West** and **East Villages** form a focus of bars, restaurants, and shops catering to students and would-be bohemians – and of course tourists. **Chelsea** is a largely residential neighborhood that is now mostly known for its gay scene and art galleries that borders on Manhattan's old **Garment District**. **Murray Hill** contains the city's largest skyscraper and most enduring symbol, the **Empire State Building**.

Beyond **42nd Street**, the main east–west artery of midtown, the character of the city changes quite radically, and the skyline becomes more high-rise and home to some of New York's most awe-inspiring, neck-cricking architecture. There are also some superb museums and the city's best shopping as you work your way north up **Fifth Avenue** as far as 59th Street. Here, the classic Manhattan vistas are broken by the broad expanse of **Central Park**, a supreme piece of nineteenth-century landscaping, without which life in Manhattan would be unthinkable. Flanking the park, the mostly residential and fairly affluent **Upper West Side** boasts Lincoln Center, Manhattan's temple to the performing arts, the American Museum of Natural History, and Riverside Park along the Hudson River. On the other side of the park, the **Upper East Side** is wealthier and more grandiose, with its nineteenth-century millionaires' mansions now transformed into a string of magnificent museums known as the "Museum Mile," the most prominent being the vast **Metropolitan Museum of Art**. Alongside is a patrician residential neighborhood that boasts some of the swankiest addresses in Manhattan, and a nest of designer shopping along Madison Avenue in the seventies. Immediately above Central Park, **Harlem**, the historic black city-within-a-city, has a healthy sense of an improving go-ahead community; a jaunt further north is most likely required only to see the unusual Cloisters, a nineteenth-century mock-up of a medieval monastery, packed with great European Romanesque and Gothic art and (transplanted) architecture.

When to go

New York's **climate** ranges from the stickily hot and humid in mid-summer to well below freezing in January and February: deep midwinter and high summer (many people find the city unbearable in July and August) are much the worst time you could come. Spring is gentle, if unpredictable, and usually wet, while fall is perhaps the best season: come at either time and you'll find it easier to get things done and the people more welcoming. Whatever time of year you come, dress in layers: buildings tend to be overheated during winter months and air-conditioned to the point of iciness in summer. Also bring comfortable and sturdy shoes – you're going to be doing a lot of walking.

| | F° | | C° | | RAINFALL | |
| | AVERAGE | | AVERAGE | | AVERAGE MONTHLY | |
	MAX	MIN	MAX	MIN	IN	MM
Jan	38	26	3	-3	3.5	89
Feb	40	27	4	3	3.1	79
March	50	35	10	2	4.0	102
April	61	44	16	7	3.8	97
May	72	54	22	12	4.4	112
June	80	63	27	17	3.6	91
July	85	69	29	21	4.4	112
Aug	84	67	29	19	4.1	104
Sept	76	60	24	16	4.0	102
Oct	65	50	18	10	3.4	86
Nov	54	41	12	5	4.4	112
Dec	43	31	6	-1	3.8	97

BASICS

BASICS

Arrival

New York's major **airports** are all within an hour from the city center by taxi or bus, depending on traffic conditions. The city's **train** and **bus** terminals are centrally located and connected to major subway stations.

BY AIR

Three major airports serve New York. International and domestic flights are handled at John F Kennedy (JFK) (☎718/244-4444), in the borough of Queens, and Newark (☎973/961-6000), in northern New Jersey; La Guardia (☎718/533-3400), also in Queens, handles domestic flights only.

Taxis are the easiest option if you are in a group or are arriving at an antisocial hour. Expect to pay $16–22 from La Guardia, a flat rate of $35 from JFK and $35–55 from Newark; you'll be responsible for the turnpike and tunnel tolls – an extra $5 or so. And don't forget a tip of fifteen to twenty percent.

Another good way into Manhattan is by **bus** (see overleaf), the two Manhattan terminals, used by all airport buses, being Grand Central Station and the Port Authority Bus Terminal.

JFK

New York Airport Service buses leave JFK for Grand Central Station, Port Authority Bus Terminal, Penn Station and midtown hotels every fifteen to twenty minutes between 6am and midnight. In the other direction, they run from the same locations every fifteen to thirty minutes between 5am and 10pm. Journeys take 45 to sixty minutes, depending on time of day; the fare is $13 (students $6) one-way when you travel from (not to) Grand Central Station. For further details on services, discounts, etc call ☎212/875-8200.

Free shuttle buses run from all terminals at JFK to the Howard Beach subway stop on the #A train; from there, one subway token ($1.50) takes you anywhere in the city. Late at night, this isn't your best choice – trains run infrequently and can be rather deserted – but in the daytime or early evening, it's a viable, if tedious, option. Travel time is at least an hour from Howard Beach.

> **For general information on getting to and from the airports, call ☎1-800/AIR-RIDE.**

NEWARK

Olympia Airport Express buses leave for Manhattan every twenty to thirty minutes (5am to 3.20am), stopping at Port Authority, Grand Central and Penn Station; going the other way, they run just as frequently (5.10am to 11.10pm); service to and from the Port Authority runs 24 hours a day. In either direction, the journey takes thirty to 45 minutes depending on the traffic, and the fare is $11. A connecting service to certain midtown hotels costs an extra $5. For details call ☎212/964-6233 or 908/354-3330.

BY AIR

LA GUARDIA

New York Airport Service buses run between Manhattan (Grand Central Station and Port Authority Bus Terminal) and La Guardia every fifteen to thirty minutes either way. The service operates 6am to midnight (to Grand Central and Port Authority), 5am to 10pm (from Grand Central), 6.40am to 9pm (from Port Authority). Buses also run to Penn Station from 6.40am to 11.40pm every thirty minutes, 10 and 40 after the hour; from Penn Station, 7.40am to 8.10pm same time-scale as above. Journey time is 45 to sixty minutes, depending on traffic, and the fare is $10 (students $6) each way. For details on services, discounts, etc call ☎212/875-8200.

The best (and least-known) bargain in New York airport transit is the #M60 bus, which for $1.50 takes you into Manhattan, across 125th Street and down Broadway to 106th Street. Ask for a transfer when you get on the bus and you can get almost anywhere. Journey time ranges from twenty minutes late at night to an hour in rush-hour traffic.

BY BUS OR TRAIN

If you come by Greyhound, Trailways, Bonanza, or any other long-distance **bus line**, you arrive at the Port Authority Bus Terminal at 42nd Street and Eighth Avenue. By Amtrak **train**, you arrive at Penn Station, 32nd Street and Seventh and Eighth avenues. (See p.357 for details on both terminals.) Both stations are well positioned for all manner of subway service.

City transportation

Getting around the city is likely to take some getting used to; public transit here is on the whole quite good, extremely cheap, and covers most conceivable corners of the city, whether by bus or subway. Don't be afraid to ask someone for help if you're confused. You'll no doubt find the need for a taxi from time to time, especially if you feel uncomfortable in an area at night; you shouldn't ever have trouble tracking one down – the ubiquitous yellow cabs are always on the prowl for passengers.

THE SUBWAY

The New York **subway** is intimidating and initially incomprehensible. It's also the fastest and most efficient way to get from A to B in Manhattan and the outer boroughs, and it is safer and more user-friendly than it once was. Put aside your qualms: Six million people ride the subway every day, quite a few for the first time.

Any subway journey costs **$1.50**, payable by **token** purchased at any booth, but if you are going to be take more than a couple of rides, it's more efficient to purchase a **MetroCard**. This allows you to transfer (for free) from subway to bus, bus to subway or bus to bus within a period of two hours. It's available, from token booths and vending machines, in several forms: cards can be bought for $3 to $80; $15 purchases allow eleven rides for the cost of ten, and $30 purchases allow 22 rides for the cost of twenty. Unlimited-ride cards allow unlimited travel for a certain period of time: a seven-day pass for $17, a thirty-day pass for $63 and a daily "Fun Pass" for $4.

A subway map can be found at the back of this book;
for subway and bus information,
call ☎718/330-1234 (24 hours daily).

BUSES

The **bus system** is simpler than the subway, and you can see where you're going and hop off at anything interesting. It also features many more crosstown routes. The major disadvantage is that they can be extremely slow – in peak hours almost down to walking pace, and extremely full to boot. In response to cries of overcrowding along several routes, the MTA recently introduced "accordion buses" – two buses attached with a flexible rubber accordion, which helps the big vehicle turn corners. However, because these run slightly less frequently than the ones they replaced, they still get crowded.

Bus maps, like subway maps, can be obtained at the main concourse of Grand Central or the Convention and Visitors Bureau at 53rd Strett and Seventh Avenue.

Anywhere in Manhattan the **fare is $1.50**, payable on entry with either a subway token, a **MetroCard** (the most convenient way) or with the correct change – no bills.

TAXIS

Taxis are always worth considering, especially if you're in a hurry or in a group or late at night. Always use medallion

BUSES • TAXIS

cabs, immediately recognizable by their yellow paintwork and medallion up top; gypsy cabs, unlicensed, uninsured operators who tout for business wherever tourists arrive, should be avoided.

Up to four people can travel in an ordinary medallion cab. Fares are $2 for the first fifth of a mile and 30¢ for each fifth of a mile thereafter or for each ninety seconds in stopped or slow traffic. The basic charge rises by 50¢ from 8pm to 6am. Trips outside Manhattan can incur toll fees; not all of the crossings cost money, however, and the driver should ask you which route you wish to take.

The tip should be fifteen to twenty percent of the fare; you'll get a dirty look if you offer less. Drivers don't like splitting anything bigger than a $10 bill, and are in their rights to refuse a bill over $20.

WALKING

Few cities equal New York for street-level stimulation. Getting around **on foot** is often the most exciting – and tiring – method of exploring. Figure fifteen minutes to walk ten north–south blocks – rather more at rush hour. However you plan your wanderings you're still going to spend much of your time walking. Footwear is important (sneakers are good for spring/summer; winter needs something waterproof). So is safety: a lot more people are injured in New York carelessly crossing the street than are mugged. Pedestrian crossings don't give you automatic right of way unless the WALK sign is on – and, even then, cars may be turning, so be prudent.

WALKING

Information and websites

The best place for **information** is the New York Convention and Visitors Bureau at 810 Seventh Ave at 53rd Street (Mon–Fri 8.30am–6pm, weekends and holidays 9am–5pm, or call one of their counselors at ☎212/484-1222, ⊛www.nycvisit.com). They have up-to-date leaflets on what's going on in the arts and elsewhere plus bus and subway maps and information on hotels and accommodation – though they can't actually book anything for you. Their quarterly *Official NYC Guide* is good too, though the kind of information it gives – on restaurants, hotels, shopping and sights – is also available in the various free tourist magazines and brochures in hotels and elsewhere. These include complete (if superficial) rundowns on what's on in the more mainstream arts, eating out, shops, etc.

The state-run I Love New York organization has free booklets and maps available from 1 Empire State Plaza, Albany, NY 12223 (☎518/474-4116). Much of their information concentrates on New York State, though; before exploring beyond the five boroughs, get their statewide map and regional guides. They do also have info on New York City, including maps and restaurant and hotel lists.

VISITORS' BUREAUS

Bloomingdale's International Visitors' Center Lexington Ave (at 59th St) ☎212/705-2098.

Harlem Visitors' Bureau 219 W 135th St (between 7th and 8th aves). Call first ☎212/283-3315.

NYU Information Center Shimkin Hall, 50 W 4th St (at Greene St/Washington Square) ☎212/998-4636.

Saks Fifth Avenue Ambassador Concierge Desk 611 5th Ave (at 49th St) ☎212/940-4141.

Times Square Visitor and Transit Information Center 1560 Broadway (between 46th and 47th sts) ☎212/869-1890.

WEBSITES

CitySearch NY ⓦwww.new york.citysearch.com. A solid search engine, weekly updated listings and tame features on this comprehensive site.

NYC Transit Authority ⓦwww.mta.nyc.ny.us. Official subway/bus/Metro-North and LIRR web site – schedules, fare info, reroutings, history and fun facts (more than 1.3 billion people ride the subway each year!).

NYC Visitors Bureau ⓦwww.nycvisit.com. Official website of the New York Convention and Visitors Bureau.

PaperMag ⓦwww.papermag.com. Updated daily and covering the cultural gamut, this hip guide has been on the cutting-edge of every trend to hit the streets.

Parks Department ⓦwww.nyc parks.org. The official word on all of the events in the city's parks.

INFORMATION AND WEBSITES

Seinfeld's Real New York
Ⓦ home.earthlink.net/~
asena/srny. Everything you
ever wanted to know about
Jerry: where he lived, ate and
got into trouble with George,
Elaine and Kramer.

Time Out New York Ⓦ www
.timeoutny.com. What's on
this week in music, clubs,
book readings, museums,
movies, and other features
from the publication.

Total NY Ⓦ www.totalny.com.
One of the few guides
sporting real New York
attitude, Total's quirky features
and eclectic listings tell you
where to go and what to do.

The Village Voice
Ⓦ www.villagevoice.com. The
best thing here, from the elder
(some say out-of-touch)
alternative weekly, is the
paper's witty listings section,
"Choices."

City tours

There are many different ways to take in the city: exploring streets and neighborhoods on your own; heading up to the tops of buildings, like the Empire State (see p.84) to get a good perspective on the lay of the land, or going on any number of city **tours**, which might let you experience New York from angles never before thought of.

If you're nervous about exploring New York,
or overwhelmed by the possibilities the city offers, look into
Big Apple Greeter, 1 Centre St, 19th floor,
NY 10007 (Ⓦ 212/669-8159 Ⓕ 669-3685,
Ⓔ information@bigapplegreeter.org,
Ⓦ www.bigapplegreeter.org), a nonprofit organization
that matches visitors with their corps of 500
trained volunteer "greeters."

BUS TOURS

Apart from equipping yourself with a decent map, perhaps the most obvious way to orient yourself to the city is to take a **bus tour**. These are extremely popular, though frankly you're swept around so quickly as to scarcely see anything. Still, the tops of double deckers are a great place to figure out what's where for later explorations. In general, an all-city tour over two days will cost $30–$45, although you can also have half-day or limited-area tours for around $25. Buses run seven days a week, from (approximately) 9am to 6pm, with special rates and times for evening tours.

Best bets are **City Sightseeing** (Coach), 1040 6th Ave, NY 10018 (℡1-800/876-9868 for tickets and locations. Terminal: 8th Ave and 53rd St), and **Gray Line Sightseeing Terminal**, Port Authority at 42nd Street and Eighth Avenue, NY 10019 (℡1-800/669-0051 for tickets and locations).

HELICOPTER TOURS

A more exciting option is to look at the city from the air, by **helicopter**. This is expensive, but you won't easily forget the experience. Liberty Helicopter Tours, at the western end of 30th Street or from the Wall Street heliport at Pier 6 (℡212/967-4550, closed on weekends), offers flights ranging from $59 (for four-and-a-half minutes) to $187 (fifteen minutes). If you leave from 30th Street, the best seat for photos is on the right in the back. Helicopters take off regularly between 9am and 9pm every day unless winds and visibility are bad; you don't need a reservation, but in high season (and nice weather) you may have quite a wait if you just show up.

TOURS ON WATER

A great way to see the island of Manhattan is a voyage on the **Circle Line ferry** (℡212/563-3200, ⓦ www.circle-line.com). Departing from Pier 83 at W 42nd Street and Twelfth Avenue, it circumnavigates Manhattan, taking in everything from the tall buildings of downtown Manhattan to the subdued stretches of Harlem and the Bronx – complete with a live wisecracking commentary; the three-hour tour is $24 ($12 for children under twelve). Another interesting option is the Harlem Spirituals Gospel Cruise, two-hour tours for $25 that depart from Pier 16 at South Street Seaport.

One of the city's true bargains is the free **Staten Island ferry** (see p.165), which leaves from South Ferry on the lower tip of Manhattan and offers great views of New York Harbor and the Statue of Liberty.

WALKING TOURS

Options for walking tours of Manhattan or the outer boroughs are many and varied. Usually led by experts, they offer fact-filled wanders through neighborhoods or focus on particular subjects. You'll find fliers for some of them at the various Visitor Centers; for what's happening in the current week, check the *New York Times* (Fri or Sun), the weekly *Village Voice* or *New York Press* (both out on Wed), or any of the free weekly papers around town. Detailed below are some of the more interesting tours: they don't all operate year-round, the more esoteric only setting up for a couple of outings at specific times of the year. Phone ahead for the full schedules.

ORGANIZATIONS

Art Tours of Manhattan
(℡ 609/921-2647). Much the best people to go with if you want firsthand accounts of the city's art scene, establishment and fringe. The custom-

designed tours include the galleries of SoHo, Chelsea, 57th St and Madison Ave, as well as a "hospitality" visit to an artist's studio, all guided by qualified – and entertaining –

art historians. Tours for up to four people cost around $225.

Big Onion Walking Tours
(T 212/439-1090, W www.bigonion.com). Big Onion specializes in tours with an ethnic and historical focus: pick one particular group, or take the "Immigrant New York" tour and learn about everyone. Cost is $10 or $8 for students and seniors; the food-included "Multi-Ethnic Eating Tour" costs $13 or $11. These last about two hours.

Bronx County Historical Society 3309 Bainbridge Ave, Bronx (T 718/881-8900, W www.bronxhistoricalsociety .org). Neighborhood tours range from strolls through suburban Riverdale to hikes across the South Bronx. Excellent value at $10 per person ($5 for society members), though tours are given the least frequently of any company listed here.

Greenwich Village Literary Pub Crawl (T 212/613-5796). A two-and-a-half-hour tour guided by actors from the New Ensemble Theater Company, who lead you to several of the most prominent pubs in literary history and read from associated works. Tours meet at the *White Horse Tavern*, 567 Hudson St, at 2pm every Sat. Reservations are highly recommended: $12, students and seniors $9.

Harlem Heritage Tours 230 W 116th St, Suite #5C (T 212/280-7888, W www.harlemheritage.com). Cultural tours of Harlem, general and specific (such as "Harlem Jazz Clubs"), are led midday and evening. Walking tours are $15–20, with the Evening Jazz Experience $30–65. Reservations are recommended. Call for details. Very helpful tour guides.

Harlem Spirituals Gospel and Jazz Tours 690 8th Ave, 2nd floor (T 212/757-0425, W www.harlemspiritual.com). Various tours of Harlem, the Bronx, and Brooklyn, ranging from Sun-morning church visits to nighttime "Soul Food and Jazz" affairs taking in dinner and a club. Professionally run and excellent value, with prices in the range of $25–75 per person (discounts for children). Reservations necessary.

Lower East Side Tenement Museum 90 Orchard St (☎ 212/431-0233, Ⓦ www.tenement.org). This museum organizes weekend walking tours of the Lower East Side April–Dec, focusing on the heritage of the various ethnic groups present, community rebuilding and relations among different groups: $9, students and seniors $7. and tickets are available for museum admission and a tour combined at a reduced price.

Municipal Arts Society 457 Madison Ave, between 50th and 51st sts (☎ 212/439-1049 or 935-3960, Ⓦ www.mas.org). Opinionated tours look at neighborhoods from an architectural, cultural, historical and often political perspective. Free (donations requested) Wed lunchtime tours of Grand Central Station start at 12.30pm from the information booth. Most other tours also start at 12.30pm, last for ninety minutes, and cost $10–15, with discounts for students and seniors. Weekend and day-long tours cost more.

The 92nd Street Y 1395 Lexington Ave, between 91st and 92nd sts (☎ 212/996-1100, Ⓦ www.92ndsty.org). None better, offering a mixed bag of walking tours ranging from straight explorations of specific New York neighborhoods to art tours, walking tours of political New York, or a predawn visit to the city's wholesale meat and fish markets. Average costs are $20–55 per person; specific tours can be organized to accommodate groups with special interests.

River to River Downtown Tours 375 South End Ave (☎ 212/321-2823). Individual and small-group tours of Lower Manhattan by New York aficionado Ruth Alscher-Green. Individual prices are $35, or $50 for two people, for a unique two-hour tour spiced with gossip and anecdotal tidbits.

Media

The days are long gone when New York could support twenty daily newspapers. Today, only **three remain**: the *New York Times* and tabloids the *Daily News* and the *New York Post*.

The *New York Times* (75¢), an American institution, prides itself on being the "paper of record" – the closest thing America has to a quality national paper. It has solid, sometimes stolid, international coverage, and places much emphasis on its news analysis. The Sunday edition ($3) is a thumping bundle of newsprint divided into a number of supplements that take days to read. The legendary crossword puzzles in Sunday's *New York Times Magazine* should keep you occupied all day.

Its archrivals concentrate on local news, usually screamed out in banner headlines. The *Daily News* (50¢) is renowned as a picture newspaper but with intelligent features and many racy headlines. The *New York Post* (25¢), the city's oldest newspaper, started in 1801 by Alexander Hamilton, has been in decline for many years. It is known for its sensationalism and conservative slant.

Of the **weekly papers**, the *Village Voice* (Wed, free in Manhattan, $1.25 elsewhere) is the most widely read, mainly for its comprehensive arts coverage and investigative features. Catch it early enough on Wednesday morning (or late Tues night at select locations around the city) and grab a free pass to a new movie the following week; look for the full-page ad that tells you where to wait in line. Its main competitor, the *New York Press*, is an edgier alternative, angrier and not afraid to offend just about everyone. Its listings are quite good.

THE GUIDE

THE GUIDE

The Statue of Liberty and Ellis Island

The tip of Manhattan Island and the enclosing shores of New Jersey, Staten Island and Brooklyn form the broad expanse of New York Harbor, one of the finest natural harbors in the world and one of the things that persuaded the first immigrants to settle here several centuries ago. Take to the water – most easily aboard the Staten Island ferry – to get the best views of the classic downtown skyline, or to get out to the **Statue of Liberty** and **Ellis Island** – two high-priority targets for a trip to the city.

At the time of writing, service on the #1 and #9 trains to South Ferry, the closest stop to the ferries, has been discontinued owing to the cleanup following the World Trade Center's collapse. The best way to reach the ferries is to take the #4 or #5 trains to Bowling Green.

FERRIES TO THE ISLANDS

Ferries, run by Circle Line, go to both the **Statue of Liberty** and **Ellis Island** and leave from the pier in Battery Park, every twenty minutes between 8.30am and 4.30pm all year long. Round-trip tickets are $8 (senior citizens $6, children 3–17 $3) and can be purchased inside Castle Clinton in Battery Park (℡212/269-5755, ⓦwww.statueoflibertyferry.com).

THE STATUE OF LIBERTY

9.30am–5pm; free; ℡212/363-7770, ⓦwww.nps.gov/stli

The **Statue of Liberty** has for a century been a monument to the American Dream, a potent reminder that the USA is a land of immigrants. It was New York Harbor where the first big waves of European immigrants arrived, their ships entering through the Verrazano Narrows to round the bend of the bay and catch a first glimpse of "Liberty Enlightening the World."

Leave as early as possible to avoid the lines, which can be long in the summer months (especially on weekends), and allow a couple of hours for the islands.

The statue, which depicts Liberty throwing off her shackles and holding a beacon to light the world, was built by Frederic Auguste Bartholdi in Paris between 1874 and 1884. Bartholdi started with a terra-cotta model and enlarged it through four successive versions to its present size, a construction of thin copper sheets bolted together and supported by an iron framework designed by Gustave Eiffel. The arm carrying the torch was exhibited in Madison Square Park for seven years, but the whole statue wasn't officially accepted on behalf of the American people until 1884, after which it was taken apart, crated up and shipped to New York. The statue was unveiled by President Grover Cleveland in 1886 in a flag-waving shindig that has never really stopped. Today you can climb 192 steps to the top of the pedestal or the entire 354 steps up to the crown (unfortunately, the cramped stairway up through the torch is closed to the public). Don't be surprised if there's an hour-long wait to get up.

ELLIS ISLAND

Just across the water, and just fifteen minutes on by ferry, sits **Ellis Island**, the first stop for over twelve million immigrants hoping to settle in the USA. The island became an immigration station in 1892, a processing point for the massive influx of mostly southern and eastern European immigrants. The station closed in 1954, and in 1990 the **Ellis Island Museum of Immigration** (daily 9.30am–5pm; free; ☎212/363-3200, ⓦwww.ellisisland.org) was opened in an ambitious attempt to recapture the spirit of the place, with films, exhibits and tapes documenting the celebration of America as the immigrant nation.

Some 100 million Americans can trace their roots back through Ellis Island and, for them especially, the museum is an engaging display. On the first floor, in the old railroad ticket office, is the excellent **"Peopling of America,"** which chronicles four centuries of American immigration, offering a statistical portrait of who the arrivals were and where they came from.

The huge, vaulted **Registry Room** on the second floor, scene of so much trepidation, elation and despair, has been left bare, with just a couple of inspectors' desks and American flags. In the side hall interview rooms recordings of those who passed through Ellis Island recall the experi-

ELLIS ISLAND

ence, along with photographs, thoughtful and informative explanatory text, and small artifacts – train timetables and familiar items brought from home.

The museum's **American Family Immigration History Center** (Ⓦwww.ellisislandrecords.org) is of great use to genealogical researchers, offering an interactive research database that contains information from ship manifests and passenger lists concerning over 22 million immigrants who passed through the Port of New York between 1892 and 1924.

On the fortified spurs of the island, names of immigrant families who passed through the building over the years are engraved in copper; paid for by a minimum donation of $100 from their descendants. This "**American Immigrant Wall of Honor**," launched in 1990, helped fund the restoration and features the names of over 600,000 individuals and families.

The Financial
District

he **Financial District** has been synonymous with
the Manhattan of the popular imagination for some
time – its tall buildings and skyline, its busy streets,
its symbols of economic strength and financial wheeling
and dealing. So when the September 11, 2001, attacks on
the World Trade Center resulted in the collapse of the Twin
Towers (see box p.28), it was no surprise the impact this
had not just on the neighborhood, but on the city and
country as well. The district will be recovering for some
time, and the celebrated skyline you've seen in movies has
been radically altered. There is still plenty to see in the area,
however, and in any case many visitors might find a pilgrimage to the site of the former Twin Towers – or as near
as you can get – hard to resist.

At the time of writing, some of the subway lines that
were running below the former World Trade Center have
not reopened; the best way to reach the Financial District is
by taking the #1, #2, #4 or #5 to Wall Street and starting
your wanderings there.

CHAPTER 2 • THE FINANCIAL DISTRICT

WALL STREET AND THE STOCK EXCHANGE

The Dutch arrived here first, building a wooden wall at the edge of New Amsterdam in 1635 to protect themselves from British settlers to the north and giving the narrow canyon of today's **Wall Street** its name. Still today, from behind the Neoclassical facade of the **New York Stock Exchange** on 8 Wall St (Map 4, E7), the purse strings of the capitalist world are pulled.

Come before noon for the best chance of getting into the **NYSE Interactive Education Center**, 20 Wall St (Mon–Fri 8.45am–4.30pm; free; ☎212/656-3000, ⓦwww.nyse.com), where the Exchange floor appears like a melee of brokers and buyers, scrambling for the elusive fractional cent on which to make a megabuck. After sitting through a glib introductory film and a small exhibition on the history of the Exchange, the hectic scurrying and constantly moving hieroglyphs of the stock prices will make more sense.

Federal Hall

Map 4, E6. 26 Wall St (Mon–Fri 9am–5pm; free; ☎212/825-6888, ⓦwww.nps.gov/feha. #1, #2, #4 or #5 trains to Wall Street.
The Federal Hall National Memorial at the street's canyon-like head, can't help but look like an Ionic temple that woke up one morning and found itself surrounded by skyscrapers. The building was built by Town and Davis as the Customs House in the 1830s and served briefly as the first capitol of the United States. There is an exhibition inside that tells the story of how democracy got its start some sixty years earlier when printer John Peter Zenger was acquitted of libel in 1735.

Trinity Church and around

At Wall Street's western end is **Trinity Church** (Map 4, E6; Mon–Sat free guided tours daily at 2pm), first built in 1698, though the current version went up in 1846. For fifty years, this was the city's tallest building, a reminder of just how relatively recent high-rise Manhattan sprung up. Trinity's cemetery is the final resting place for such luminaries as the first secretary of the Treasury, Alexander Hamilton, steamboat king Robert Fulton, signer of the Declaration of Independence Francis Lewis and many others.

Trinity Church is an oddity amid its office-building neighbors, several of which are worth nosing into. **One Wall Street**, immediately opposite the church, is among the best, with an Art Deco lobby in red and gold. East down Wall Street, the **Morgan Guaranty Trust Building**, at no. 23, bears the scars of a weird happening on September 16, 1920 when a horse-drawn cart exploded in front. The explosion remains unexplained to this day and the pockmark scars on the building's wall have never been repaired.

THE FEDERAL RESERVE PLAZA AND AROUND

Take Nassau Street north of Wall to Maiden Lane, where you'll find Phillip Johnson and John Burgee's **Federal Reserve Plaza**, which complements the original 1924 Federal Reserve Bank (Map 4, E6). Eighty feet below the somber neo-Gothic interior of the bank are most of the "free" world's gold reserves. It is possible – but tricky – to tour; contact the Public Information Department, Federal Reserve Bank, 33 Liberty St, New York, NY 10045 (⊤212/720-6130, ⊚www.ny.frb.org) several weeks ahead – tickets have to be mailed.

THE WORLD TRADE CENTER 1972–2001

On September 11th, 2001, a hijacked airline slammed into the north tower of the World Trade Center at 8.45am; eighteen minutes later another hijacked plane struck the south tower. As thousands looked on in horror – in addition to millions more viewing on TV – the south tower collapsed at 9.50am, its twin about half an hour later. That afternoon, a smaller building in the World Trade Center complex also crumbled, and the center was reduced to a monument of steel, concrete and glass rubble.

The devastation was staggering. While most of the 50,000 working in the towers had been evacuated before the towers fell, many never made it out; hundreds of firemen, policemen and rescue workers who arrived on the scene when the planes struck were crushed when the buildings collapsed. In all, around 3000 perished in what was easily the largest attack on America in history.

In the days after the attack, downtown was basically shut down, and the seven-square-block vicinity immediately around the WTC – soon to be known as Ground Zero – was the obvious focus of the rescue effort. New Yorkers lined up to give

Retrace your steps along Nassau to **Liberty Street**, which leads west toward Liberty Plaza. At no. 1, you'll find the **US Steel Building** (Map 4, E6). When the World Trade Center collapsed, many of the US Steel Building's windows popped out, and it was feared that the building itself would tumble.

St Paul's Chapel and south on Broadway

The oldest church in Manhattan, **St Paul's Chapel** (Map 4, E5) dates from 1766 – eighty years earlier than Trinity Church, almost prehistoric by New York standards. George

blood and volunteer to help the rescue workers; vigils were held throughout the city, most notably in Union Square, which became peppered with all manner of candles and makeshift shrines; and all city hospitals were on red alert to receive injured victims. Precious few came, and as weeks passed, reality began to sink in. Through it all Mayor Giuliani cut a highly composed and reassuring figure as New Yorkers struggled to come to terms with the physical and emotional assault on their city. It was more than just sheer numbers – the lives lost, the expected $60 billion cost of insurance payouts, property value loss, cleanup (expected to take a full year) – things were irrevocably changed.

The chief suspect in the attacks was Osama bin Laden's many-headed terrorist network that he operated from the mountains of Afghanistan. In October 2001, the US government struck back against Afghanistan's ruling Taliban group, known to harbor and support bin Laden.

An observation platform, overlooking the former World Trade Center, has been erected on Broadway and Fulton Street.

Washington worshipped here and his pew, zealously treasured, is on show. Heading south along Broadway, a most impressive leftover of the confident days before the Wall Street Crash is the old **Cunard Building** (Map 4, D8), at no. 25. Its marble walls and high dome once housed a steamship's booking office – hence the elaborate, whimsical murals of variegated ships and nautical mythology splashed around the ceiling. Today, it houses a post office – one that's been fitted with little feeling for the exuberant space it occupies. On the second floor is the **New York City Police Museum** (Tues–Sat 10am–6pm; free; ☎212/301-4440, ⓦwww.nycpolicemuseum.org), housing a collection of 250 years worth of memorabilia of the New York Police Department, the largest and oldest in the country.

At 26 Broadway, located in the former headquarters of **John D. Rockefeller's Standard Oil Company**, is the **Museum of American Financial History** 28 Broadway (Tues–Sat 10am–4pm; $2; ℡212/908-4110, ⓦwww.financialhistory.org). This is the largest public archive of financial documents and artifacts in the world, featuring such finance-related objects as the bond signed by Washington bearing the first dollar sign ever used on a Federal document. On Fridays, the museum also offers a "World of Finance" walking tour ($15).

BOWLING GREEN

Map 4, E7. #4 or #5 train to Bowling Green.

Broadway comes to a gentle end at **Bowling Green Park**, originally the city's meat market, but in 1733 turned into an oval of turf used for the game by colonial Brits on a lease of "one peppercorn per year." In 1626, the green had been the location of one of Manhattan's more memorable business deals, when Peter Minuit, first director general of the Dutch colony of New Amsterdam, bought the whole island from the Indians for a bucket of trade goods worth sixty guilders (about $24). The other side of the story (and the part you never hear) was that these particular Indians didn't actually own the island.

The green sees plenty of office folk picnicking in the shadow of Cass Gilbert's **US Customs House**, a heroic monument to the Port of New York and home of the **Smithsonian National Museum of the American Indian**, 1 Bowling Green (daily 10am–5pm; free; ℡212/514-3700, ⓦwww.si.edu/nmai). This excellent collection of artifacts from almost every tribe native to the Americas was largely assembled by one man, George Gustav

Heye (1874–1957), who traveled throughout the Americas picking up such works for over fifty years. Built in 1907, the Customs House itself was intended to pay homage to the booming maritime market. The four **statues** were sculpted by Daniel Chester French, who also created the Lincoln Memorial in Washington, DC. As if French foresaw the House's current use, the sculptor blatantly comments on the mistreatment of Indians in his statues.

BATTERY PARK AND CASTLE CLINTON

Map 4, D8. #4 or #5 train to Bowling Green.

Due west, lower Manhattan lets out its breath in **Battery Park**, a bright and breezy space with tall trees, green grass, lots of flowers and views overlooking the panorama of the Statue of Liberty, Ellis Island and Governors Island. Various monuments and statues ranging from Jewish immigrants to Celtic settlers to the city's first wireless telegraph operators adorn the park.

Before a landfill closed the gap, **Castle Clinton**, the 1811 fort on the west side of the park, was on an island, one of several forts defending New York Harbor. Later it acted as a pre-Ellis Island dropoff point for arriving immigrants. Today, the squat castle is the place to buy tickets for and board ferries to the Statue of Liberty and Ellis Island (see p.22).

BATTERY PARK CITY

Map 4, C7. #4 or #5 train to Bowling Green.

The hole dug for the foundations of the Twin Towers threw up a million cubic yards of earth and rock; these excavations were dumped into the Hudson to form the 23-acre base of **Battery Park City**, a self-sufficient island of office blocks, apartments, chain boutiques, and landscaped esplanade that feels a far cry from much of Manhattan indeed.

At its very southern end is the entrance to **Robert F. Wagner Jr. Park** – Zen-like in its peacefulness away from the ferry crowds and winner of a National Honor Award for Urban Design in 1998. In the park, a hexagonal, pale-granite building designed in 1997 by Kevin Roche will catch your eye. That's the **Museum of Jewish Heritage**, 18 First Place (Map 4, C8; Sun–Wed 9am–5pm, Thurs until 8pm, Fri 9am–5pm, closed Jewish holidays; $7, children $5; ☎212/509-6130, ⓦwww.mjhnyc.org), was created as a memorial to the Holocaust. Three floors of exhibits feature historical and cultural artifacts ranging from the practical accoutrements of everyday Eastern European Jewish life to the prison garb survivors wore in Nazi concentration camps, along with photographs, personal belongings and narratives.

WATER AND PEARL STREETS

Retrace your steps through Robert F. Wagner Park to **Water Street** and turn east down Old Slip. The pocket-size palazzo, which was once the **First Precinct Police Station**, slots easily into the narrow strip, a cheerful throwback to a different era. A little to the south, off Water Street, stands the **Vietnam Veterans' Memorial**, an assembly of sad and often haunting mementos. A recent renovation has made the place a peaceful spot for contemplation – and enjoying a nice view of the East River.

The eighteenth-century **Fraunces Tavern Museum**, 54 Pearl St at Broad Street (Map 4, F8; Mon–Fri 9am–5pm; $3, children, seniors, students $2; ☎212/425-1778, ⓦwww.frauncestavernmuseum.org), has survived extensive modification, several fires and nineteenth-century use as a hotel. The Tavern's second floor re-creates the site's history with a series of illustrated panels.

At 6 Pearl St, you'll find **New York Unearthed** (Mon–Fri noon–6pm; free; ☏212/748-8628), the South Street Seaport Museum's tiny, hands-on, annex devoted to the city's archeology.

SOUTH STREET SEAPORT

Map 4, H6. #A, #E, #J, #M, #1, #2, #4 or #5 train to Fulton Street–Broadway Nassau.

At the eastern end of Fulton Street, the **South Street Seaport** is a mixed bag – a fair slice of commercial gentrification that was necessary to woo developers and tourists, plus the presence of a centuries-old working fish market that has kept things real. It dates back to the 1600s, when this stretch of the waterside was New York's sailship port. When the FDR Drive was constructed in the 1950s, the Seaport's decline was rapid, but private initiative beginning in 1967 rescued the remaining warehouses and saved the historic seaport just in time.

Regular guided tours of the Seaport run from the **Visitors' Center**, located at 12–14 Fulton St.

The Seaport Museum

Map 4, G5. 207 Water St. Daily: April–Sept 10am–6pm, Oct–March 10am–5pm; $5, includes all tours, films, galleries and museum-owned ships, as well as New York Unearthed; ☏212/748-8600, ⓦwww.southstseaport.org.

Housed in a series of painstakingly restored 1830s warehouses, the **South Street Seaport Museum** offers a collection of refitted ships and chubby tugboats (the largest collection of sailing vessels – by tonnage – in the US). It also features a handful of maritime art and trades exhibits, a museum store and info about the Fulton Fish Market.

For a stellar view of the Brooklyn Bridge, have a seat on the benches or have your photo taken in front of one of the most beautiful backdrops New York City has to offer.

The Fulton Fish Market

Map 4, H5. #A, #E, #J, #M, #1, #2, #4 or #5 train to Fulton Street–Broadway Nassau.

The elevated East Side Highway forms a suitably grimy gateway to the Fulton Fish Market, the city's oldest and largest wholesale outlet. Business has been done on this site since 1835 and now generates over a billion dollars in revenues annually. If you can manage it, the best time to visit is around 5am when buyers' trucks park up beneath the highway to collect the catches. Otherwise, tours can be arranged through the South Street Seaport Museum the first and third Wednesday of the month, April–Oct (☏212/748-8786). The market will move to Hunts Point in the Bronx in 2003.

Pier 17 and the rest of the seaport

Map 4, H6.

To many, **Pier 17**, right next to the Fish Market, has become the focal point of the district, created from the old fish market pier demolished and then restored in 1982. A three-story glass-and-steel **pavilion** houses all kinds of restaurants and shops; a bit more interesting is the outdoor promenade, always crowded in the summer, when you can listen to free music, tour historic moored ships or book cruises with the New York Waterway (two-hour cruises $12; ☏1-800/533-3779, ⓦwww.nywaterway.com).

Just across South Street, there's an assemblage of upmarket chain shops. Yet keep your eyes peeled for some unusual buildings preserved here, like at **203 Front St**; this giant J. Crew store was an 1880s hotel that catered to unmarried laborers on the dock. Not far away, cleaned-up **Schermerhorn Row** is a unique ensemble of Georgian-Federal-style early warehouses, dating to about 1811.

City Hall
and TriBeCa

Since the city's early days, the seats of New York's federal, state and city government have been located around City Hall Park, and though many of the original buildings no longer stand, great examples of the city's finest architecture can be found here. While neighboring TriBeCa, to the west, does not hold the same historical allure, it does feature some of New York's most vibrant galleries, chic restaurants and bars, and complements a visit to New York's civic center nicely, especially if you arrive in the evening.

CITY HALL

Map 4, E4. #N or #R to City Hall, the #6 to Brooklyn Bridge or the #2 or #3 to Park Place.

Broadway and Park Row form the apex of **City Hall Park**, a noisy, pigeon-splattered triangle of green that marks the center of the jumble of municipal offices and courts. At the park's northern head stands **City Hall** (tours available Mon–Fri at 10am, 11am and 2pm; reservations are required at least two weeks prior; tours are available only for parties of between 10 and 35 people; admission is free; ☎212/788-6865), whose interior is an elegant meeting of arrogance and authority, with the sweeping spiral staircase delivering you to the precise geometry of the Governor's Room. In 1865, Abraham Lincoln's body lay in state here for 120,000 New Yorkers to file past. Later, after the city's 1927 feting of the returned aviator Charles Lindbergh, it became the traditional finishing point for Broadway tickertape parades given for astronauts, returned hostages and triumphant sports teams.

This triangular wedge is dotted with **statues**, not least of which is one of Horace Greeley, founder of the *New York Tribune* newspaper, and in front of whose bronzed countenance a farmer's market is held each Tuesday and Friday (April–Dec 8am–6pm). Prize position among the patriotic statues here goes to **Nathan Hale** who, in 1776, was captured by the British and hanged for spying, but not before he'd spat out his gloriously and memorably famous last words: "I regret that I only have but one life to lose for my country."

THE WOOLWORTH BUILDING

Map 4, E4.
At one side of the park the venerable **Woolworth Building** looks on. Money, ornament and prestige mingle in the 1913 "Cathedral of Commerce," whose soaring, graceful lines are fringed with Gothic decoration more for fun than any portentous allusion. Within, vaulted ceilings ooze honey-gold mosaics – even the brass mailboxes are magnificent. The whole building has a well-humored panache more or less extinct in today's architecture.

THE MUNICIPAL BUILDING AND AROUND

Straddling Chambers Street, which runs across the top of City Hall Park, the **Municipal Building** (Map 4, F4) stands like an oversized chest of drawers. Built between 1907 and 1914, the building was architects McKim, Mead and White's first skyscraper. Atop it, an extravagant pile of columns and pinnacles signals a frivolous conclusion to a no-nonsense building that houses public records; below, though not apparent, subway cars travel through its foundation.

To walk across the Brooklyn Bridge, take the footpath that emerges in the middle of Centre Street just in front of the Municipal Building ; it should take about 45 minutes to reach the Brooklyn side (see p.150).

At 100 Centre St, the 1939 Art Deco **Criminal Courts Building**, reminiscent of a Babylonian temple, houses the **Manhattan Detention Center of Men**, which is nicknamed "the Tombs," after the funereal Egyptian-style building that once stood across the street. Where "the Tombs" used to be, the White Street Correctional Facility houses up to 500 maximum-security inmates, and the "bridge of sighs" towering over White Street connects the two facilities. All courts are open to the public (Mon–Fri 9am–5pm), yet the Criminal Courts are your best bet for viewing the ponderous New York City justice system in action.

TRIBECA

#1 or #2 train to Franklin Street.

Head north and west from City Hall and you're in **TriBeCa** (Try-beck-a) – the *Tri*angle *Be*low *Ca*nal Street, an area that was rapidly transformed from a wholesale garment district to an upscale community that mixes commercial establishments with loft residences, studios, galleries and chic eateries. Less a triangle than a crumpled rectangle – the area bounded by Canal and Murray streets, Broadway and the Hudson River – it takes in spacious industrial buildings whose upper layers have become the apartments of TriBeCa's new gentry.

Despite rising rents, commercial space in TriBeCa is also cheaper than SoHo or the Villages, so creative industries have been moving to the area en masse. Galleries, such as the **Moving Image Gallery**, at 414 Broadway (Tues–Fri 10am–2pm; ☎212/966-4741, ◎www.movingimage gallery.com), which features new art technologies, have made themselves at home here. So have recording studios, computer graphics companies, photo labs and even the film industry; the **TriBeCa Film Center** (Map 4, C2), at 375 Greenwich St, and TriBeCa Productions, is a screening facility and production company that is co-owned by Robert De Niro.

Exploring TriBeCa

To get a feel for TriBeCa's mix of old and new, go to **Duane Park**, a sliver of green between Hudson and Greenwich streets. Around the Park's picturesque perimeter you'll see the former depots of New York's egg, butter and cheese distribution center wedged between new residential apartments, where the World Trade Center buildings used to guard the skyline like sentinels.

Take a left out of Duane Park and follow Greenwich toward Canal Street. In this main strip restaurants from the affordable (*Yaffa's*) to the expensive (*TriBeCa Grill*) line the street. Parallel to Greenwich lies Hudson Street, which catches the overflow of fancy restaurants then, in sharp contrast, peters out into still-active warehouses, whose denizens do the same work they have for decades.

TRIBECA

For restaurant and gallery listings
for TriBeCa, see pp.212 and 333.

West Broadway is one of TriBeCa's main thoroughfares and has a few interesting, if nonessential sites to check out. On its northeast corner with White Street stands a rare remaining Federal-era store, in continuous use since 1809, and now home to the *Liquor Store* bar. **Ladder Company 8**, between Varick and North Moore streets, a turn-of-the-nineteenth century brick-and-stone firehouse, is dotted with white stars. The closest firehouse to the World Trade Center, it suffered many casualties on September 11, 2001.

Chinatown

With more than 200,000 residents (125,000 of them Chinese and the rest other Asian ethnicities), 7 Chinese newspapers, 12 Buddhist temples, around 150 restaurants and over 300 garment factories, **Chinatown** is Manhattan's most populous ethnic neighborhood, one of busy restaurants and exotic street markets. Since the Eighties, it has pushed its boundaries north across Canal Street into Little Italy and sprawls east into the nether fringes of the Lower East Side around Division Street and East Broadway.

The Chinese community has been careful to preserve its own way of dealing with things, preferring to keep affairs close to the bond of the family and allowing few intrusions into a still-insular culture. And while insularity means that much of Chinatown's character survives relatively unspoiled – especially on streets such as Canal, Pell, Mott and Bayard – it has also meant non-union sweatshop labor and poor overcrowded tenements ill-kept by landlords. However, unless you stay in Chinatown for a considerable length of time it's unlikely you'll see much of this seamier side. Most tourists, like most New Yorkers, come here not to get the lowdown on Chinese politics but to eat excellent Chinese **food** or to hunt for bargains along **Canal Street**.

The best way to reach Chinatown is to take the #J, #M, #N, #Q, #R, #W, #Z or #6 train to Canal Street.

CHINESE NEW YEAR

Chinatown bursts open during the Chinese New Year festival, held each year on the second full moon after the winter solstice (usually between mid-Jan and mid-Feb) when a giant cloth and papier mache dragon runs down Mott Street. The firecrackers that traditionally accompanied the festival are now banned by the city as a fire hazard (much to local chagrin), yet the gutters still run with ceremonial dyes.

MOTT STREET

Mott Street is the area's most obvious tourist restaurant row, although the streets around – Canal, Pell, Bayard, Doyers and Bowery – host a glut of restaurants, tea and rice shops and grocers. Cantonese cuisine predominates, but there are also many restaurants that specialize in the spicier Szechuan and Hunan cuisines, along with Fukien, Soochow and the spicy Chowchou dishes. Just remember that most Chinese restaurants start closing up around 9.30pm – best to go early if you want friendly service and atmosphere. If you're looking for specific recommendations (especially for BYOB lunchtime dim sum), some of the best are detailed in Chapter 26, "Restaurants."

Besides scoffing down Asian delights, the lure of Chinatown lies in wandering amid the exotica of the shops and absorbing the neighborhood's vigorous street life. Meandering comes highly recommended, though, and there are several interesting, vaguely structured routes to take. Mott Street, again, is the obvious starting point: follow it from Worth Street and there's **Chinatown Fair** at the southern end, on the site of the district's first Chinese shop. Once a bona fide museum, this is now little more than a bizarre and very popular video arcade, where a predominantly male crowd gathers to smoke, prowl and play anything from pinball to 1950s Test Your Own Strength machines and the most modern interactive video phenomena.

Further north along Mott Street, a rare edifice predating the Chinese arrival dominates the corner of Mott and Mosco streets. It's the early nineteenth-century green-domed Catholic school and **Church of the Transfiguration** (Map 7, G3), an elegant building that has been undergoing massive renovations since 1999. Masses are held here daily in Cantonese and English, with additional services in Mandarin on Sunday. Just across from the church is picturesquely crooked **Doyers Street**, once known as "Bloody Angle" for its reputation as a dumping ground for dead bodies.

MUSEUM OF CHINESE IN THE AMERICAS

Map 4, G2. Tues–Sat noon–5pm; $3, children $1; ☏212/619-4785, Ⓦwww.moca-nyc.org

One block west of Mott is Mulberry Street, where, at no. 70, you'll find the double red doors of the community center right on the corner. Two floors up lies the tiny, but fascinating, **Museum of Chinese in the Americas** dedicated to documenting the experiences of Chinese immigrants in the Americas as well as reclaiming and preserving Chinese history in the West. The displays include Chinese photographs and cultural memorabilia; temporary exhibits of Asian American art; and the museum also offers historical group tours of Chinatown ($10, three weeks advance booking required).

The Museum of Chinese in the Americas sells a Historic Walking Tour Map, ideal for touring Chinatown.

CANAL AND GRAND STREETS

Mulberry Street runs north to **Canal Street**, at all hours a
crowded thoroughfare crammed with jewelry shops and
kiosks hawking sunglasses, T-shirts and fake Rolexes. The
Pearl River Department Store, at no. 277 (the corner of
Canal and the Bowery, though scheduled to move to 477
Broadway in 2003), is the closest you'll ever get to a
Shanghai bazaar without going to China. Specialties here
include all sorts of embroidered slippers and silk clothing,
rice cookers, pottery and beautiful lacquered paper
umbrellas. Across the street at no. 308, housed in an imposing red-and-white-painted turn-of-the-nineteenth-century
warehouse, are the many floors of **Pearl Paint**, which
claims to be the largest art supply store in the world.

Take Mott or Mulberry north to **Grand Street**, where
outdoor fruit, vegetable and live seafood stands line the
curbs – offering snow peas, bean curd, fungi, oriental cabbage and dried sea cucumbers to the passersby. Ribs, whole
chickens and Peking ducks glisten in the storefront windows nearby: the sight of them can put more than a vegetarian off his food. Perhaps even more fascinating are the
Chinese herbalists. The roots and powders in their boxes,
drawers and glass are century-old remedies, but, to those
accustomed to Western medicine, may seem like voodoo
potions.

Little Italy and NoLita

S igns made out of red, green and white tinsel effusively welcome visitors here, a signal perhaps that today's **Little Italy** is light years away from the solid ethnic enclave of old. The neighborhood is a lot smaller and more commercial than it once was, and the area settled by New York's huge nineteenth-century influx of Italian immigrants is encroached upon a little more each year by Chinatown (see p.41). In fact, if you walk north from Canal Street along Mulberry or Mott streets to get here, the transition from the cultural heart of Chinatown to Little Italy's Big Tomato tourist schmaltz can be a little difficult to stomach. Few Italians still live here and some of the restaurants cater to tourists with valet parking and by piping the music of NY's favorite Italian son, Frank Sinatra, onto the street.

But that's not to advise missing out on Little Italy altogether. Some original bakeries and *salumerias* (Italian specialty food stores) do survive, and here, amid the imported cheeses, sausages and salamis hanging from the ceiling, you can buy sandwiches made with slabs of mozzarella or eat slices of homemade focaccia.

The best way to access Little Italy is by taking the #N, #R, #J, #M, #Z or #6 train to Canal Street and walking up Mulberry Street.

Restaurant and café options for Little Italy are listed on pp.209–210 and pp.193–194.

MULBERRY STREET

Mid-September's ten-day Festa di San Gennaro is a wild and tacky celebration of the day of the patron saint of Naples. Italians from all over the city converge on **Mulberry Street**, Little Italy's main strip, and the area is transformed by street stalls and numerous Italian fast-food and snack outlets. The festivities center around the **Church of the Most Precious Blood**, just off Canal at 109 Mulberry St, and provide a rare chance to see this quaint church and its courtyard, normally closed up and protected from the public gaze.

Few of the restaurants around here really stand out, but the former site of **Umberto's Clam House**, on the corner of Mulberry and Hester streets, was quite notorious in its time: it was the scene of a vicious gangland murder in 1972, when Joe "Crazy Joey" Gallo was shot dead while celebrating his birthday with his wife and daughter. Gallo, a big talker and ruthless businessman, was alleged to have offended a rival family and so paid the price. *Umberto's Clam House* has since relocated to 386 Broome St.

Old St Patrick's Cathedral

Map 5, G6.

In striking counterpoint to the lawlessness of the Italian underworld, the **Old St Patrick's Cathedral** at 263

Mulberry St was the first Catholic cathedral in the city and the parent church to its much more famous offspring on Fifth Avenue and 50th Street. The interior has been restored to its former glory and plans are afoot to add spires to its 100-year-old roof. Mass is still held in the cathedral and it is open to the public, unlike the walled cemetery behind, which is unfortunately almost always locked.

A description of St Patrick's Cathedral
can be found on p.90.

Old Police Headquarters

Map 5, G7.
Reaction to Little Italy's illicit past can be found at the corner of Centre and Broome streets, where you'll find the **Old Police Headquarters**, a palatial 1909 Neoclassical confection meant to cow would-be criminals into obedience with its high-rise dome and lavish ornamentation. The police headquarters moved to a bland modern building around City Hall in 1973, and the overbearing palace was converted in the late Eighties into upmarket condominiums, some of which have been called home by Steffi Graf, Winona Ryder and Christy Turlington.

NoLita

Map 5, G6. #N or #R to Prince Street.
Just east of Broadway and south of Houston, fashion, style and nonchalant living have found fertile new breeding ground. Lining the streets are fresh, creative and independent designer boutiques, coffeehouses and cafés, establishing this area as the latest in chic. Referred to as **NoLita**, this section north of Little Italy, which extends east from

Lafayette, Mott and Elizabeth streets between Prince and Houston, is great for only-in-New York, hip accessory shopping. NoLita is not cheap by any means, but the young, artsy and restless hanging outside the area's proliferation of trendy stores, bars and restaurants make it an excellent place for a late-afternoon drink and a spot of beautiful-people watching.

The Lower East Side

Historically the epitome of the American melting pot, the **Lower East Side** is one of Manhattan's most enthralling downtown neighborhoods. A little-known quarter that began to attract attention toward the end of the nineteenth century when it became an insular slum for over half a million **Jewish immigrants** – and the most densely populated spot in the world. Coming here from Eastern Europe, refugees sought a better life, scratching out a living in the neighborhood's sweatshops. Since then, the area has become considerably depopulated and better maintained, and while up until recently the inhabitants were largely working-class Puerto Rican or Chinese, these days you are just as likely to find students, artsy types and other refugees from the overly gentrified areas of SoHo and the nearby East Village. Below Houston, today's Lower East Side is one of the most hip areas around for shopping, drinking, dancing and (what else?) food. Along East Broadway or Grand Street, however, it is still a bit seedy.

To reach the Lower East Side, take the #F, #S or #6

train to Broadway-Lafayette Street, or the #F or #V to Delancey Street.

HOUSTON STREET TO GRAND STREET

In the first half of the nineteenth century the streets immediately South of Houston were known as *Kleine Deutschland*, home to the well-off German merchants and then, as they moved away, the poorest of the Jewish immigrants fleeing poverty and pogroms in Eastern Europe. Even now it still holds the remnants of its Jewish past, such as the area's homemade kosher cuisine and its ritual bathhouse for women who are "unclean." Some outsiders are drawn to the area for the **bargain shopping**. You can get just about anything at cut-price in the stores: clothes on **Orchard Street**, lamps and shades on the **Bowery**, ties and shirts on Allen Street, underwear and hosiery on **Grand Street**, textiles on Eldridge. And, whatever you're buying, people will if necessary haggle down to the last cent.

Ludlow and Orchard streets

Ludlow Street, where a half-dozen or so bars, such as the popular *Local 138* at no. 138 and *Max Fish* at no. 178, sparked the hipster migration south of the East Village, dot the block. A number of secondhand stores offer kitsch items – especially retro furniture - and slightly worn treasures. Around the intersection of Allen and Stanton streets are several bar/performance spaces. (For more on this area's excellent bar scene, see pp.250–251.)

On the corner of Ludlow and East Houston you'll find *Katz's Deli* (Map 5, K5), a delicatessen famous for its assembly-line counter service and lauded by locals as one of the best in New York. If it looks familiar, don't be surprised:

this was the scene of Meg Ryan's faked orgasm in *When Harry Met Sally*. There are a variety of Jewish delicacies available on East Houston: *Russ & Daughters*, at no. 179, specializes in smoked fish, herring and caviar, and *Yonah Schimmel*, further west at no. 137, has been making some of New York's best knishes since 1910.

Continue east on Houston and you'll arrive at **Orchard Street**, center of the so-called Bargain District, which is filled with stalls and storefronts hawking discounted designer clothes and bags.

The best time to visit the Orchard Street Market is Sunday morning, when you'll catch the vibrancy of the Lower East Side at its best.

The Lower East Side Tenement Museum

Map 5, K7. Tues, Wed & Fri 1–5pm, Thurs 1–8pm, Sat & Sun 11am–4.30pm; ☎212/431-0233, ⓦwww.tenement.org. #F or #V to Delancey Street.

If you haven't got the time to tour the Lower East Side extensively, make sure to visit the **Lower East Side Tenement Museum**, at 90 Orchard St, a fully intact and wonderfully preserved 1863 tenement which does a rilliantly imaginative job of bringing to life the neighborhood's immigrant past and present. Guided tours are available ($9) on the hour and half-hour, but come early on the weekend as they often sell out.

DELANCEY, ESSEX AND CLINTON STREETS

Orchard Street leads to **Delancey Street** – once the horizontal axis of the Jewish Lower East Side, now a tacky boulevard – and all the way east to the **Williamsburg**

Bridge, which you can walk across to the Williamsburg section of Brooklyn (see p.157). Look for the neon signs of *Ratner's Dairy Restaurant*, at 138 Delancey, a staple of the Jewish Lower East Side and one of the neighborhood's most famous dairy restaurants.

On either side of Delancey sprawls the **Essex Street Market**. Here you'll find all sorts of fresh fruit, fish and vegetables, along with random clothing bargains and the occasional trinket. At no. 35 is The Essex Street (Guss') Pickle Products, where people line up outside the storefront to buy fresh homemade pickles and olives from barrels of garlicky brine.

East of Essex Street, the atmosphere changes from a smorgasbord of ethnic treats to an edgy melting pot of white kids and long-established locals. Here the inhabitants are largely Latino, mostly Puerto Ricans but with a fair smattering of immigrants from other Latin American countries. **Clinton Street** – a mass of cheap Hispanic retailers, restaurants, travel agents and the occasional upscale trendy restaurant, such as *Clinton Fresh Food* at no. 71 – is in many ways the central thoroughfare of the Puerto Rican Lower East Side.

The Bowery

The **Bowery** (from *bouwerij*, the Dutch word for farm) spears north out of Chinatown, running a mile from Chatham Square up to Cooper Square on the edge of the East Village. The city's only thoroughfare never to have been graced by a church, it is still – in some sections – a skid row for the city's drunk and derelict. Such days are probably limited, however, as the demand for apartments continues and the tide of gentrification sweeps its way south through the Lower East Side.

BETWEEN DELANCEY AND EAST BROADWAY

Although the southern half of **East Broadway** is now almost exclusively Chinese, the street used to be the hub of the Jewish Lower East Side. For the old feel of the quarter – where the synagogues remain active – best explore north of here, starting with **Canal Street**. The recently renovated **Eldridge Street Synagogue** on 12 Eldridge St (Map 5, J9), built in 1886, was in its day one of the neighborhood's most grand with its brick and terra-cotta hybrid of Moorish arches and Gothic rose window.

Tours of the Eldridge Street Synagogue's majestic interior are offered Tues & Thurs 11.30am and 2.30pm, Sun hourly noon–4pm; $4.

East Broadway, Essex and Grand streets frame the pie-slice-shaped complex that comprises **Seward Park** (Map 5, L8 and its neighboring apartment blocks. Constructed in 1899 by the city to provide a bit of green space in the over-burdened precincts of the Lower East Side, the park boasted the first public playground in New York and is still sur-rounded by benevolent institutions set up for the benefit of ambitious immigrants.

A few blocks west, you'll pass the **Church of St Mary**, at 440 Grand St, the third-oldest Catholic church (1832) in the city. It's now a favorite resting spot of elderly Jewish couples, who sit on the benches outside and watch the world go by.

SoHo

ince the mid-1960s, **SoHo**, the grid of streets that runs **So**uth of **Ho**uston Street, has meant art. As the West Village increased in price and declined in hipness, artists moved into the loft spaces and cheap-rental studios. Galleries were established, quickly attracting the city's art crowd, as well as trendy clothes shops and some of the city's best restaurants. Gentrification soon followed. What remains is a mix of chichi antique shops, often overpriced art and chain clothiers from around the world – in other words, earthy industry and high living.

Yet although SoHo now carries the veneer of the establishment – a loft in the area means money (and lots of it) – no amount of gloss can cover up SoHo's quintessential appearance, its dark alleys of paint-peeled former garment factories fronted by some of the best cast-iron facades in the country. Nowadays, few artists or experimental galleries are left in the area: the late-1980s art boom drove up rents, and only the more established or consciously "commercial" galleries can afford to stay. Yet still, in many ways, SoHo is a place to see and be seen.

Houston Street (pronounced *How*ston rather than *Hew*ston) marks the top of SoHo's trellis of streets, any exploration of which entails crisscrossing and doubling back. **Greene Street** is a great place to start, highlighted all along by the nineteenth-century cast-iron facades that, in part if not in whole, saved SoHo from the bulldozers. **Prince Street**, **Spring Street** and **West Broadway** hold the best selection of shops and galleries in the area. Take the #N or #R trains to Prince Street or the #6 to Spring Street.

SOHO'S CAST-IRON ARCHITECTURE

The technique of cast-iron architecture was used simply as a way of assembling buildings quickly and cheaply, with iron beams rather than heavy walls carrying the weight of the floors. The result was the removal of load-bearing walls, greater space for windows and remarkably decorative facades. Almost any style or whim could be cast in iron and pinned to a building, and architects created the most fanciful of fronts for SoHo's sweatshops.

The SoHo Cast Iron Historic District runs roughly north–south from Houston to Canal and east–west from West Broadway to Broadway. Have a look at 72–76 Greene St, an extravagance whose Corinthian portico stretches its entire five stories, all in painted metal, and at the elaborations of its sister building at nos 28–30. These are some of the best examples, but from Broome to Canal streets most of the fronts on Greene Street's west side are either real (or mock) cast iron.

At the northeast corner of Broome Street and Broadway is the magnificent Haughwout Building (Map 5, G7), perhaps the ultimate in cast-iron architecture. Rhythmically repeated motifs of colonnaded arches are framed here behind taller columns in a thin sliver of a mock-Venetian palace. In 1904, Ernest Flagg took the possibilities of cast iron to their conclusion in his "Little Singer" Building (Map 5, F6), at 561 Broadway (at Prince St), a design whose use of wide window frames points the way to the glass curtain wall of the 1950s.

PRINCE STREET

SoHo celebrates its architecture in Richard Haas's smirky **mural** at 114 Prince St (corner of Greene St), also the venue of one of SoHo's affordable **markets** (there's another at the meeting of Spring and Wooster streets). Many of the clothes and antique shops around are beyond reasonable budgets, although Prince and the other SoHo streets have their fair share of chain clothing stores you'd find in any reputable mall. Bargain treasures and pure bric-a-brac can also be found at the **Antique Flea Market**, held every weekend on the southeast corner of Grand Street and Broadway.

See Chapter 32, "Shops and Markets," for further shopping options and Chapter 33, "Commercial Galleries," for more gallery listings.

What you'll find in SoHo's **galleries** is similarly over-priced, but no one minds you looking in for a while, and doing this is also a sure way of bumping into the more visible eccentrics of the area. Most of the galleries are concentrated on West Broadway and Prince Street, though a fair share have opened on Grand between West Broadway and Broadway. They're generally open from Labor Day to Memorial Day, Tuesday–Saturday 10/11am–6pm, Saturdays being most lively.

The New Museum of Contemporary Art

Map 5, F6. 583 Broadway (between Prince and Houston sts). Wed & Sun noon–6pm, Thurs–Sat noon–8pm; $6, students, seniors and artists $3, under 18s free, free Thurs 6–8pm; ☎212/219-1222, ⓦwww.newmuseum.org. #N or #R to Prince Street, or #6 to Spring Street.

Regularly changing exhibitions by contemporary American and international artists. Offbeat and eclectic, the **New Museum** will mount risky works that other museums are unable – or unwilling – to show. Pick up the museum's calendar for details on current and forthcoming exhibits and lectures.

Guggenheim Museum SoHo

Map 5, F6. 575 Broadway (at Prince St). Thurs–Mon 11am–6pm; $5, students and seniors $3, children under 12 free; ⊤212/423-3500, ⓦwww.guggenheim.org.

An outpost for the **Guggenheim Museum's** permanent collection, this aims to have exhibitions with an emphasis on single-artist retrospectives and in-depth interpretations of the collection, particularly postwar art. Entrance to the museum is through the museum store, which offers an excellent range of art books, jewelry and contemporary design.

For a description of the Guggenheim
Museum uptown, see p.127.

Museum for African Art

Map 5, F6. 593 Broadway (between Houston and Prince sts). Tues–Fri 10.30am–5.30pm, Sat & Sun noon–6pm; $5, students and kids $2.50, free Sun and every third Thurs 5.30–8.30pm; ⊤212/966-1313, ⓦwww.africanart.org.

Two floors of changing exhibitions of the best of modern and traditional African art; paintings, sculpture, masks, sacred objects and more.

PRINCE STREET

SOUTH TO CANAL STREET

Loosely speaking, SoHo's diversions get grittier as you drop south. Still, Broome and Grand streets, formerly full of dilapidated storefronts and dusty windows, have recently become home to a small band of boutiques, galleries, cafés and eclectic restaurants. The ultrachic (and ultraexpensive) *SoHo Grand Hotel* occupies the corner of Canal and West Broadway. If you don't want to fork out the dough for a room, at least look around the lobby, designed by Larry Bogdanow, or have a cocktail at the bar. Canal Street links the **Holland Tunnel** with the Manhattan Bridge and marks SoHo's southern entrance, though in truth the street is in look and feel more Chinatown than any other area.

The West Village

When the *Village Voice*, NYC's most venerable listings/comment/investigative magazine, began life as a chronicler of Greenwich Village nightlife in the 1960s, "the Village" really had a dissident, artistic, vibrant voice. While the nonconformist image of Greenwich Village, more commonly known today as the **West Village**, survives to an extent, the tag is no longer truly accurate. Though still one of the more progressive neighborhoods in the city, the West Village has attained a moneyed status over the last four decades and is firmly for those who have Arrived.

There's still a European quaintness here that is genuine and enjoyable and makes for a great day of walking through a grid of streets that doesn't even attempt to conform to the rest of the city's established numbered pattern. **Washington Square** is a hub of enjoyably aimless activity throughout the year, and a natural place to start explorations.

Elsewhere the Village is quiet and residential, yet the neighborhood has a busy streetlife that lasts later than in many other parts of the city. There are more restaurants per head here than any other neighborhood, and bars, though never cheap, clutter every corner, especially around **Bleecker Street**, while **Christopher Street** is the main artery of the city's gay life.

The West Village is easily reached by taking the #1 to Christopher Street or the #A, #C, #E, #F and #S to West Fourth Street.

WASHINGTON SQUARE

Map 5, E3.

The ideal way to see the Village is to walk, and by far the best place to start is its natural center, **Washington Square**, commemorated in the 1880 novel of that title by Henry James and haunted by many of the Village's illustrious past residents. It is not an elegant-looking place – too large to be a square, too small to be a park – but it does retain its northern edging of red-brick rowhouses (the "solid, honorable dwellings" of Henry James' novel). More imposing is the impossible-to-miss **Triumphal Arch**, built in 1892 to commemorate the centenary of George Washington's inauguration as president. In 1913, Marcel Duchamp climbed atop the arch to declare the Free Republic of Greenwich Village – but don't plan on re-creating his stunt; the arch has been cordoned off around its perimeter in an effort to ward off graffiti.

Nowadays, the square is rife with undercover police officers, part of a (mildly) successful effort to clear drug dealers. More effective than the cops, perhaps, is the fact that the park itself is closed after 11pm, a curfew that is strictly enforced, though you should not really be worried about your safety here. As soon as the weather gets warm, the square becomes a running track, performance venue, chess tournament and social club, boiling over with life as skateboards flip, dogs run, and acoustic guitar notes crash through the urgent cries of performers calling for the crowd's attention. At times like this, there's no better square in the city.

Around Washington Square

Eugene O'Neill, one of the Village's most acclaimed residents, lived (and in 1939 wrote *The Iceman Cometh*) at 38 Washington Square S and consumed vast quantities of ale at **The Golden Swan Bar**, which once stood on the corner of Sixth Avenue and W 4th Street. *The Golden Swan* was best known in O'Neill's day for the dubious morals of its clientele and the playwright drew many of his characters from his drinking buddies here. It was nearby, also, that he got his first dramatic break, with a company called the Provincetown Players who, on the advice of author John Reed, had moved down here from Massachusetts and set up shop at 177 MacDougal St.

Some of the best street basketball you'll ever see is played on the court between W 4th and W 3rd streets on Sixth Avenue before an ever-present crowd of spectators and the occasional TV crew.

In the NYU Student Center at Washington Square South and LaGuardia Place lies **Madame Katherine Blanchard's House of Genius**, a former boarding house that Willa Cather, Theodore Dreiser and O'Henry all called home. From the southwest corner of the park, follow MacDougal Street south, pausing for a detour down Minetta Lane until you hit **Bleecker Street**; a vibrant junction with mock-European sidewalk cafés that have been literary hangouts since Modernist times. The **Café Figaro**, made famous by the Beat writers in the 1950s, is always thronged throughout the day: it's still worth the price of a cappuccino to people-watch for an hour or so. Afterwards, you can follow Bleecker Street one of two ways – east toward the solid towers of Washington Square Village, or west right through the hubbub of West Village life.

WASHINGTON SQUARE

West of Sixth Avenue

Sixth Avenue itself is mainly tawdry stores and plastic eating houses, but on its west side, across Father Demo Square and up Bleecker, are some of the Village's prettiest residential streets. Turn left on **Leroy Street** and cross over Varick Street, where, confusingly, Leroy Street becomes St Luke's Place for a block. The houses here, dating from the 1850s, are among the city's most graceful, one of them (recognizable by the two lamps of honor at the bottom of the steps) is the ex-residence of **Jimmy Walker**, mayor of New York in the 1920s. Walker was for a time the most popular of mayors, a big-spending, wisecracking man who gave up his work as a songwriter for the world of politics and lived an extravagant lifestyle that rarely kept him out of the gossip columns.

BEDFORD AND GROVE STREETS

Retrace your steps across Varick Street and take a left on **Bedford Street**, pausing to peer into **Grove Court**, a typical secluded West Village mews. Along with nearby Barrow and Commerce streets, Bedford is one of the quietest and most desirable Village addresses – Edna St Vincent Millay, the poet and playwright, lived at no. 75 1/2 – said to be the narrowest house in the city, nine feet wide and topped with a tiny gable. Built in 1799, the clapboard structure next door claims to be the **oldest house** in the Village, but much renovated since and probably worth a considerable fortune now. Further down Bedford, at no. 86, the former speakeasy *Chumley's* (see "Drinking," p.252) is recognizable only by the metal grille on its door – a low profile useful in Prohibition years that makes it hard to find today.

Turn right off Bedford onto **Grove Street**, following it

towards Seventh Avenue and looking out for **Marie's Crisis Café** at no. 59 (see p.299). Now a gay bar, it was once home to Thomas Paine, English by birth but perhaps *the* most important and radical thinker of the American Revolutionary era, and from whose *Crisis Papers* the café takes its name. Grove Street meets Seventh Avenue at one of the Village's busiest junctions, **Sheridan Square** (Map 5, C3) – not in fact a square at all unless you count Christopher Park's slim strip of green, but simply a wide and hazardous confluence of several busy streets. The square was named after General Sheridan, cavalry commander in the Civil War, and holds a pompous-looking statue to his memory. It is better known, however, as the scene of one of the worst and bloodiest of New York's Draft Riots (see "History" in Contexts, p.363), when a marauding mob assembled here in 1863 and attacked members of the black community, several of whom were lynched.

CHRISTOPHER STREET

Christopher Street, one of the main thoroughfares of the West Village, leads off from here – the traditional heartland of the city's gay community. Scenes of violence also erupted in 1969, when the **gay community** wasn't as readily accepted as it is now. The violence on this occasion was provoked by the police, who raided the *Stonewall* gay bar, and started arresting its occupants – for the local gay community the latest in a long line of harassment from the police. Spontaneously, word went around to other bars in the area, and before long the *Stonewall* was surrounded, resulting in a siege that lasted the better part of the night and sparked up again the next two nights. The riot ended with several arrests and a number of injured policemen. Though hardly a victory for their rights, it was the first time that gay men had stood up en masse to the persecutions of the city police and, as such, formally inaugurated the gay rights movement. The event is honored by the annual **Gay Pride march** (held on the last Sun in June).

Nowadays, the gay community is much more a part of West Village life; indeed for most the Village would seem odd without it, and from Seventh Avenue down to the Hudson is a tight-knit enclave – focusing on Christopher Street – of bars, restaurants and bookstores used specifically, but not exclusively, by gay men. The scene along the Hudson River itself, along and around West Street and the river piers, is considerably raunchier at night: only the really committed or curious should venture. But on the far east stretch of Christopher Street, things crack off with the accent less on sex and more on excessive, fun camp. Among the more accessible gay bars here are *The Monster* on Sheridan Square itself and *Marie's Crisis Café* on Grove Street (see overleaf).

See Chapter 30, "Gay and lesbian New York,"
for more bar and nightlife options.

Patchin Place

At the eastern end of Christopher Street, Sixth Avenue is met by **Greenwich Avenue**, one of the neighborhood's major shopping streets. Look out for **Patchin Place** (Map 5, C2) – opening onto W 10th Street by the Jefferson Market Courthouse – a tiny mews whose neat, gray row-houses are yet another Village literary landmark, home to the reclusive Djuna Barnes for more than forty years. Barnes' longtime neighbor e. e. cummings used to call her "just to see if she was still alive." Patchin Place was at various times also home to Marlon Brando, John Masefield, Theodore Dreiser, Reed and O'Neill.

Across the street, the gourmet food store **Balducci's** offers pricey yet irresistable delicacies and a respite to your wanderings.

The East Village

Like the Lower East Side, which it abuts, the **East Village**, stretching between Houston and 14th streets and Broadway and Avenue D, was once a refuge of immigrants and solidly working class. It became home to New York's nonconformist intelligentsia in the early part of the twentieth century, and ever since has hosted its share of celebrated artists, politicos and literati. W.H. Auden lived at 77 St Mark's Place, the neighborhood's main artery. In the 1950s, the East Village was the New York haunt of the Beats – Kerouac, Burroughs, Ginsberg, et al – who would get together at Ginsberg's house on E 7th Street for declamatory poetry readings. Later, Andy Warhol debuted the Velvet Underground at the now-defunct *Fillmore East*, which played host to just about every band you've ever heard of – and forgotten. Still kicking, however, is the infamous **CBGB** (Map 5, H5) club on the **Bowery**, where the likes of the Ramones, Talking Heads, Blondie and Patti Smith made their indelible marks in the Seventies.

During the nineties, escalating rents forced many people out, and the East Village is no longer the hotbed of dissidence and creativity it once was. Nevertheless, the area remains one of downtown Manhattan's most vibrant neighborhoods, with boutiques, thrift stores, record shops, bars and restaurants, populated by a mix of old-world

Ukrainians, students, punks, artists and burn-outs feeding continuous energy through the streets 24 hours a day. Despite the vaudevillian circus of **St Mark's Place** and corporate attempts to turn the whole neighborhood into a *Starbucks*, principled resistance to the status quo can still be found.

To reach the East Village, take the #6 train to Astor Place, or the #N or the #R to 8th Street and Broadway.

ST MARK'S PLACE, COOPER SQUARE AND AROUND

It's best to use **St Mark's Place** (aka 8th St) as a base and branch out from here. Start between Second and Third avenues, where independent book and discount record stores struggle for space amid hippy-chic clothiers and head shops in a somewhat contrived atmosphere of MTV cool. **Seventh Street** boasts used-clothing stores as well as several original boutiques, while 6th Street, between First and Second avenues – also known as **"Indian Row"** – offers endless choices of all things curry.

On **Cooper Square** (Map 5, H3), a busy crossroads formed by the intersection of the Bowery, Third Avenue and Lafayette Street, countless teenage style-gods and hipsters from out of town mill around. The square is dominated by the seven-story brownstone mass of **Cooper Union**, erected in 1859 by the wealthy industrialist/inventor Peter Cooper as a college for the poor, and the first New York structure to be hung on a frame of iron girders. It's best known as the place where, in 1860, Abraham Lincoln wowed an audience of top New Yorkers with his so-called "might makes right" speech, in which he criticized the pro-slavery policies of the Southern states and helped propel himself to the White House later that year.

ASTOR PLACE AND AROUND

Just west of Cooper Square lies **Astor Place**, named after John Jacob Astor and, during the 1830s, just before high society moved west to Washington Square, one of the city's most desirable addresses. The old-fashioned kiosk of the Astor Place subway station, bang in the middle of the junction, discreetly remembers Astor on the platforms, its colored mosaic reliefs depicting beavers recalling Astor's first big killings – in the fur trade. The orange-brick Astor Building (housing one of the city's ubiquitous *Starbucks* on its lower level) with arched windows, is where John Jacob Astor III conducted business. It's currently being converted into $1 million loft apartments, despite intense neighborhood resistance – one indication of the speed of East Village gentrification.

Lafayette Street and Broadway

Today, it's hard to believe that Astor Place was once home to wealth and influence. **Lafayette Street** is an undistinguished thoroughfare, steering a grimy route along the edge of the East Village and down into SoHo. All that's left to hint that this might once have been more than a down-at-heel gathering of industrial buildings is **Colonnade Row**, just south of Astor Place. This strip of four 1832 Greek Revival houses with a Corinthian colonnade is now home to the Colonnade Theater. The **Public Theater**, at no. 425 (Map 5, H3), is legendary both as a forerunner of Off-Broadway theater and as the original venue of hit musicals like *Hair*. For years it was run by the director Joseph Papp, who pioneered Shakespeare in the Park. On the ground floor you'll find the celeb-studded performance space/restaurant/bar, *Joe's Pub*, named in his honor.

Head one block west to Broadway and look north: filling

a bend in the street is the lacy marble of **Grace Church** (Map 5, G2), on the corner of 10th Street, which was built and designed in 1846 by James Renwick (of St Patrick's Cathedral fame) in a delicate neo-Gothic style. Dark and aisled, with a flattened, web-vaulted ceiling, it's one of the city's most successful churches – and, in many ways, one of its most secretive escapes.

EAST TOWARD TOMPKINS SQUARE PARK

Go east along 10th Street until you reach **St Mark's-in-the-Bowery** (Map 5, I2), a box-like church on the corner of Second Avenue originally built in 1799 but with a Neoclassical portico added half a century later. In the 1950s, the Beat poets gave readings here, and it remains an important literary rendezvous, with regular readings, dance performances and music recitals, where you can often catch the likes of Lou Reed, Patti Smith and Sonic Youth's Lee Ranaldo do their thing.

Continue along Tenth, past the old redbrick **Tenth Street Russian and Turkish Bath**, whose steam and massage services have been active back into the nineteenth century. Venture further east and you'll catch up with Avenue A, which will lead you south to the once-sketchy, now-safe **Tompkins Square Park** (Map 5, K3) and which buzzes with thrift stores and trendy bars.

ALPHABET CITY

In the late 1980s and early 1990s, the lettered avenues forming Alphabet City formed a notoriously unsafe corner of town, run by drug pushers and gangsters. Most of this was brought to a halt with "Operation Pressure Point," a massive police campaign to clean up the area and make it a place where people would want to live. Crime is way down, the old buildings have been renovated and supplemented by ugly new ones, and today the streets have become the haunt of moneyed twenty-somethings and tourist youth. Go beyond Avenue C and you may get hassled, but – during the day at least – you're unlikely to be mugged, and avenues A, B and C have some of the coolest bars, cafés and stores in the city.

At the *NuYorican Poets Café* at 236 E 3rd St
(☎212/505-8183), you may catch some of the biggest stars
of the spoken-word scene.

COMMUNITY GARDENS

Over the past three decades, East Village residents have begun reclaiming neglected and empty lots of land, turning burnt out rubble into some of the prettiest and most verdant spaces in lower Manhattan and providing a focus for residents in what was traditionally a down-at-heel part of Manhattan. Though the city decreed that these spaces should be used for real estate, several have survived. In summer, there is no nicer way to while away an evening than to relax, eat a sandwich or read a book surrounded by lush trees and carefully planted foliage.

Of particular note is the 6th Street and Avenue B affair, overgrown with wildflowers, vegetables, trees, and roses and home to a spectacular four-story-high sculpture. Other gardens nearby include the very serene 6BC Botanical Garden, on 6th Street between B and C; Miracle Garden on 3rd Street between A and B; El Sol Brillante on 12th Street between A and B; and the Liz Christie Garden, on Houston Street and Second Avenue.

ALPHABET CITY

Chelsea

A low-built, sometimes seedy grid of tenements, rowhouses and warehouses, **Chelsea** lies between 14th and 23rd streets to the west of Broadway. It's here that the neighborhood has become a commercial player, mostly boosted by spillover from SoHo and the Village and the arrival of affluent gay and artistic communities. These days, trendy stores, chichi restaurants and a few notable tourist attractions pepper the scene, along with increasingly upmarket real estate.

If you do come and you want to stay, try to make the **Chelsea Hotel** your home, and don't forget to check out the cutting-edge, top-quality **Chelsea art scene**. Chelsea can be reached by taking the #1 to 18th or 23rd in Broadway, or by taking the #C or #E to 23rd and Eighth Avenue.

EIGHTH, NINTH AND TENTH AVENUES

If Chelsea has a main drag it's **Eighth Avenue**, where the transformation of the neighborhood is most pronounced. This area has a vibrant retail energy to rival the fast-moving traffic in the street. A spate of bars, restaurants, healthfood stores, gyms, bookstores and clothes shops have opened in the last five years, and while it's not exactly a picturesque route, a few minor diversions into the crosstown streets will suffice to restore faith in the architectural beauty of New York.

One of the best places in the city to see modern dance is the Art Deco-style Joyce Theater at 175 Eighth Ave (Map 6, E8), where the accomplished Feld Ballet is in residence.

Just round the corner on **Ninth Avenue**, the redbrick **Chelsea Market** (Map 6, C9), housed in an old Nabisco factory, is an emporium of fresh gourmet produce filling an entire block between 15th and 16th streets.

Further north the cross streets between Ninth and Tenth avenues, specifically 20th, 21st and 22nd streets, constitute the **Chelsea Historic District**. Although the label "district" is a bit grand for an area of three blocks, it boasts a great variety of predominantly Italianate and Greek Revival rowhouses in brick and various shades of brownstone. At the corner of 22nd Street and Tenth Avenue, the nineteenth century meets the modern era in the aluminum-sided **Empire Diner**, built in the 1930s.

Between Ninth and Tenth avenues and 20th and 21st streets lies one of Chelsea's secrets: the **General Theological Seminary** (Map 6, D7). Clement Clarke Moore donated the land to the institute where he formerly taught, and today the harmonious assembly of ivy-clad Gothicisms surrounding a restive green feels like part of an elite college campus. Though the buildings, most of which were completed in the nineteenth century, still house a working seminary, it's possible to explore the park on weekdays and Saturday lunchtimes, as long as you sign in and keep quiet (the entrance is via the modern building on Ninth Avenue). And if you're at all interested in theological history, you should check out their collection of Latin bibles – it's one of the largest in the world.

CHELSEA

THE CHELSEA PIERS

Map 6, A8.

Head west along 23rd Street and brave crossing the West Side Highway to one of Manhattan's most ambitious waterfront projects, **Chelsea Piers** (Ⓦwww.chelseapiers.com), a $100 million, 1.7-million-square-foot development along four Hudson River piers. Opened in 1910, this was the place where the great transatlantic liners would disembark their passengers – the *Titanic* was en route when it sank in 1912. In the 1960s, the piers fell into disuse and decay, but a recent infusion of money has transformed them into a thriving sports complex, with ice rinks and a landscaped golf driving range (see Chapter 34, "Sports and outdoor activities"). Perhaps the best part of the development is its emphasis on **public spaces**, including a waterfront walkway of over a mile, and the pleasant park at the end of Pier 62.

THE CHELSEA ART SCENE

Back over the West Side Highway and along 22nd Street are the galleries and warehouse spaces that house one of New York's most vibrant art scenes. You'll find an especially strong presence along West 22nd Street between Tenth and Eleventh avenues. The Dia Center for the Arts, a Chelsea pioneer, with space here since 1987, has its main exhibition gallery at 548 W 22nd St, featuring a dramatic open-air space on top. See Chapter 33, "Commercial galleries," for more listings.

THE CHELSEA HOTEL

Map 6, F7.

Double back east along 23rd Street, past Eighth Avenue to find one of the neighborhood's major claims to fame – the

Chelsea Hotel at no. 222. The undisputed watering hole of the city's (often hard-up) literati, it has lodged Mark Twain and Tennessee Williams, while Brendan Behan and Dylan Thomas staggered in and out during their New York visits. Thomas Wolfe assembled *You Can't Go Home Again* from thousands of pages of manuscript he had stacked in his room; in 1951, Jack Kerouac, armed with a specially adapted typewriter (and a lot of Benzedrine), typed the first draft of *On the Road* nonstop onto a 120-foot roll of paper. William Burroughs completed *Naked Lunch* and Arthur C. Clarke wrote *2001: A Space Odyssey* while in residence.

In the 1960s, the *Chelsea* entered a wilder phase. Andy Warhol and his doomed protégés Edie Sedgwick and Candy Darling walled up here and made the film *Chelsea Girls* as a twisted homage. Nico, Hendrix, Zappa, Pink Floyd, Patti Smith and various members of the Grateful Dead passed through, and in 1978, Sid Vicious stabbed Nancy Spungen to death in their suite.

With a pedigree like this it's easy to forget the hotel itself, which has a down-at-heel Edwardian grandeur all of its own, and, incidentally is also an affordable place to stay; (see p.179).

NORTH CHELSEA

Heading north above 23rd Street, away from Chelsea's heart, the city's largest **antiques market** (and surrounding junk sales) takes place on weekends in a few open-air parking lots centered around Sixth Avenue and 26th Street (see Chapter 32, "Shops and markets"). The area around 28th Street is Manhattan's **Flower Market**: not really a market as such, but rather a collection of warehouses where potted plants and cut flowers are stored before brightening offices and atriums across the city.

The Garment District

Muscling in between Sixth and Eighth avenues from 34th to 42nd streets, the **Garment District**, which takes in the twin modern monsters of Penn Station and Madison Square Garden, offers little of interest to the casual tourist. The majority of people who cross the Garment District do so for a specific reason – to catch a train or bus, to watch wrestling or basketball, or to work – and it's only a wedge of stores between Herald and Greeley squares that attracts the out-of-towner.

Three-quarters of all the women's and children's clothes in America are made here, though you'd never believe it: outlets are strictly wholesale with no need to woo customers, and the only clues to the industry inside are the racks of clothes shunted around on the street and occasional bins of offcuts that give the area its look of an open-air rummage sale. Every imaginable button, bow, boa and bangle is on display. The Garment District can best be reached by taking the #1, #2, #3, #A, #C and #E to Penn Station or the #N, #R, #Q and #W to Herald Square.

MADISON SQUARE GARDEN AND AROUND

Map 6, E4.

The most prominent landmark of the Garment District is the **Pennsylvania Station and Madison Square Garden complex**, a combined box-and-drum structure that swallows up millions of commuters into its train station belly while housing Knicks basketball and Rangers hockey games. There's nothing memorable about the railway station, which has incurred a fair amount of resentment because the original Penn Station, demolished in 1963 to make way for it, is now hailed as a lost masterpiece, one that brought an air of dignity to the neighborhood. As 1960s architectural historian Vincent Scully lamented following the passing of the original, "through it one entered the city like a god... one now scuttles in like a rat."

Ticket details for the Knicks, Rangers or for other Madison Square Garden events are described on p.339.

A whimsical reminder of the old days is the **Hotel Pennsylvania** on the corner of Seventh Avenue and 33rd Street. A main venue for Glenn Miller and other big swing bands of the 1940s, it keeps the phone number that made it famous – ☏212/736-5000 (under the old system, "PENNsylvania 6-5000") the title of Miller's affectionate hit. It has recently been refurbished, and now bravely claims to offer "New York's newest rooms."

GREELEY AND HERALD SQUARES

One block east of Penn Station, Sixth Avenue collides with Broadway at seedy **Greeley Square**. Perhaps Horace Greeley, founder of the *Tribune* newspaper deserves better than this triangle. Known for his rallying call to the youth of the nineteenth century to explore the continent ("Go West, young man!"), he also supported the rights of women and trade unions, denounced slavery and capital punishment and commissioned a weekly column from Karl Marx. His paper no longer exists and the square named after him is one of those bits of Manhattan that looks ready to disintegrate at any moment.

Herald Square opposite is perhaps best recognized as the one George M. Cohan asked to be remembered to in his 1904 hit song. These days its grimy mediocrity wouldn't inspire anyone to sing about it, and the area's unkempt and seedy nature is tempered only by that American temple of commercialism, **Macy's** (Map 6, G3), the world's largest department store, on the corner below (see Chapter 32, "Shop's and markets," for more).

THE GENERAL POST OFFICE AND AROUND

Map 6, D4.

Immediately west of Penn Station, the **General Post Office** is a 1913 structure that survived from an era when municipal pride was all about making statements – though to say that the Post Office is monumental in the grandest manner still seems to underplay it. The old joke is that it had to be this big to fit in the sonorous inscription above the columns – "Neither snow nor rain nor heat nor gloom of night stays these couriers from the swift completion of their appointed rounds" – a highly incredible claim. In early 2001, Fraport AG, a German architectural firm, won the highly contested and much-delayed contract to create a new Penn Station for Amtrak in the General Post Office building, an edifice that will aim to expiate the destruction of the original structure.

Belying its tawdry reputation as a hideout for the desperate and lonely in the area, the **Port Authority Terminal**

Building (Map 6, E1), at 40th Street and Eighth Avenue, is a spruced-up and efficiently run modern bus station. Greyhound leaves from here, as do regional services out to the boroughs, and (should you arrive in the early hours) it's a remarkably safe place, station staff keeping the winos and weirdos in check. Incidentally, the station holds an exceptional (if expensive) bowling alley, (see p.340 for more details). To the west of Port Authority, at 330 W 42nd St, is the **McGraw-Hill Building** (Map 6, D1), a greeny-blue radiator built in 1972 that architects raved over: "proto-jukebox modern," the critic Scully called it. The lobby should definitely be seen.

Union Square and Gramercy Park

Broadway forms a dividing line between Chelsea to the west and the area that comprises **Union Square** and **Gramercy Park**. It is here, between the great avenues – Third, Park and Fifth – that midtown Manhattan's skyscrapers begin to rise from the low-lying buildings. Before heading on to those jaw-droppers, like the Empire State Building (see p.84), it's certainly worth at least a jaunt around the more genteel parts of these two neighborhoods, which offer some decent architecture themselves, like the **Flatiron Building**. The #N, #R, #Q, #L, #W, #4, #5 and #6 trains all stop at Union Square.

UNION SQUARE

Map 6, J9.

Once the elegant center of the city's theatrical and shopping scene, **Union Square**, where Broadway, Fourth and Park avenues meet between 14th and 18th streets, invites you to stroll its paths, feed the squirrels and gaze at its array

THE FARMERS' MARKET

On Mondays, Wednesdays, Fridays and Saturdays from 7am until 6pm, the park plays host to the city's best and most popular greenmarket on its northern edge. Farmers and other food producers from upstate New York, Long Island, New Jersey and as far as Pennsylvania Dutch country sell fresh fruit and vegetables, baked goods, cheeses, eggs, meats, fish, plants and flowers. The quality of the produce is generally very high and buying picnic fodder from the market to concoct a feast is one of the finest things you can do here on a spring or summer's day.

of statuary. Unfortunately, the proliferation of chain cafés and superstores around make it impossible to forget you are on the fringes of the most commercial part of New York, but the park is still a welcome respite from the crazed taxi drivers and rushed pedestrians just south. Following September 11, 2001, Union Square was the scene of candlelight vigils attended by thousands.

Irving Place and around

Just one block east of Union Square, the six graceful blocks of **Irving Place** (named for *The Legend of Sleepy Hollow* author Washington Irving, who never actually lived here) lead north toward Gramercy Park. Before reaching the park, digress on 20th Street, where, at no. 28, you will find **Theodore Roosevelt's birthplace** (Map 6, I8; Wed–Sun 9am–5pm; $2; ☎212/260-1616), or at least a reconstruction of it: in 1923, the house was rebuilt as it would have been when Roosevelt was born there in 1858. The rather somber mansion contains many original furnishings, some of Teddy's hunting trophies and a small gallery documenting the president's life, viewable on an obligatory guided tour.

GRAMERCY PARK

Map 6, K7.

Manhattan's clutter suddenly breaks into the ordered open space of **Gramercy Park**, a former swamp between 21st and 22nd streets that divides Irving Place and Lexington Avenue. It is one of the city's prettiest squares. Its center is beautifully planted and completely empty for much of the day, for it is the city's last private park and the only people who can gain access are those rich or fortunate enough to live here. Famous past key holders have included Mark Twain and Julia Roberts, never mind all those Kennedys and Roosevelts.

Have a walk around the square to get a look at the many early-nineteenth century townhouses. **The Players** at 16 Gramercy Park S was created in 1888 when actor Edwin Booth turned his home into a private club for play and socializing, at a time when theater types were not accepted into regular society. Members have included Irving Berlin, Frank Sinatra and Winston Churchill – women were not admitted until 1989.

Next door, at no. 17, the **School of Visual Arts** occupies the former home of Joseph Pulitzer, while at the northeastern corner of the square, no. 38, is the mock Tudor building in which John Steinbeck, then a struggling reporter, lived between 1925 and 1926. At 52 Gramercy Park N stands the imposing 1920s bulk of the old-fashioned **Gramercy Park Hotel**, whose early elite residents included Mary McCarthy, a very young John F. Kennedy and Humphrey Bogart with first wife, Mayo Methot. Lining Gramercy Park West is a splendid row of brick Greek Revival townhouses from the 1840s.

GRAMERCY PARK

Madison Square and the Flatiron Building

Map 6, I7. #N or #R to 23rd Street.

Northwest of Gramercy Park, where Broadway and Fifth Avenue meet, lies **Madison Square**. Though a maelstrom of cars and cabs, buses and dodging pedestrians all around, the grandiose architectural quality of the surrounding buildings and the newly renovated park-space in the square's center lend it a neat seclusion that Union Square has long since lost. Rumor has it that baseball as we know it was invented here in 1845, when the Knickerbocker Base Ball Club played the first game to adhere to Alexander Cartwright's rules.

The lofty, elegant yet decidedly anorexic **Flatiron Building** (originally the Fuller Construction Company, later renamed in honor of its distinctive shape), set on a triangular plot of land on the square's southern side, is one of the city's most well-known buildings. It's now hard to believe that this was the city's first true skyscraper, hung on a steel frame in 1902, its full twenty stories dwarfing all the other structures around.

North of Madison Square

Lexington Avenue begins its long journey north at Gramercy Park: if you're heading uptown on the East Side from here, you'll pass the lumbering **69th Regiment Armory** at 25th Street, the site of the celebrated Armory Show of 1913, which brought modern art to New York. It is now a venue for antiques shows and art fairs. Between 27th and 30th streets, one of Manhattan's most condensed ethnic enclaves, **Little India**, aligns Lexington. Blink, and you might miss this altogether: most of New York's 180,000 Indians live in Queens, yet there's still a sizeable handful of restaurants and fast-food places – slightly outnumbered by those down on E 6th Street – and a pocket of spice shops and fabric stores.

The Empire State Building and Murray Hill

The East 30s are mostly celebrated for what is likely Manhattan's most elegant skyscraper, the **Empire State Building**, a must on almost everyone's New York itinerary. The blocks that surround it are uneventful, as is the neighborhood to the east, **Murray Hill**, a tenuously tagged residential area that has little to recommend it besides the **Morgan Library**.

THE EMPIRE STATE BUILDING

Map 6, H4. Daily 9.30am–midnight, last trip 11.30pm; $9, $4 for under 12s; $7 for seniors, free for children under 5; combined tickets for New York Skyride and the Observatory $17, $10 for under 12s; ☎212/736-3100, ⓦwww.esbnyc.com.

With the destruction of the World Trade Center, the **Empire State Building**, is once again the city's tallest skyscraper. Nestling in a whole city block between 33rd and 34th Streets, it is easily the most potent and evocative symbol of New York, and has been since its completion in 1931. Its 103 stories and 1454 feet – toe to TV mast – rank the Empire State Building behind only the Sears Tower in Chicago and the Petronas Towers in Kuala Lumpur, Malaysia, but its height is deceptive, rising in stately tiers with steady panache.

Standing on Fifth Avenue below, it's easy to walk right by without even realizing that it's there; only the crowds serve as an indicator of what stretches above. Skip the eight-minute simulated flight **New York Skyride** (daily 10am–10pm; $13.50, $10.50 kids and seniors; ☎212/299-4922 or 1-888/SKY-RIDE, ⊛www.skyride.com), which soars above skyscrapers and among other New York landmarks, but will leave the weak-hearted merely dizzy and the strong-willed wondering why they wasted their cash. Better to save your pennies for the ascent to the top of the world.

- -

Because the 102nd-floor Observatory is closed on weekends during the summer, be sure to go during the week if you want to reach the very top.

- -

The first elevators, alarmingly old and rickety, take you to the 86th floor, summit of the building before the radio and TV mast was added. The views from the outside walkways here are as stunning as you'd expect. If you're feeling brave – and can stand the wait for the tight squeeze into the single elevator – you can go up to the building's last reachable zenith, a small cylinder at the foot of the TV mast that was added as part of a harebrained scheme to erect a mooring post for airships.

THE EMPIRE STATE BUILDING

SKYSCRAPERS

Manhattan is one of the best places in the world in which to view skyscrapers, its puckered, almost medieval skyline of towers the city's most familiar and striking image. In fact, there are only two main clusters of skyscrapers, but they set the tone for the city – the Financial District, where the combination of narrow streets and tall buildings forms slender, lightless canyons, and midtown Manhattan, where the big skyscrapers, flanking the wide central avenues between the 30s and the 60s, have long competed for height and prestige.

New York's first skyscraper was Madison Square's 1902 Flatiron Building (see p.82), so called because of the obvious way its triangular shape made the most of the new iron-frame technique of construction that had made such structures possible. In 1913, the sixty-story Woolworth Building on Broadway (see p.37) gave New York the world's tallest building, and the city later produced such landmarks as the Chrysler Building (p.96), the Empire State Building, and the recently destroyed World Trade Center (p.28).

Styles have changed over the years, perhaps most influenced by the stringency of the city's zoning laws, which, early in the twentieth century, placed restrictions on the types of building permitted. At first skyscrapers were sheer vertical monsters, maximizing the floor space possible from any given site with no regard to how this affected neighboring buildings. City authorities later invented the concept of "air rights," limiting how high a building could be before it had to be set back from its base. This constraint forced skyscrapers to be designed in a series of steps – a law most elegantly adhered to by the Empire State Building, which has no less than ten steps in all – and forms a pattern you will see repeated all over the city.

THE EMPIRE STATE BUILDING

THE MORGAN LIBRARY

Map 6, J3. 29 E 36th St (at Madison Ave); Tues–Thurs 10.30am–5pm, Fri 10.30am–8pm, Sat 10.30am–6pm, Sun noon–6pm; suggested donation $8, $6 students and seniors, free for children under 12; ℡212/685-0610, ⓦwww.morganlibrary.org.

When Madison Avenue was on a par with Fifth as the place to live, Murray Hill came to be dominated by the Morgan family, the crusty old financier J.P. and his offspring, who at one time owned a clutch of property here. The **Morgan Library** was built for the old crustacean in 1906. A gracious Italian Renaissance-style mansion, it houses one of New York's best small museums.

Originating with Morgan's own impressive collection of manuscripts, the museum has grown to include nearly 10,000 drawings and prints (including works by Rembrandt da Vinci, Degas and Dürer), and an extraordinary array of historical, literary and musical manuscripts. The exhibits change so frequently that it's impossible to catalog what visitors will see – but a copy of the 1455 Gutenberg Bible (the museum owns a magnificent three out of the eleven surviving manuscripts) is always on display. There are also original scores by Mahler, Beethoven, Schubert and Gilbert and Sullivan; the only complete copy of Thomas Malory's *Morte d'Arthur*; and letters from the likes of Vasari, Mozart and George Washington, and the literary manuscripts of Dickens, Jane Austen and Thoreau.

Fifth Avenue

F or the last two centuries, a **Fifth Avenue** address has signified social position, prosperity and respectability. Whether around its lower reaches on Washington Square or far uptown around the Harlem River, the street has been the home to Manhattan's finest mansions, hotels, churches and stores. Between 42nd and 59th streets, Fifth Avenue has always drawn crowds – particularly during Christmas, when department-store windows are filled with elaborate displays – to gaze at what has become the automatic image of wealth and opulence, or to visit **Rockefeller Center**, **Radio City Music Hall** or the **Museum of Modern Art**.

Fifth Avenue is home to most of the city's parades
and processions, many of which are detailed in
Chapter 31, "Parades and festivals."

ROCKEFELLER CENTER

Map 7, H8. #E or #F train to 5th Ave–53rd St.

Filling the whole block west of Fifth Avenue between 49th and 50th streets, **Rockefeller Center** was built between 1932 and 1940 by John D. Rockefeller, son of the oil mag-

nate. It's one of the finest pieces of urban planning anywhere – office space with cafés, a theater, underground
concourses and rooftop gardens work together with a rare
intelligence and grace.

You're lured into the center from Fifth Avenue down the
gentle slope of the **Channel Gardens** to the **GE
Building**, focus of the center. Rising 850 feet, this monumental structure is softened by symmetrical setbacks. At its
foot, the **Lower Plaza** holds a sunken restaurant and bar in
the summer months, linked visually to the downward flow
of the building by Paul Manship's sparkling *Prometheus*
sculpture; in winter it becomes an ice rink, giving skaters a
chance to show off their skills to passing shoppers. Inside,
the GE Building's lobby are José Maria Sert's murals,
American Progress and *Time*, which are faded but eagerly in
tune with the 1930s Deco ambience.

NBC STUDIOS

Among the many office ensembles in the GE Building is NBC
Studios, home of the network's long-established late-night
comedy show *Saturday Night Live*, which simply refuses to
die, among other programs. Get a backstage look at NBC's
studios on the NBC Experience Tour (Mon–Sat 8.30am–
5.30pm, Sun 9.30am–4.30pm; $17.50, seniors and children
$15, under 6 not allowed on tour; ☎212/664-3700). Tours
leave from the NBC Experience Store on 49th Street between
Fifth and Sixth avenues.

For an early-morning TV thrill, you can gawk at NBC's *Today
Show*, which broadcasts live from 7am to 9am weekday morn-
ings from glass-enclosed studios in the new NBC News
Building on the southwest corner of 49th and Rockefeller
Plaza.

ROCKEFELLER CENTER

Radio City Music Hall

Map 7, G7. Tours daily 10am–6pm; $15, children under 12 $9; ⓣ212/631-4345, ⓦwww.radiocity.com.

Just northwest of Rockefeller Center, at Sixth Avenue and 50th Street, is **Radio City Music Hall**, an Art Deco jewel box that represents the last word in 1930s luxury. The staircase is regally resplendent with the world's largest chandeliers and the huge auditorium looks like an extravagant scalloped shell or a vast sunset. Believe it or not, Radio City was nearly demolished in 1970, and the outcry this caused resulted in its being designated a National Landmark.

St Patrick's Cathedral

Map 7, H7. #E or #F train to 5th Ave–53rd St.

Between 50th and 51st streets, bone-white **St Patrick's Cathedral** sits among the glitz like a misplaced bit of moral imperative, and seems the result of a painstaking academic tour of the Gothic cathedrals of Europe: faultless in detail, lifeless in spirit. In the peaceful **Lady Chapel** at the back of the cathedral, however, the graceful, simple, altar captures the spirituality that its big sister lacks. Nevertheless, St Patrick's is an essential part of the midtown landscape, and perhaps the most important Catholic church in America. The Gothic details are perfect and the cathedral is certainly striking – and made all the more so by the backing of the sunglass-black **Olympic Tower**. Across the street, at 611 Fifth Ave, are the striped awnings of **Saks Fifth Avenue**, one of the last of New York's premier department stores.

THE MUSEUM OF MODERN ART

Map 7, G7. 11 W 53rd St (between 5th and 6th aves) Sat–Tues & Thurs 10.30am–6pm, Fri 10.30am–8.30pm, closed Wed; $9.50, students $6.50, Fri 4.30–8.15pm pay what you wish; recorded audio tour $4. Free gallery talks held Mon, Tues, Thurs, Sat & Sun 1pm & 3pm; Fri 3pm, 6pm & 7pm; ☏212/708-9480, ⊛www.moma.org. #E or #F train to 5th Ave–53rd St.

A major renovation is currently underway at **MoMA** (as the museum is usually called), starting in the summer of 2002 and ending by summer 2005, in time for the museum's 75th anniversary. The expansion will allow MoMA to display more of its permanent collection, as well as mount even larger temporary exhibits. During the reconstruction, the museum will move to Long Island City in Queens, in a spot known as **MoMAQNS**, 45-20 33rd St at Queens Blvd (subway #7 to 33rd St stop; ☏212/708-9400; inquire what's on view when).

The collection is indeed impressive, offering one of the finest and most complete accounts of late nineteenth- and twentieth-century art you're likely to find, with a permanent collection of over 100,000 paintings, sculptures, drawings, prints, photographs, architectural models and design objects, as well as a world-class film archive. Painting highlights include Post-Impressionist masterworks, such as **Cézanne**'s *Bather*, **Monet**'s *Water Lilies* and paintings by **Gauguin**, **Seurat** and **Van Gogh**, including his celebrated *Starry Night*. Cubism is represented particularly by **Derain**, **Braque** and **Picasso** whose *Demoiselles d'Avignon*, a jagged, sharp and then revolutionary clash of tones and planes, is held to be the embodiment of Cubist principles.

The late-modern and contemporary painting collection has a more American slant, with paintings such as **Wyeth**'s *Christina's World*, and works by **Hopper**, including *House by the Railroad* and *New York Movie*, potent and atmospheric pieces that give a bleak account of 1930s and 1940s American life. Equally notable are more abstract pieces, such as **Gorky**'s Miró-like doodles, and the anguished scream of **Bacon**'s *No. 7 from 8 Studies for a Portrait*.

THE MUSEUM OF MODERN ART

●

Some of the biggest draws are the paintings from the New York School – large-scale canvases meant to be viewed from a distance. The finest examples are the paintings of **Pollock** and **de Kooning** – wild and, in Pollock's case, textured patterns with no clear beginning or end. MoMA also features several well-known examples of Pop Art, including **Warhol**'s *Gold Marilyn Monroe* and the familiar *Campbell Soup* canvas.

Museum of Television & Radio

Map 7, H7. 25 W 52nd St (between 5th and 6th aves) Tues, Wed, Fri–Sun noon–6pm, Thurs noon–8pm; $6, students $4, under 13 $3; ☎212/621-6600, ⓦwww.mtr.org. #E or #F train to 5th Ave–53rd St.

This museum holds an archive of 100,000 mostly American TV shows, radio broadcasts and commercials, any of which are available for your personal viewing. The museum's excellent computerized reference system allows you to research news, public affairs, documentaries, sporting events, comedies, advertisements and other aural and visual selections. The MTR becomes unbearably crowded on weekends, so plan to visit at other times.

NORTH TOWARD CENTRAL PARK

Here comes the glitz: **Cartier**, **Gucci** and **Tiffany and Co.** are among many gilt-edged storefronts that will jump out at you between 53rd and 59th streets. If you're keen to do more than merely window-shop, Tiffany's, at no. 727, is worth a perusal, its soothing green marble and weathered wood interior best described by Truman Capote's fictional Holly Golightly: "It calms me down right away . . . nothing very bad could happen to you there."

Topping all of this off is **F.A.O. Schwarz**, a block north at no. 767, a colossal emporium of children's toys. Fight the kids off and there's some great stuff to play with – once again, the best (and biggest, including gas-powered cars, life-sized stuffed animals and Lego creations) that money can buy. Across 58th Street, Fifth Avenue broadens into **Grand Army Plaza** and the fringes of Central Park. Looming impressively on the plaza is, aptly enough, the copper-edged **Plaza Hotel** (Map 7, H6), recognizable from its many film appearances. Wander around to soak in the (slightly faded) gilt-and-brocade grandeur; the snazzy **Oak Room** bar, is worth a snoop too.

42nd Street

Though its western side holds few attractions, east of Fifth Avenue **42nd Street** is home to some of the city's most distinctive buildings, ranging from great Beaux Arts palaces like **Grand Central Station**, to white elephants like the **United Nations Building** at the street's eastern end. In between lie gems such as that definitive New York icon, the **Chrysler Building**. Surrounded by superb architecture and breathtaking views down such great avenues as Fifth, Madison, Lexington and Third, this section of New York is one of the most distinctive parts of the city.

BRYANT PARK AND THE NEW YORK PUBLIC LIBRARY

Map 6, H1. #7, #B, #D, #F or #V to 42nd Street and Fifth Avenue.

One block east of **Times Square** (see p.104), **Bryant Park**, Sixth Avenue between 40th and 42nd streets, is a lush grassy square block filled with slender trees and inviting green chairs. As well as free jazz in summer months and several outdoor eateries, there's also a rather aggressive happy hour singles scene at the *Bryant Park Café*. Just across from the park, at 40 W 40th St, the Radiator Building, designed in 1924 for the American Radiator Company, commands attention for its Gothic tower and polished black-granite facade.

In summer, free outdoor movies are shown in Bryant Park on Monday evenings (℗212/768-4242, ⓦwww.bryantpark.org).

Bryant Park forms the backyard of the **New York Public Library** (Mon & Thurs–Sat 10am–6pm, Wed 11am–7.30pm; ℗212/870-1630, ⓦwww.nypl.org), whose Fifth Avenue entrance is guarded by two majestic lion statues. The library boasts 88 miles of books, which are stored on eight levels of stacks – a collection that makes this the largest research library with a circulation system in the world. Tours of the building are available (Mon–Sat 11am & 2pm; free), the highlight of which is the large coffered **Reading Room**.

GRAND CENTRAL STATION

Map 7, I9. #7, #4, #5, #6 or #S train to Grand Central Station.

A masterful piece of urban planning, the 1903 **Grand Central Station**, between Madison and Lexington avenues, mainly serves commuters speeding out no further than Connecticut or Westchester County. A Beaux Arts monument to the power of the railways, Grand Central was the symbolic gateway in the nineteenth century to an undiscovered continent. Today, the most spectacular aspect of the building is its size. Its main concourse is one of the world's finest and most imposing open spaces, 470 feet long and 150 feet high, the barrel-vaulted ceiling speckled like a Baroque church with a painted representation of the winter night sky. Stand in the middle and you realize Grand Central represents a time when stations were humbling preludes to great cities.

Take an excellent free tour of Grand Central run by the
Municipal Arts Society (see p.16).

THE CHRYSLER BUILDING

Map 7, J9. #7, #4, #5, #6 or #S train to Grand Central Station.

Occupying the block between Lexington and Third avenues, the **Chrysler Building** dates from an era (1930, though renovated in 2000 by Philip Johnson) when architects carried off prestige with grace and style. The building was for a fleeting moment the world's tallest – until it was surpassed by the Empire State Building in 1931 – and, since the rediscovery of Art Deco a decade or so ago, has become easily Manhattan's best loved. Its car-motif friezes, a spire resembling a car radiator grill and hood-ornament gargoyles jutting from the setbacks all recall the golden age of motoring. The **lobby**, once a car showroom, has opulently inlaid elevators, walls covered in African marble and on the ceiling a realistic, if rather faded, study showing airplanes, machines and the brawny builders who worked on the tower, which, unfortunately, is not open to the public.

East of the Chrysler Building

Flanking Lexington Avenue on the south side of 42nd Street are two more buildings that repay consideration. The **Chanin Building** on the west side is another Art Deco monument, cut with terra-cotta carvings of leaves, tendrils and sea creatures. More interestingly, the design on the outside of the weighty **Mobil Building** (Map 6, K1) across the street is deliberately folded in such a manner that it can be cleaned automatically by the movement of the wind.

East of here is the somber yet elegant former **Daily**

News Building (Map 6, L1), whose stone facade fronts a surprising Deco interior. The most impressive remnant of the original 1923 decor is a large globe encased in a lighted circular frame (with updated geography), made famous by the film *Superman*, in which the Daily News Building housed the *Daily Planet*.

Further east still, 42nd Street grows more tranquil. Between Second and First avenues, the **Ford Foundation Building** provides one of the most peaceful spaces of all. Built in 1967, this was the first of the atriums that are now commonplace across Manhattan, and it is certainly the most lush. It's a giant greenhouse, with two walls of offices visible through the windows. 42nd Street is no more than a murmur outside.

At the east end of 42nd Street, steps lead up to the 1925 ensemble of **Tudor City**, which rises behind a tree-filled parklet. With its coats of arms, leaded glass and neat neighborhood shops, it is the very picture of self-contained residential respectability, and an official historic district. Trip down the steps from here and you're plum opposite the **United Nations** (see p.102).

Midtown East

If there is a stretch that is immediately and unmistakably New York, it is the area that runs east of Fifth Avenue in the 40s and 50s. The great avenues of **Madison**, **Park**, **Lexington** and **Third** reach their richest heights as the skyscrapers line up in neck-cricking vistas, the streets choke with yellow cabs and office workers, and Con Edison vents belch steam from old heating systems. More than anything else, buildings define this part of town. Many house anonymous corporations and supply excitement to a skyline that was largely formed during the 1960s build-'em-high glass-box bonanza. Others, like the **Sony Building** and the **Citicorp Center**, don't play that game; and enough remains from the pre-box days to maintain variety. The commercial properties largely disappear as midtown slinks toward the East River, giving way to the quietly affluent residential **Beekman** and **Sutton places** as well as the unappealing mass of the **United Nations complex**, which anchors itself like a barnacle to the eastern edge of the city.

MADISON AVENUE

Madison Avenue shadows Fifth, offering some of its sweep but less excitement. It is a little removed from its 1960s and 70s prime, when it was internationally recognized as the epicenter of the advertising industry. A few good stores – notably those specializing in men's haberdashery, shoes and cigars – can be found here.

Madison's most interesting buildings come in a four-block strip above 53rd Street. The **Sony Building** (Map 7, H6), between 55th and 56th streets, followed the postmodernist theory of eclectic borrowing from historical styles: a modernist skyscraper sandwiched between a Chippendale top and a Renaissance base. The building has its fans, but in popular opinion the tower doesn't work, and it's unlikely to stand the test of time. The first floor is well worth ducking into to soak in the brute grandeur, though.

The **IBM Building**, next door at 590 Madison Ave, has a far more inviting plaza, the calm glass-enclosed atrium and tropical foliage making for a far less ponderous experience. Across 57th Street, as the first of Madison's clothes stores appear, the **Fuller Building** is worth catching – black-and-white Art Deco, with a fine entrance and tiled floor. Cut east down 57th Street to find the **Four Seasons Hotel**, notable for its I.M. Pei-designed foyer and lobby, ostentatious in its sweeping marble.

PARK AVENUE

"Where wealth is so swollen that it almost bursts," wrote Collinson Owen of **Park Avenue** in 1929, and things aren't much changed: corporate headquarters jostle for prominence in a triumphal procession to capitalism, pushed apart by Park's broad avenue that was built to support elevated rail tracks. Whatever your feelings, it's one of the city's most awesome sights. Looking south from anywhere above 42nd St, everything progresses to the high altar of the New York Central Building (now renamed the **Helmsley Building**, Map 7, I8), a delicate, energetic construction with a lewdly excessive Rococo lobby.

Despite Park Avenue's power, an individual look at most of the skyscrapers reveals the familiar glass box, and the first few buildings to stand out do so exactly because that's what they're not. Wherever you placed the solid **Waldorf-Astoria Hotel** (Map 7, I8), it would hold its own, a resplendent statement of Art Deco elegance. Duck inside to stroll through the sweeping marble and hushed plushness. Crouching across the street, **St Bartholomew's Church** is a low-slung Byzantine hybrid that by contrast adds immeasurably to the street scene, giving the lumbering skyscrapers a much-needed sense of scale. The spiky-topped **General Electric Building** (Map 7, I7) behind seems like a wild extension of the church, its slender, carved red-marble shaft rising to a meshed crown of abstract sparks and lightning strokes that symbolizes the radio waves used by its original owner, RCA. The lobby with its vaulted ceiling (entrance at 570 Lexington Ave) is yet another Art Deco delight.

The Seagram Building

Map 7, I7. #E or #V to Lexington Ave–53rd St.

Among all this it's difficult at first to see the originality of the **Seagram Building** between 52nd and 53rd streets. Designed by Mies van der Rohe and built in 1958, this was the seminal curtain-wall skyscraper, the floors supported internally rather than by the building's walls, allowing a skin of smoky glass and whiskey-bronze metal, now weathered to a dull black. It was the supreme example of modernist reason, deceptively simple and cleverly detailed, and its opening was met with a wave of approval. The **plaza**, an open forecourt designed to set the building apart from its neighbors and display it to advantage, was such a success as a public space that the city revised the zoning laws to encourage other high-rise builders to supply plazas.

Across Park Avenue between 53rd and 54th, **Lever**

PARK AVENUE

●

House (Map 7, I7) was the building that set the modernist ball rolling on Park Avenue in 1952. Then, the two right-angled slabs that form a steel and glass bookend seemed revolutionary compared to the traditional buildings that surrounded it.

LEXINGTON AVENUE AND CITICORP CENTER

Lexington Avenue is always active, especially around the mid-40s, where commuters swarm around Grand Central Station and the **post office** on the corner of 50th Street. Just as the Chrysler Building dominates the lower stretches of the avenue, the chisel-topped **Citicorp Center** (Map 7, J7) anchors and governs the 50s. Finished in 1979, the building, now one of New York's most conspicuous landmarks, looks as if it is sheathed in shiny graph-paper, while the slope of tower resembles a linear representation of a mathematical equation. The slanted roof was designed to house solar panels and provide power, but the idea was ahead of the day's technology and Citicorp had to content itself with adopting the distinctive top as a corporate logo. The atrium of stores known as **The Market** is pleasant enough, with some enticing food options.

THIRD, SECOND AND FIRST AVENUES

Citicorp provided a spur for the development of **Third Avenue**, though things really took off when the old elevated railway that ran here was dismantled in 1955. Until then Third had been a strip of earthy bars and run-down tenements, in effect a border to the more salubrious midtown district. After Citicorp went up, other office buildings sprouted, revitalizing the flagging fortunes of midtown Manhattan in the late 1970s. The best section is between 44th and 50th streets – look out for the sheer marble monument of the **Wang Building** between 48th and 49th, whose cross-patterns reveal the structure within.

All this office space hasn't totally removed interest from the street, but most life, especially at night, seems to have shifted across to **Second Avenue** – on the whole lower, quieter, more residential and with any number of bars to crawl between. The area from Third to the East River in the upper 40s is known as **Turtle Bay**, and there's a scattering of brownstones alongside chirpier shops and industry that disappear as you head north.

First Avenue has a certain raggy looseness that's a relief after the concrete claustrophobia of midtown, and **Beekman Place**, 49th to 51st streets between First Avenue and the East River, is quieter still, a beguiling enclave of garbled styles. Similar, though not quite as intimate, is **Sutton Place**, a long stretch running from 53rd to 59th between First and the river. Originally built for the lordly Morgans and Vanderbilts in 1875, Sutton increases in elegance as you move north and, for today's crème de la crème, **Riverview Terrace** (Map 7, L5) is a (very) private enclave of five brownstones.

THE UNITED NATIONS

Map 7, L9. First Avenue at 46th Street; one-hour tours leave every 20min from General Assembly Lobby, 9.15am–4.45pm; $7.50, $4.50 students; ☎212/963-7539. #4, #5, #6, #7 or #S train to Grand Central Station.

Some see the United Nations complex as one of the major sights of New York; others, usually those who've been there, are not so complimentary. Whatever the symbolism of the UN, there can be few buildings that are quite so dull to walk around. What's more, as if to rationalize years of UN impotence in war and hunger zones worldwide, the (obligatory) guided tours emphasize that the UN's main purpose is to promote dialogue and awareness rather than enforcement.

For the determined, the complex consists of three main buildings – the thin glass-curtained slab of the Secretariat, the sweeping curve of the General Assembly Building and, just between, the low-rise connecting Conference Wing. Tours take in the main conference chambers of the UN and its constituent parts, the foremost of which is the General Assembly Chamber itself.

THE UNITED NATIONS

Midtown West

The area west of Fifth Avenue in midtown Manhattan takes **Times Square** as its center, an exploded version of the East Side's more tight-lipped monuments to capitalism. Though in some ways it cannot compete with the richer avenues and enclaves to the east, the area north of the once "naughty, bawdy 42nd Street," with its **Theater District** and **Restaurant Row**, is well worth exploring. Most of Times Square's pornography and crime is gone, replaced in part by products of Disney imagination, modern high-rise office buildings and hotels that threaten to spoil the square's historic greasy appeal. The further west you head, the fewer tourist attractions you'll find, with the notable exception of a retired US aircraft carrier that encompasses the massive **Intrepid Sea-Air-Space Museum**.

TIMES SQUARE

Times Square occupies the streets between 42nd and 47th, where Seventh Avenue and Broadway collide. This is the center of the Theater District, where the pulsating neon suggests a heart for the city itself. Since the major cleanup launched by the city and by business interests like Disney, the ambience here has changed dramatically. Traditionally a melting pot of debauch, depravity and fun, the area became increasingly edgy, a place where out-of-towners supplied easy pickings for petty criminals, drug dealers and prostitutes. Most of the peep shows and sex shops have been pushed out, and Times Square is now a largely sanitized universe of consumption. The neon signs seem to multiply at the same rate as coffee bars, and Disney rules the roost on the stretch of 42nd between Seventh and Eighth avenues, home to the remaining palatial Broadway "houses" and movie palaces.

Times Tower at the Square's southernmost edge was originally headquarters of the *New York Times*, the city's (and America's) most respected newspaper. It's here that the alcohol-fueled masses gather for New Year's Eve, to witness the giant sparkling ball drop from the top of the Tower. The newspaper itself has long since moved around a corner to a handsome building with globe lamps on 43rd Street; walk past in the early hours of the morning and you'll see the newspaper coming hot off the presses.

Dotted around Times Square are most of New York's great **theaters**, such as the majestic 1927 clock-and-globe-topped **Paramount Building** at 1501 Broadway, between 43rd and 44th streets. The **New Amsterdam** and the **New Victory**, both on 42nd Street between Seventh and Eighth avenues, have been refurbished to their original splendor, one of the truly welcome results of the massive changes here. The **Lyceum**, at 149 W 45th St, has its original facade, while the **Shubert** Theater, which hosted *A Chorus Line* during its twenty-odd-year run, occupies its own small space at 225 W 44th St. At 432 W 44th St is the **Actors' Studio**, where Lee Strasberg, America's leading proponent of Stanislavski's method-acting technique, taught his students. Among the oldest is the **Belasco**, on 111 W 44th St, between Sixth and Seventh avenues, which was also the first of Broadway's theaters to incorporate machinery into its stagings.

See Chapter 29, "The performing arts
and film," for theater listings.

Duffy Square is the northernmost island in the heart of
Times Square and offers an excellent panoramic view of the
square's lights, megahotels, theme stores and theme restaurants metastasizing daily. The nifty canvas-and-frame stand
of the **TKTS booth**, modest in comparison, sells half-
price, same-day tickets for Broadway shows. A lifelike statue
of Broadway's doyen **George M. Cohan** looks on –
though if you've ever seen the film *Yankee Doodle Dandy* it's
impossible to think of him as other than a swaggering
Jimmy Cagney.

HELL'S KITCHEN

To the west of Times Square lies **Hell's Kitchen**, an area
centered on the engaging slash of restaurants, bars and ethnic delis of **Ninth Avenue**. Extending down to the
Garment District and up to the low 50s, this was once one
of New York's most violent and lurid neighborhoods, made
up of soap and glue factories, slaughterhouses and the like.
Gangs roamed the streets, and though their rule ended in
1910 after a major police counteroffensive, the area
remained a bit dangerous until fairly recently, when musicians and Broadway types began moving in.

Head to it from Eighth Avenue (which now houses the
porn businesses expelled from the square) down 46th Street
– the so-called **Restaurant Row** that is the area's preferred
haunt for pre- and post-theater dining. Here you can begin
to detect a more pastoral feel, which only increases on
many of the side streets around Ninth and Tenth avenues.

HELL'S KITCHEN

Intrepid Sea-Air-Space Museum

Map 7, A8. April–Sept Mon–Fri 10am–5pm, Sat–Sun 10am–7pm; Oct 1–March 31 Tues–Sun 10am–5pm, last admission 1 hour prior to closing; $12, children 12–17 $9, children 6–11 $6, children 3–5 $2, under 2 years free; ☎212/245-0072, ⊛www.intrepidmuseum.org. Continue west down 46th Street until you hit the Hudson River at Pier 86 and you'll spot the grey hulk of the **Intrepid Sea-Air-Space Museum**. This old aircraft carrier has a long and distinguished history, including hauling capsules out of the ocean following *Mercury* and *Gemini* space missions. It holds an array of modern and vintage air and sea craft including the A-12 Blackbird, the world's fastest spy plane, and the USS *Growler*, a guided missile submarine.

North of Times Square

Heading north from Times Square, the **West 50s** between Sixth and Eighth avenues are emphatically tourist territory. Edged by Central Park in the north and the Theater District to the south, and with Fifth Avenue and Rockefeller Center in easy striking distance, the area has been invaded by overpriced restaurants and cheapo souvenir stores.

One sight worth searching out, however, is the **Equitable Center** (Map 7, F7). The building itself, at 757 Seventh Ave, is dapper if not a little self-important, with Roy Lichtenstein's 68-foot *Mural with Blue Brush Stroke* poking you in the eye as you enter.

SIXTH AVENUE

Sixth Avenue is properly named **Avenue of the Americas**, though no New Yorker ever calls it this: the

SIXTH AVENUE

DIAMOND ROW

One of the best things about New York City is the small hidden pockets abruptly discovered when you least expect them. W 47th Street between Fifth and Sixth avenues is a perfect example: Diamond Row is a strip of shops chock-full of gems and jewelry, largely managed by Hassidic Jews who seem only to exist in the confines of the street. Maybe they are what gives the street its workaday feel – Diamond Row seems more like the Garment District than Fifth Avenue, and the conversations you overhear on the street or in the nearby delicatessens are memorably Jewish.

only manifestation of the tag are lamppost flags of Central and South American countries. If nothing else, Sixth's distinction is its width, a result of the elevated railway that once ran along here, now replaced by the Sixth Avenue subway. In its day the Sixth Avenue "El" marked the border between respectability to the east and shadier areas to the west, and in a way it's still a dividing line separating the glamorous strips of Fifth, Madison and Park avenues from the brasher western districts. At 1133 Sixth Ave (at 43rd St) is the **International Center of Photography** (Map 7, G9; Tues–Thurs 10am–5pm, Fri 10am–8pm, Sat & Sun 10am–6pm; $8, students $6, free Fri 5–8pm), whose glassy confines generally present interesting exhibits. Further up, in the AXA Financial Building at no. 1290, look out for Thomas Hart Benton's *America Today* murals, which dynamically and magnificently portray ordinary American life in the days before the Depression.

Towards 57th Street

By the time Sixth Avenue reaches midtown Manhattan, it has become a dazzling showcase of corporate wealth.

There's little of the ground-floor glitter of Fifth or the razzmatazz of Broadway, but the **Rockefeller Center Extension** strikes an impressive note. Following the **Time & Life Building** at 50th Street, three near-identical blocks went up in the 1970s, and if they don't have the romance of their predecessors they at least possess some of their monumentality. At street level, things can be just as interesting – the broad sidewalks allow peddlers of food and handbills, street musicians, mimics and actors to do their thing.

Carnegie Hall

Map 7, F6. #N, #R, #Q or #W to 57th Street.

At 154 W 57th St stands stately **Carnegie Hall**, one of the world's greatest concert venues, whose superb acoustics ensure full houses most of the year. Tchaikovsky conducted the program on opening night and Mahler, Rachmaninov, Toscanini, Frank Sinatra and Judy Garland all played here. If you attend a performance, catch one of the engaging tours (Oct–June Mon–Tues, Thurs–Fri 11.30am, 2pm & 3pm, $6, $5 students; ☎212/247-7800). Alternatively, you can sneak in through the stage door on 56th Street for a look – no one minds as long as there's not a rehearsal in progress.

A few doors down at no. 150 W 57th St, the *Russian Tea Room* (see p.232 for review) reigns as one of those places to see and be seen at, ever popular with "in" names from the entertainment business, its revolving doors ushering in a well-heeled crowd.

SIXTH AVENUE

●

Central Park

"**A**ll radiant in the magic atmosphere of art and taste." So raved *Harper's* magazine on the opening of **Central Park** in 1876, and though that was a slight overstatement, today few New Yorkers could imagine life without it. At various times and places, the park functions as a beach, theater, singles' scene, athletic activity center, and animal behavior lab, both human and canine. In bad times and good New Yorkers still treasure it more than any other city institution.

In spite of the advent of motorized traffic, the sense of disorderly nature the park's nineteenth-century designers, Frederick Law Olmsted and Calvert Vaux, intended largely survives, with cars and buses cutting through the park in the sheltered, sunken transverses originally meant for horse-drawn carriages, mostly unseen from the park itself. The midtown skyline, of course, has changed, and buildings thrust their way into view, sometimes detracting from the park's original pastoral intention, but at the same time adding to the sense of being on a green island in the center of a magnificent city.

GETTING AROUND THE PARK

At 840 acres, Central Park – which runs from 59th to

110th streets and is flanked by Fifth Avenue to Central Park West – is so enormous that it's almost impossible to miss and nearly as impossible to cover in one visit. Nevertheless, the intricate **footpaths** that meander with no discernible organization through the park are one of its greatest successes; after all, the point here is to lose yourself . . . or at least to *feel* like you can. **To figure out exactly where you are**, find the nearest **lamppost** – the first two digits on the post signify the number of the nearest cross street.

Orientation

The **Reservoir** divides Central Park in two. The larger and more familiar **southern park** holds most of the attractions (and people), but the **northern park** (above 86th St) is worth a visit for its wilder natural setting and its dramatically different ambience.

As for **safety**, you should be fine during the day, though always be alert to your surroundings and try to avoid being alone in an isolated part of the park. After dark, it's safer than it used to be but still not advisable to walk around. The exception to this rule is in the case of a public evening event such as a concert or Shakespeare in the Park; just make sure you leave when the crowds do.

BICYCLE RENTAL

One of the best ways to see the park is to **rent a bicycle** from either the Loeb Boathouse (see p.113). Bikes from the Boathouse are $9 and require a $250 cash or credit card refundable deposit.

GETTING AROUND THE PARK

THE SOUTHERN PARK

Entering at **Grand Army Plaza** (Fifth Ave and 59th St), to your left lies the **Pond** and a little further north you'll find the **Wollman Memorial Rink** (Map 7, G5). Sit or stand above the rink to watch skaters and contemplate the view of Central Park South's skyline emerging above the trees. Or **rent skates** of your own: rollerblades, the most popular mode of park transportation, and ice skates are each available here in season.

Northeast of the skating rink lies the small zoo, or **Central Park Wildlife Center** at 64th Street and Fifth Avenue (Map 7, H4; Mon–Fri 10am–5pm, Sat, Sun & holidays 10am–5.30pm; $3.50, 3–12 50¢, under 3 free; ☎212/439-6500). Its collection is based on three climatic regions – the Tropic Zone, the Temperate Territory and the Polar Circle, and the complex also boasts the **Tisch Children's Zoo**, with interactive displays and a petting zoo.

The next point to head for is the **Dairy** (65th Street at mid-park), a kind of Gothic toy ranch building built in 1870 and originally stocked with cows (and milkmaids) for the purpose of selling milk and other dairy products to mothers with young children. It now houses one of the park's **Visitor Centers** (Tues–Sun 10am–5pm; ☎212/794-6564), which distributes free leaflets and organizes weekend walking tours.

Just west of the Dairy stands the **Carousel** at 64th Street at mid-park (Mon–Fri 10am–6pm, Sat & Sun 10am–7pm; $1). Built in 1903 and moved from Coney Island to the park in 1951, this is one of fewer than 150 left in the country (one of the others is at Coney Island). The Carousel offers a ride on hand-carved jumping horses accompanied by the music of a military band organ.

Straight ahead and north past the Dairy, you'll come to the **Mall**, the park's most formal stretch, where you'll witness every manner of street performer. To the west lies the **Sheep Meadow** (Map 7, F3; 66th–69th sts, West Side), fifteen acres of commons where sheep grazed until 1934; today the area is usually crowded with picnic blankets, sunbathers and Frisbee players.

On warm weekends, an area between the Sheep Meadow and the north end of the Mall is filled with colorfully attired rollerbladers dancing to loud funk, disco and hip-hop music – one of the best free shows around. Just west of the Sheep Meadow is the once-exclusive, still-expensive, but now rather tacky landmark restaurant and finishing point of the annual New York City Marathon, **Tavern on the Green** (67th St and Central Park W).

At the northernmost point of the Mall lie the **Bandshell**, **Rumsey Playfield**, site of the free SummerStage performance series (see box, p.116), and the **Bethesda Terrace and Fountain** (72nd St at mid-park). Bethesda Terrace overlooks the lake; beneath it is an **Arcade** whose tiled floors are currently being restored.

Take a break from your wanderings on the lake's eastern bank at the **Loeb Boathouse** (Map 7, G2). Here, you can go for a gondola ride or rent a rowboat (March–Nov daily 10am–6pm, weather permitting; rowboats $10 for the first hour, $2.50 each 15min after, with a $30 refundable deposit; gondola rides available 5–10pm for $30 per 30min per group and require reservations; ☎212/517-2233).

The Great Lawn and around

If you continue north you will reach the backyard of the **Metropolitan Museum of Art** (Map 8, H8) to the east at 81st Street (see p.118) and the **Obelisk** to the west, an 1881 gift from Egypt that dates back to 1450 BC. Also nearby is the **Great Lawn** (Map 8, F8), recently reopened after a massive two-year, $18.5 million renewal program.

STRAWBERRY FIELDS

At 72nd St and Central Park West, Strawberry Fields (Map 7, E2) is a peaceful region of the park dedicated to the memory of John Lennon, who in 1980 was murdered in front of his home at the Dakota Building, across the street on Central Park West (see p.137). Strawberry Fields draws people here to remember Lennon, as well as picnickers and seniors resting on the park benches. Near the W 72nd Street entrance to the area is a round Italian mosaic with the word "Imagine" at its center, donated by Yoko Ono and invariably covered with flowers. Every year without fail on December 8th, the anniversary of Lennon's murder, Strawberry Fields is packed with his fans, singing Beatles songs and sharing their grief, even after all these years.

Now reseeded, it hosts free New York Philharmonic and Metropolitan Opera concerts (see p.116). The lawn features eight softball fields and, at its northern end, new basketball and volleyball courts, and a 1/8-mile running track.

Southwest of the Great Lawn is the **Delacorte Theater** (Map 8, F9), site of the annual free Shakespeare in the Park festivals. Next door, the tranquil **Shakespeare Garden** claims to hold every species of plant mentioned in the Bard's plays. East of the garden is **Belvedere Castle**, a mock medieval citadel first erected in 1869 as a lookout, but now the home of the Urban Park Rangers (who provide walking tours and educational programs). The highest point in the park, and a wonderful viewpoint, the castle also houses the NY Meteorological Observatory's weather center, which provides the "official" Central Park temperature of the day, and makes for a lovely backdrop for the Delacorte's performances.

THE NORTHERN PARK

There are fewer attractions, but more open space, above the Great Lawn. Much of it is taken up by the **Reservoir** (86th–87th streets at mid-park, main entrance at 90th St and Fifth Ave), around which disciplined New Yorkers faithfully jog. The raised track is a great place to get breathtaking 360-degree views of the midtown skyline – just don't block any jogger's path or there will be hell to pay. If you see nothing else above 86th Street in the park, don't miss the **Conservatory Garden** (Map 8, H3), between E 103rd and 106th streets along Fifth Avenue, a pleasing, six-acre space made up of three formal, terraced gardens filled with flowering trees and shrubs, planted flower beds, fanciful fountains, and shaded benches. The main iron-gated entrance at 104th Street and Fifth Avenue is a favorite spot for weekend wedding party photographs.

**The Conservatory Garden is a terrific
place to pause for a picnic.**

At the northeast corner of the park is the **Charles A. Dana Discovery Center** (Map 8, G2; Tues–Sun 10am–5pm, 4pm in winter; ☎212/860-1370), an environmental education and Visitor Center, with free literature, changing visual exhibits, bird walks every Saturday at 11am in July and August, and multicultural performances (see box overleaf). Crowds of locals fish in the adjacent **Harlem Meer**. The center provides free bamboo poles and bait, though you'll have to release your catch of the day.

SEASONAL EVENTS AND ACTIVITIES

SummerStage concerts are held at the Rumsey Playing Field near 72nd St and 5th Ave (☎212/360-2777, ⓦwww.summerstage.org). Shakespeare in the Park takes place at the open-air Delacorte Theater, near the W 81st Street entrance to the park, where tickets are distributed daily at 1pm for that evening's performance, but you'll probably have to get in line well before. Tickets are also distributed downtown at the Public Theater (425 Lafayette St) between 1pm and 3pm the day of the performance. Call the Shakespeare Festival (☎212/539-8750) for more information.

New York Philharmonic in the Park (☎212/875-5709) and Metropolitan Opera in the Park (☎212/362-6000) hold several evenings of classical music in the summer.

Claremont Riding Academy, 175 W 89th St ☎212/724-5100. Mon–Fri 6.30am–10pm, Sat & Sun 6.30am–5pm. Horseback riding lessons are available, as are rentals for riders experienced in the English saddle. $42 for a 30min lesson, $35 for a ride on Central Park's bridlepaths.

The Harlem Meer Festival, 110th St between 5th and Lenox aves ☎212/860-1370. Fairly intimate and enjoyable free performances of jazz and salsa music outside the Dana Discovery Center on Sundays from 4 to 6pm throughout the summer.

General information

General Park Information ☎212/360-3444. Also ☎1-888/NYPARKS for special events information.

Founded in 1980, the Central Park Conservancy is a nonprofit organization dedicated to preserving and managing the park. It operates four Visitor Centers, with free maps and other helpful literature, as well as special events. All are open Tues–Sun 10am–5pm: The Dairy (mid-park at 65th St; ☎212/794-6564); Belvedere Castle (mid-park at 79th St; ☎212/772-0210); North Meadow Recreation Center (mid-park at 97th St; ☎212/348-4867; also open Mon); and the Dana Discovery Center (110th St off Fifth Ave; ☎212/860-1370).

Restrooms are available at Hecksher Playground, the Boat Pond (Conservatory Water), Mineral Springs House (northwest end of Sheep Meadow), Loeb Boathouse, the Delacorte Theater, the North Meadow Recreation Center, The Conservatory Garden and the Dana Discovery Center.

In case of emergency, use the emergency call boxes located throughout the park and along the Park Drives (they provide a direct connection to the Central Park Precinct), or dial 911 at any pay phone.

SEASONAL EVENTS AND ACTIVITIES

The Metropolitan Museum of Art

A massive slab of a building on the eastern edge of Central Park between 80th and 84th Streets, the **Met**, as the museum's usually called, is the foremost museum in America and one of the great museums of the world. The Met's collection takes in over two million works of art. Any overview of the museum is out of the question: the Met demands many and specific visits or, at least, self-imposed limits.

MUSEUM PRACTICALITIES

Map 8, H8. Fifth Avenue at 82nd Street, set into Central Park. Tues–Thurs & Sun 9.30am–5.15pm, Fri & Sat 9.30am–8.45pm; suggested donation $10, students $5 (includes admission to the Cloisters, see p.147, on the same day); recorded "acoustiguide" tours of the major collections $5; free conducted tours, "Highlights of the Met," daily; also highly detailed tours of specific galleries; several restaurants and excellent book and gift shops; ℡212/879-5500 or 535-7710 for recorded information. #4, #5 or #6 train to 86th St–Lexington Ave.

Broadly, the museum breaks down into **seven major collections**: European Arts-Painting and Sculpture; Asian Art; American Painting and Decorative Arts; Egyptian Antiquities; Medieval Art; Ancient Greek and Roman Art; and the Art of Africa, the Pacific and the Americas.

Among the less famous Met collections are its Islamic Art (possibly the largest display anywhere in the world); European Decorative Arts; Greek and Roman Art; Arms and Armor Galleries (the largest and most important in the Western Hemisphere); a Musical Instrument Collection (containing the world's oldest piano); and the spectacular Costume Institute.

Despite the museum's size, initial orientation is not too difficult. There is just one main entrance, and once you've passed through it you find yourself in the **Great Hall**, a deftly lit Neoclassical cavern where you can consult plans, check tours and pick up info on the Met's excellent lecture listings.

EUROPEAN ART

The Met's **European Art** galleries are at their best in the Dutch painting section, with major works of **Rembrandt** (a superb *Self-Portrait*), **Hals**, and especially **Vermeer**, whose *Young Woman with a Water Jug* and *A Girl Asleep* display the artist at his most complex and the Met at its most fortunate. Continue on, and as you loop back to the entrance to the painting galleries you'll pass through another smattering of works by Spanish, French and Italian painters, most notably **Goya** and **Velázquez**. The latter's piercing and somber *Portrait of Juan de Pareja* shouldn't be missed. A whole room is dedicated to the formidable works of **El Greco**. His extraordinary *View of Toledo* – all brooding intensity as the skies seem about to swallow up the ghost-like town – is perhaps the best of his works anywhere in the world.

The **Italian Renaissance** isn't spectacularly represented, but there's a worthy selection from the various Italian schools; these works consist largely of narrative panels or altarpieces, and gold paint is often used, either for the background or for the haloes of the religious figures. Highlights include an early *Madonna and Child Enthroned with Saints* by **Raphael**, a late **Botticelli** (the crisply linear *Three Miracles of Saint Zenobius*), **Filippo Lippi**'s *Madonna and Child Enthroned with Two Angels*, and **Michele de Verona**'s handsome *Madonna and Child with the Infant John the Baptist*, in which the characters are almost sculpturally rendered.

IMPRESSIONIST AND POST-IMPRESSIONIST PAINTING

On its second floor the Met has a startling array of Impressionist and Post-Impressionist art. Chief works include **Manet**'s *Young Lady in 1866*, **Courbet**'s *Young Ladies from the Village* and **Degas**' *Dancers Practicing at the Bar*. There are three superb works by **Monet** – *Rouen Cathedral*, *The Houses of Parliament (Effect of Fog)* and *The Doge's Palace Seen from San Giorgio Maggiore* – which show the beginnings of his final phase of near-abstract Impressionism. **Renoir** is perhaps the best represented among the remaining Impressionists, though his most important work here dates from 1878, when he began to move away from the mainstream techniques he'd learned while working with Monet. *Mme Charpentier and her Children* is a likeable enough piece, one whose affectionate tone manages to sidestep the sentimentality of Renoir's later work.

Also here is **Cézanne**'s masterpiece *The Card Players*. All of this scratches little more than the surface of the galleries. Look out for major works by **Van Gogh** (including *Irises*,

Woman of Arles and *Sunflowers*), **Rousseau**, **Bonnard**, **Pissarro** and **Seurat**.

MODERN ART

The Met's **modern art** collection, housed on the second-floor Lila Acheson Wallace Wing, is a fascinating and relatively compact group of paintings. Picasso's *Portrait of Gertrude Stein* and his blue-period *The Blind Man's Meal* are here, alongside works by **Klee**, **Modigliani**, **Braque** and **Klimt**. Other highlights include **Hopper**'s *Views From Williamsburg Bridge* and **O'Keefe**'s, sumptuous, erotic *Black Iris*, **Pollock**'s masterly *Autumn Rhythm (Number 30)* and **Warhol**'s *Last Self-Portrait*, which dates from 1986.

THE CANTOR ROOF GARDEN

From May through October, you can ascend to the Cantor Roof Garden (accessible by elevator from the first floor) on top of the Wallace Wing, which displays contemporary sculpture against the dramatic backdrop of New York's midtown skyline. In October this is a great place to see the colorful fall foliage in Central Park. Drinks and snacks are served, perhaps on the expensive side – though the breathtaking views make up for it.

ASIAN ART

The second floor's **Asian Art** galleries gather an impressive and vast array of Chinese, Japanese, Indian and Southeast Asian sculpture, painting, ceramics and metalwork, as well as an indoor replica of a Chinese garden. Fourteen recently renovated and expanded galleries showcase Chinese painting, calligraphy, jade, lacquer and textiles, making this collection one of the largest in the world.

The highlight is the **Chinese Garden Court**, a serene, minimalist retreat enclosed by the galleries, and the adjacent **Ming Room**, a typical salon decorated in period style with wooden lattice doors. The naturally lit garden is representative of one found in Chinese homes – a pagoda, small waterfall and stocked goldfish pond landscaped by limestone rocks, trees and shrubs conjure up an inordinate sense of peace.

AMERICAN PAINTING

The **American paintings** galleries, on the second floor of the American Wing, begin in a maze of rooms on the second floor with eighteenth-century portraits (look out for the heroics of **Leutzes**'s *Washington Crossing the Delaware*), but really get going with **West**'s allegorical *The Triumph of Love* and the nineteenth-century landscape painters of the Hudson Valley School, who glorified the landscape in their vast lyrical canvases. **Cole**, the school's doyen, is represented by *The Oxbow*, his pupil **Church** by an immense *Heart of the Andes* – combining the grand sweep of the mountains with minutely depicted flora. Also here are several striking portraits by **Sargent** including the magnificent *Portrait of Madam X*.

Winslow Homer is allowed most of a gallery to himself – fittingly for a painter who so greatly influenced the late-nineteenth-century artistic scene in America. Homer began his career illustrating the day-to-day realities of the Civil War – there's a good selection here that shows the tedium and sadness of that era. His talent in recording detail carried over into his late, quasi-Impressionistic studies of seascapes of which *Northeaster* is one of the finest.

THE EGYPTIAN COLLECTION

The **Egyptian collection**, to the north end of the Great Hall, holds 35,000 objects in its collection and nearly all are on lavish display. The large statuary are the most immediately striking of the exhibits, but it's the smaller sculptural pieces that hold the attention longest. Look out for the dazzling collection of Princess **Sit-Hathor-yunet's jewelry**, a pinnacle in Egyptian decorative art from around 1830 BC. Most striking of all is the **Temple of Dendur**, moved here during the construction of the Aswan High Dam in 1965 and marvelously illuminated by night.

ART OF AFRICA, THE PACIFIC AND THE AMERICAS

The Rockefeller Wing holds the Met's comprehensive collection of art from **Africa, the Pacific and the Americas**. It's a superb set of galleries, the muted, understated decor throwing the exhibits into sharp and often dramatic focus. The African exhibit has a particularly awe-inspiring display of art from the Court of Benin in present-day Nigeria – tiny carved-ivory statues and vessels, created with astonishing detail. The Pacific collection covers the islands of Melanesia, Micronesia, Polynesia and Australia, and contains a wide array of objects such as wild, somewhat frightening, wooden masks with piercing all-too-realistic eyes.

The Upper East Side

The defining characteristic of Manhattan's **Upper East Side**, a two-square-mile grid scored with the great avenues of **Madison**, **Park** and **Lexington**, is wealth. While other neighborhoods are affected by incursions of immigrant groups, artistic trends, and the like, this remains primarily an enclave of the well-off, with tony shops, clean and relatively safe streets, well-preserved buildings and landmarks. It also has some of the city's finest **museums**, all in a compact strip running on or near Fifth Avenue, known as Museum Mile: the **Frick Collection** and the **Guggenheim Museum** are the best (and best known), but the **Whitney Museum of American Art**, the **Jewish Museum** and the **Museum of the City of New York** each command attention.

FIFTH AVENUE

Fifth Avenue has been the haughty patrician face of Manhattan since the opening of Central Park in 1876 lured the Carnegies, Astors, Vanderbilts, Whitneys and other capitalists north from lower Fifth Avenue and Gramercy Park to build their fashionable Neoclassical residences along the park's eastern edge. A great deal of what you see, though, is third- or fourth-generation building: through the latter part of the nineteenth century, fanciful mansions were built at vast expense, to last only ten or fifteen years before being demolished for even wilder extravagances or, more commonly, grand apartment blocks. Rocketing land values made the chance of selling at vast profit irresistible.

Grand Army Plaza to the Frick

Grand Army Plaza (Map 7, H5) is the southernmost point of introduction to all this, an oval at the junction of Central Park South and Fifth Avenue that marks the division between Fifth as a shopping district to the south and a residential boulevard to the north. This is one of the city's most dramatic public spaces, boasting a fountain and a gold statue of Civil War victor General Sherman, and flanked by the extended copper-lined chateau of the **Plaza Hotel**, with the darkened, swooping television-screen facade of the **Solow Building** behind. Two more hotels, the high-necked **Sherry Netherland** and **Pierre**, luxuriate nearby. Many of the rooms here have permanent guests; needless to say, they're not on welfare.

Take away Fifth Avenue's museums and a resplendent though fairly bloodless strip remains. On the corner of Fifth Avenue and 65th Street, America's largest reform synagogue, the **Temple Emanu-El** (Map 7, H4; Mon–Fri & Sun 9am–5pm), strikes a sober aspect, a brooding Romanesque–Byzantine cavern that manages to be bigger inside than it seems out. The interior melts away into mysterious darkness, making you feel very small indeed.

FREE MUSEUMS HOURS

The following museums are free at the stated times:

Tuesday Cooper-Hewitt (5–9pm), International Center of Photography (5–8pm, pay what you wish), Jewish Museum (5–9pm).

Thursday Asia Society Gallery (6–8pm), New Museum of Contemporary Art (6–8pm).

Friday Guggenheim (6–8pm, pay what you wish), Museum of Modern Art (4.30–8.15pm, pay what you wish), Whitney (6–9pm, pay what you wish).

The Frick Collection

Map 7, H3. 1 E 70th St. Tues–Sat 10am–6pm, Sun 1–6pm, closed Mon; $10, students $5, under 10 are not admitted; ☎212/288-0700, ⓦwww.frickcollection.org. Admission includes the use of ArtPhone, a dial-up audio guide to the rooms and exhibition pieces. A 22min audiovisual presentation is given every hour on the half-hour. #6 to 68th St–Lexington Ave.

Housed in the former mansion of Henry Clay Frick, the immensely enjoyable **Frick Collection** comprises the art treasures hoarded by this most ruthless and hated of New York's robber barons. However, the legacy of his ill-gotten gains is a superb collection of works, and as good a glimpse of the sumptuous life enjoyed by New York's early industrialists as you'll find.

Opened in the mid-1930s, the museum has been largely kept as it looked when the Fricks lived there. Much of the furniture is heavy eighteenth-century French, but the nice thing about the place – and many people rank the Frick as their favorite New York gallery because of this – is that it strives hard to be as unlike a museum as possible.

There's a magnificent array of works here by **Rembrandt** (including a set of piercing *Self-Portraits*),

FIFTH AVENUE

Goya and **Whistler**, as well as an early (and suggestive) **Vermeer**, *Officer and Laughing Girl*, and one of **van Eyck**'s last works, a *Virgin and Child*.

The **West Gallery** is the Frick's major draw, holding some of its finest paintings in a truly magnificent setting – a long elegant room with a concave glass ceiling and ornately carved wood trim. Two **Turners**, views of Cologne and Dieppe, hang opposite each other, each a blaze of orange and creamy tones; **Van Dyck** pitches in with a couple of uncharacteristically informal portraits of Frans Snyders and his wife – two paintings reunited only when Frick purchased them; and there are several portraits by **Frans Hals**, and *Vincenzo Anastagi* by **El Greco**, a stunning portrait of a Spanish soldier resplendent in green velvet and armor.

The Guggenheim Museum

Map 8, H7.1071 5th Ave (at 88th St). Sun–Wed 9am–6pm, Fri & Sat 9am–8pm; $12, seniors, students $7, under 12 free, Fri 6–8pm pay what you wish; ☎212/423-3500, ⊛www.guggenheim.org. #4, #5 or #6 to 86th St–Lexington Ave.

Whatever you think of the **Guggenheim Museum**'s collection of paintings, it's the upturned beehive building, designed by Frank Lloyd Wright that steals the show, looking wildly out of place amidst the solemn facades of Fifth Avenue. Solomon R. Guggenheim was one of America's richest men and he collected modern paintings with fervor, buying wholesale the paintings of **Kandinsky**, adding works by **Chagall**, **Klee**, **Léger** and others, and exhibiting them to a bemused American public in the 1920s. Subsequent donations include masterworks by **Cézanne**, **Degas**, **Gauguin**, **Manet**, **Toulouse-Lautrec**, **Van Gogh** and **Picasso**, among others, greatly enhancing the museum's Impressionist and Post-Impressionist holdings. The Robert Mapplethorpe Foundation recently gave 196

FIFTH AVENUE

photographs that bridge the artist's entire career, which are now housed in a brand new **Mapplethorpe** gallery on the fourth floor.

Since the circular galleries increase upward at a not-so-gentle slope, it may be preferable to start at the top of the museum and work your way down; most of the temporary exhibits are planned that way.

Jewish Museum

Map 8, H6. 1109 5th Ave (92nd St). Sun 10am–5.45pm, Mon–Thurs 11am–5.45pm, Tues until 9pm, Fri 11am–3pm; $8, students $5.50, under 12 free, free Tues 5–9pm; ⊤ 212/423-3200, ⊛www.jewishmuseum.org. #4, #5 or #6 to 96th St–Lexington Ave.

This is the largest museum of Judaica outside Israel. Its centerpiece is a permanent exhibition on the Jewish experience that seeks to answer the question, "What constitutes the essence of Jewish identity?" with a presentation of the basic ideas, values and culture developed over four thousand years. A collection of **Hanukkah lamps** is one of the highlights. More vibrant, however, are the changing displays of works by major international artists, and theme exhibitions (for example, a recent major show on Freud containing nearly 200 artifacts from his Vienna offices). The Jewish Museum sponsors a varied media program, including a film festival.

Museum of the City of New York

Map 8, H3. 1220 5th Ave (103rd St). Wed–Sat 10am–5pm, Sun noon–5pm, Tues 10am–2pm for pre-registered tour groups only; suggested donation $7, students $4, families $12; ⊤212/534-1672, ⊛www.mcny.org. #6 to 103rd St–Lexington Ave.

Spaciously housed in a neo-Georgian mansion, the permanent collection of this museum provides a history of the city from Dutch times to the present. Prints, photographs, costumes and furniture are displayed on four floors, and a film about the city's history runs continuously. One of its permanent exhibits is **New York Toy Stories**, an engaging trip from the late 1800s to today that consists of all manner of motion toys, board games, sports equipment, and doll houses. This is a comprehensive, worthwhile and fascinating look at the evolution of a city. (The museum is scheduled to relocate downtown to the Tweed Courthouse in the spring of 2003.)

Museo del Barrio

Map 8, H3. 1230 5th Ave (at 104th St). Wed–Sun 11am–5pm; suggested donation $5, students $3; ⊤212/831-7272, ⊛www.elmuseo.org. #6 to 103rd St–Lexington Ave.

Literally translated as "the neighborhood museum," the **Museo** was founded in 1969 by a group of Puerto Rican parents, educators and artists from Spanish Harlem who wanted to teach their children about their roots. Now, although the emphasis remains largely Puerto Rican, the museum embraces the whole of Latin America and the Caribbean, with five major loan exhibits of painting, photographs and crafts each year, by both traditional and emerging artists.

MADISON AVENUE

Immediately east of Fifth Avenue lies **Madison Avenue**, a strip that was entirely residential until the 1920s. Today it is mainly an elegant shopping street, lined with top-notch designer clothes stores, some of whose doors are kept locked. The only key sight along its Upper East Side stretch is the Whitney Museum.

The Whitney Museum of American Art

Map 7, I2. 945 Madison Ave (at 75th St). Tues–Thurs & Sat–Sun 11am–6pm, Fri 1–9pm; $10, seniors and students $8; Fri 6–9pm pay what you wish; ☎212/570-3600, ⊛www.whitney.org. Excellent free gallery talks Wed–Sun, call for times. #6 to 77th St–Lexington Ave.

Located in a heavy arsenal-like building, the **Whitney** is a great forum for one of the pre-eminent collections of twentieth-century American art.

Currently, the museum owns over 12,000 modern paintings, sculptures, photographs and films, the best overview of which is contained in the **Highlights of the Permanent Collection** on the second and fifth floors. The collection is particularly strong on **Hopper** and several of his best paintings are here: *Early Sun Morning* is typical, a bleak urban landscape, uneasily tense in its lighting and rejection of topical detail. Other major bequests include a significant number of works by **Avery**, **Demuth** and **O'Keefe**. The Abstract Expressionists are featured strongly, with great works by **Pollock** and **de Kooning**. In a different direction there's work by **Warhol**, **Johns** (the celebrated *Three Flags*) and some of **Oldenburg**'s *Soft Sculptures*.

Every other year there is an exhibition – the **Whitney Biennial** – designed to give a provocative overview of what's happening in contemporary American art. It is often panned by critics (sometimes for good reason) but always packed with visitors. Catch it if you can between March and June in even-numbered years.

PARK AVENUE

A block east of Madison, **Park Avenue** is stolidly comfortable and often elegant. In the low 90s, the large black shapes of the **Louise Nevelson sculptures** stand out on the traffic islands. Just above 96th Street the neighborhood abruptly transforms into **Spanish Harlem** at the point where the subway line emerges from underground. One of the best features of this boulevard is the sweeping view south, as Park Avenue coasts down to the **New York Central** and **Met Life** (originally Pan Am) buildings.

Dominating a square block between 66th and 67th streets is the **Seventh Regiment Armory** (Map 7, I4), built in the 1870s with pseudo-medieval crenellations and the only surviving building from the era before the New York Central's railroad tracks were roofed over and Park Avenue became an upscale residential neighborhood. There are two surviving interiors inside the Veterans' Room and the Library; call ahead for a tour (℡212/744-8180). Frequent art and antique shows provide an opportunity to gawk at the enormous drill hall inside.

Asia Society Museum

Map 7, I3. 725 Park Ave (at 70th St). Tues–Sat 11am–6pm, Thurs until 8pm, Sun noon–5pm; $4, students and seniors $2; free Thurs 6–8pm; ℡212/517-ASIA, ℗www.asiasociety.org . #6 to 68th St–Lexington Ave.

A prominent educational resource on Asia founded by John D. Rockefeller 3rd, the **Asia Society** offers an exhibition space dedicated to both traditional and contemporary art from all over Asia; in addition to the usually worthwhile temporary exhibits, intriguing performances, political roundtables, lectures, films and free events are frequently held.

LEXINGTON AVENUE AND EAST

Lexington Avenue is Madison without the class; as the west became richer, property developers rushed to slick up real estate in the east. Much of the East 60s and 70s now house young, unattached and upwardly mobile professionals – as the number of "happening" singles bars on Second and Third avenues will attest.

At 421 E 61st St, between York and First avenues, the **Mount Vernon Hotel Museum and Garden** (Map 7, L5; Sept–July daily 11am–4pm, Sun 1–5pm; $4, students and senior citizens $3, under 12 free; ℡212/838-6878) is a Federal-period structure restored by the Colonial Dames of America. The furnishings, knickknacks and the serene little park out back are more engaging than the house itself, but there's an odd sort of pull if you're lucky enough to be guided around by a chattily urbane Colonial Dame.

Much further north **Gracie Mansion** (Map 8, N7; $4, $3 for seniors; ℡212/570-4751), one block east of York at East End Avenue and 88th Street, was built in 1799 as a country manor house. It is one of the best-preserved colonial buildings in the city, and has been the official residence of the mayor of New York City since 1942, though "mansion" is a bit overblown for what is really a rather cramped clapboard cottage. Gracie is open for tours April through November, usually on Wednesday, though you need to book far enough in advance to receive a mailed confirmation.

The Upper West Side

T he **Upper West Side** has always had a more unbut-
toned vibe than its counterpart across the park. It is
now one of the city's most desirable addresses, and
tends to attract what might be called New York's cultural
elite and new-money types – musicians, writers, journalists,
curators and the like – though there is also a small but visible homeless presence.

The Upper West Side is bordered by Central Park to the
east, the Hudson River to the west, **Columbus Circle** at
59th Street to the south, and 110th Street (the northernmost point of Central Park) to the north. The main artery
is **Broadway** and, generally speaking, the further you stray
east or west the wealthier things become, until you reach
the pinnacle of prosperity, the historic apartment buildings
of **Central Park West** and **Riverside Drive**. **Lincoln
Center**, New York's most prestigious palace of performing
arts, lies in the region's southern streets, and along with the
superlative **American Museum of Natural History**,
forms the Upper West Side's greatest draw. North of 110th
Street finds you in **Morningside Heights**, home to the

Cathedral Church of St John the Divine and Columbia University.

COLUMBUS CIRCLE AND AROUND

Map 7, E5. #A, #B, #C, #D, #1, or # 2 to 59th Street.

Columbus Circle, at the intersection of Broadway, Central Park West and 59th Street, is a pedestrian's worst nightmare but a good place to start investigating the Upper West Side nonetheless.

You'll immediately spy the glittering **Trump International Hotel**, a new luxury hotel and residential condo, that was touted as "The World's Most Prestigious Address" – just the most recent example of Donald Trump's extraordinary hubris.

For relief, go west a few blocks and contemplate the **Church of St Paul the Apostle**, 9th Avenue between 59th and 60th streets, a beautiful Old Gothic structure housing Byzantine basilica features.

At 2 Lincoln Square (at Broadway and 66th St) the **Museum of American Folk Art** (Map 7, D4; Tues–Sun 11.30am–7.30pm; suggested admission $3; ☎212/595-9533, ⓦwww.folkartmuseum.org) has occasionally interesting (if the recondite) exhibitions of multicultural folk art from all over the US, with a permanent collection that includes over 3500 works from the seventeenth to twentieth centuries.

LINCOLN CENTER

Map 7, D4. #1 to 66th St-Broadway.

Broadway continues north from Columbus Circle to the **Lincoln Center for the Performing Arts**, an imposing group of buildings arranged around a large plaza and fountain, on the west side between 63rd and 66th streets. Built in the mid-1960s on a site that formerly held some of the city's poorest slums, Lincoln Center is home to the Metropolitan Opera and the New York Philharmonic, as well as a host of other smaller companies. See pp.286–287 for ticket details.

Lincoln Center is home to a variety of free entertainment, ranging from the Autumn Crafts Fair in early September, and folk and jazz bands at lunchtime throughout the summer. Call ☎212/875-5000 for specifics.

The New York State Theater and Avery Fisher Hall

The spare and elegant **New York State Theater** (☎212/870-5570), on the south side of the plaza, is home to the New York City Ballet, the New York City Opera and the famed annual December performances of *The Nutcracker Suite*. The ballet season runs from late November through February, and from early April through June; the opera season starts in July and runs through mid-November.

Avery Fisher Hall (☎212/875-5030), on the north side of the plaza, does not possess the magnificence of the auditorium across the way, and the most exciting thing about the hall is its foyer, dominated by a huge hanging sculpture. The New York Philharmonic performs here from September through May; the less expensive *Mostly Mozart* concerts take place here in July and August.

The Metropolitan Opera House

Known as "the Met," the **Metropolitan Opera House** (☎212/362-6000) is the focal point of the plaza, with

LINCOLN CENTER ●

enormous crystal chandeliers and red-carpeted staircases designed for grand entrances in gliding evening wear. Behind two of the high-arched windows hang **murals** by Marc Chagall and the opera house's elegant interior says opulence, pure and simple. **Backstage tours** of the Met cost $9 ($4 for students) and are given daily October through June, at 3.45pm and at 10am on Saturday.

The rest of Lincoln Center

To the south of the Met lies Damrosch Park, a large space with rows of chairs facing the **Guggenheim Bandshell**, where you can catch free summer lunchtime concerts and various performances. To the north, you will find a lovely, smaller plaza facing the **Vivian Beaumont Theater**. Across 66th Street is **Alice Tully Hall**, a recital hall that houses the Chamber Music Society of Lincoln Center, and the **Walter E. Reade Theater**, which features foreign films and retrospectives and, together with the Avery Fisher and Alice Tully halls, hosts the annual **New York Film Festival** in September. The famed **Juilliard School of Music** is in an adjacent building.

BROADWAY

The Upper West Side has seen a lot of changes in the last few years and **Broadway**, the neighborhood's main drag, reflects them. Gentrification is creeping northward, sometimes for the better, often not. The turnover of establishments here is often astounding, but one stalwart is **Zabar's**, at 2254 Broadway, between 80th and 81st streets, (Map 8, B9). The Upper West Side's principal gourmet shop, this area landmark offers more or less anything connected with food.

A few blocks north at 212 W 83rd St, between Broadway

BROADWAY

THE DEATH OF JOHN LENNON

Most people know the Dakota Building as the former home of John Lennon – and present home of his wife Yoko Ono, who owns a number of the apartments. It was outside the Dakota, on the night of December 8, 1980, that Lennon was murdered by Mark David Chapman, who had been hanging around outside the building all day to get Lennon's autograph.

and Amsterdam Avenue, the **Children's Museum of Manhattan** (Map 8, C8; Tues–Sun 10am–5pm; children and adults $5, under 1 free; ☏212/721-1234, ⓦwww .cmom.org) offers interactive exhibits that stimulate learning, in a fun, relaxed environment for kids (and babies). The Dr. Seuss exhibit and the storytelling room (filled with books kids can choose from) are particular winners.

CENTRAL PARK WEST

On Central Park West at 72nd Street, the **Dakota Building** (Map 7, E2), with its turrets, gables and other odd details, was built to persuade wealthy New Yorkers that life in an apartment could be just as luxurious as in a private house. Over the years there have been few residents here not publicly known in some way: big-time tenants included Lauren Bacall and Leonard Bernstein, and in the 1960s the building was used as the setting for Roman Polanski's film *Rosemary's Baby*. But the most famous recent resident of the Dakota was **John Lennon**, remembered in a memorial just across the street in Central Park (see p.114).

The New-York Historical Society

Map 7, E1. 2 W 77th St at Central Park W; Tues–Sun 11am–5pm, Summer Tues–Fri only; suggested donation $5, students and seniors $3, children free; ☎212/873-3400, ⊛www.nyhistory.org. #B or #C to 81st St–Central Park West.

The often overlooked **New-York Historical Society** is more a museum of American than New York history, and its temporary exhibitions are more daring than you'd expect, mixing high and low culture with intelligence and flair. On the second floor, **James Audubon**, the Harlem artist and naturalist who specialized in lovingly detailed watercolors of birds, is the focus of one room (the collection holds all 432 original watercolors of Audubon's *Birds of America*); other galleries hold a broad sweep of **nineteenth-century American painting**.

The American Museum of Natural History

Map 8, E9. Central Park W at 79th St. Sun–Thurs 10am–5.45pm, Fri & Sat 10am–8.45pm; suggested donation (including the Rose Center) $10, students $7.50, children $6; IMAX films, the Hayden Planetarium and certain special exhibits cost extra; ☎212/769-5100, ⊛www.amnh.org. #B or #C to 81st St–Central Park West.

An enormous complex of buildings full of fossils, gems, skeletons and other natural specimens, along with a wealth of man-made artifacts from indigenous cultures worldwide, the **American Museum of Natural History** is one of the best and largest museums of its kind, with 32 million items on display. There's a fantastic amount to see, but be selective; depending on your interests, anything from a highly discriminating couple of hours to half a day should be ample.

On the **second** (entry-level) **floor** are the **Hall of Asian People** and **Hall of African People**, each filled with fascinating art and artifacts. Another highlight of this floor is the lower half of the **Hall of African Mammals** – don't miss (though how can you?) the life-size family of elephants in the center of the room.

The fourth floor is almost entirely taken up with the wildly popular **Dinosaur Exhibit**; covering five spacious, well-lit, and well-designed halls, it is the largest collection in the world, with more than 120 specimens on display.

On the first floor, the **Hall of Gems and Minerals** includes some strikingly beautiful crystals – not least the *Star of India*, the largest blue sapphire ever found. More captivating, however, is the new **Hall of Biodiversity**, whose centerpiece is a living re-creation of a Central African Republic rainforest that you can walk through, to the sounds of birdcalls.

Across from the Hall of Biodiversity lies the first installation of the **Rose Center for Earth and Space** – the spanking new **Hall of Planet Earth**, containing the **Dynamic Earth Globe**, where visitors seated below the globe are able to watch the earth via satellite go through its full rotation.

RIVERSIDE PARK AND RIVERSIDE DRIVE

At the western edge of 72nd Street **Riverside Park** and **Riverside Drive** begin. Riverside Drive winds north, flanked by palatial townhouses and multistory apartment buildings put up in the early part of the twentieth century by those not quite rich enough to compete with the folks on Fifth Avenue. A number of landmarked districts lie along it, particularly in the mid-70s, mid-80s, and low-100s.

Riverside Park, one of only eight designated scenic landmarks in New York City, is not as imposing or spacious as Central Park, though it was designed by the same team of architects and took 25 years to complete. Between 72nd and 79th streets, the park is at its narrowest and not as scenic as it becomes farther north. However, along Riverside Drive are lovely turn-of-the-nineteenth-century townhouses, many with copper-trimmed mansard roofs and private terraces or roof gardens.

A delightful place for a break is the 79th Street Boat Basin in Riverside Park, with paths leading down to it located on either side of 79th Street at Riverside Drive. It's one of the city's most peaceful locations, with views across the Hudson of New Jersey.

Further north on Riverside Drive between 105th and 106th streets is a lovely block of historic apartments. It begins with 330 Riverside Drive, now the **Riverside Study Center**, a glorious five-story Beaux-Arts house built in 1900 – note the copper mansard roof, stone balconies and delicate iron scrollwork.

MORNINGSIDE HEIGHTS

Morningside Heights, just north of the Upper West Side, is the last gasp of Manhattan's wealth before Harlem. Marked at the edge by the monolithic **Cathedral of St John the Divine**, the area is filled largely with students and professors from **Columbia University**, as well as middle-class families and a mix of whites, blacks, Latinos and Asians.

The Cathedral Church of St John

Map 8, D1. #1 to 110th Street- Broadway.
The Cathedral Church of St John the Divine, Amsterdam Avenue at 112th Street, rises out of the urban landscape with a sure, solid kind of majesty – far from finished, but still one of New York's most impressive sights.

Work on the Episcopal church began in 1892 to the specifications of a Romanesque design that, with a change of architect in 1911, became French Gothic. Work progressed quickly for a while but stopped with the outbreak of war in 1939 and only resumed again in the mid-1980s. The church declared bankruptcy in 1994, fraught with funding difficulties and hard questioning by people who thought the money might be better spent on something of more obvious benefit to the local community, and has since launched a massive international fund-raising drive in the hope of resuming building work soon.

The cathedral appears complete at first glance (despite the ever-present scaffolding), but when you gaze up into its huge, uncompleted towers, you realize how much is left to do. Only two-thirds of the cathedral is finished, and completion isn't due until around 2050 – even assuming it goes on uninterrupted. Still, if finished, St John the Divine will be the largest cathedral structure in the world, its floor space – at 600 feet long and at the transepts 320 feet wide – big enough to swallow both the cathedrals of Notre Dame and Chartres whole.

Walking the length of the **nave**, you can see the melding of the Romanesque and Gothic styles. This blending is particularly apparent in the choir, which rises from a heavy arcade of Romanesque columns to a high, light-Gothic vaulting, the temporary dome of the crossing to someday be replaced by a tall, delicate Gothic spire.

In December 2001, a fire broke out in the cathedral's gift shop. The damage was confined to the shop as well as several tapestries along the north wall – relatively little harm considering the events of the year.

Columbia University and north

Map 9, B9. #1 to 116th Street–Broadway.
The **Columbia University** campus fills six blocks between Broadway and Morningside Drive from 114th to 120th streets, with its main entrance at Broadway and 116th Street

(tours of the campus leave from the **information office** here Mon through Fri; call ☎212/854-4900 for information). It is one of the most prestigious academic institutions in the country, ranking with the other Ivy League colleges and boasting a campus laid out in grand Beaux Arts style. Of the buildings, the domed and colonnaded **Low Memorial Library** (built in 1902) stands center-stage at the top of a wide flight of stone steps, a focus for somewhat violent demonstrations during the Vietnam War.

Riverside Church (Map 9, B8), on Riverside Drive between 120th and 121st streets (daily 9am–4.30pm, Sun service 10.45am), has a graceful French Gothic Revival tower. Take the elevator to the 20th floor and ascend the steps around the carillon (the largest in the world, with 74 bells) for some classic spreads of Manhattan's skyline, New Jersey and the hills beyond.

Up the block from the church at 122nd Street is **Grant's Tomb** (Map 9, B8; daily 9am–5pm; free), a Greek-style memorial and the nation's largest mausoleum in which conquering Civil War hero and blundering President Grant really is interred with his wife, in two black-marble Napoleonic sarcophogi.

Harlem and
north Manhattan

Harlem, which stretches from the top of Central Park to the 140s, has long been synonymous with racial conflict and urban deprivation, though as a visit will reveal, that's only part of a much bigger picture, one often simplified and jaundiced by some media hostility to the black culture here. Though Harlem has its problems, it's a far less dangerous neighborhood than its reputation suggests, especially in light of solid city and neighborhood improvement efforts as of late. If you intend to tour Harlem, it will serve you well to feel comfortable about where you're going beforehand, stick to the well-trodden streets and be relaxed once there.

Continuing northwest, **Hamilton Heights** is largely residential, with an old Federal-style mansion. Further uptown, **Washington Heights** is a patchy neighborhood with little in the way of attractions. You still want to pass through because the **Cloisters Museum**, a mock-medieval monastery that holds the Metropolitan Museum's superlative collection of medieval art, lies very near the top end of the island.

125TH STREET

125th Street between Broadway and Fifth Avenue is the working center of Harlem and serves as its main commercial and retail drag. The #2 and #3 trains let you out here at 125th Street and Lenox Avenue, and the **Adam Clayton Powell, Jr. State Office Building** on the corner of Seventh Avenue provides a looming concrete landmark. Walking west along 125th, you'll encounter the **Studio Museum in Harlem**, at no. 144 (Map 9, D8; Wed–Thurs noon–6pm, Fri noon–8pm, Sat–Sun 10am–6pm; $5, students and seniors $3, under 12 $1; ☎212/864-4500, ⓦwww.studiomuseuminharlem.org), an exhibition space dedicated to contemporary African-American painting, photography and sculpture. The permanent collection is displayed on a rotating basis and includes works by Harlem Renaissance-era photographer James Van Der Zee, and paintings and sculptures by postwar artists.

Just west is the **Apollo Theatre** (Map 9, D8) at no. 253, which, though not much to look at from the outside, was, from the 1930s to the 1970s, the center of black entertainment in New York City and northeastern America. Almost all the great figures of jazz and blues played here along with singers, comedians and dancers. Past winners of its renowned Amateur Night have included Ella Fitzgerald, Billie Holiday, The Jackson Five, Sarah Vaughan, Marvin Gaye and James Brown.

The Apollo offers daily 45-minute tours (call ☎212/531-5337).

POWELL BOULEVARD

Above 110th Street, Seventh Avenue becomes **Adam**

SUNDAY GOSPEL

Gospel music tours are big business in Harlem, often pricey yet usually covering transportation uptown and brunch afterwards. You can, however, easily go it on your own. The choir at the Abyssinian Baptist Church is arguably the best in the city, but others of note include Metropolitan Baptist Church, 151 W 128th St at Adam Clayton Powell Jr Boulevard (☎212/663-8990), Mount Moriah, 2050 5th Ave between W 126th and 127th streets (☎212/289-9448) and Mount Nebo,1883 7th Ave at W 114th St (☎212/866-7880). Keep in mind that worship is taken especially seriously, so dress accordingly.

Clayton Powell Jr Boulevard, a broad sweep pushing north between low-built houses that for once in Manhattan allow the sky to break through. As with the rest of Harlem, Powell Boulevard shows years of decline in its graffiti-splattered walls and storefronts punctuated by demolished lots. The recent injection of funds into this area should change it for the better; in fact if the current investments don't make some difference, it's hard to say what will.

At 132 W 138th St stands the **Abyssinian Baptist Church** (Map 9, D6), noted primarily because of its long-time minister, the **Reverend Adam Clayton Powell Jr**, who was instrumental in the 1930s in forcing the white-owned stores of Harlem to employ the blacks who ensured their economic survival. Later, he became the first black on the city council, then New York's first black representative in Congress, sponsoring the country's first minimum-wage law.

Strivers Row

Map 9, D6. #B or #C to 135th St–Frederick Douglass Blvd.
Near the Abyssinian Baptist Church at 138th Street

POWELL BOULEVARD

between Powell and Eighth avenues (aka Frederick Douglass Blvd) are what many consider the finest blocks of rowhouses in Manhattan – **Strivers Row**. Commissioned during the 1890s housing boom, Strivers Row constitutes a uniquely harmonious, dignified Renaissance-derived strip, that's an amalgam of simplicity and elegance. At the turn of the nineteenth century, this came to be the desirable place for ambitious professionals to reside – hence its nickname.

HAMILTON AND WASHINGTON HEIGHTS

Running down Convent Avenue to City College in the 130s, the **Hamilton Heights Historic District** was populated during the Depression by black professionals, who looked down on lesser Harlemites. The Heights' greatest historic lure is the 1798 house of Alexander Hamilton, flamboyant first Secretary to the Treasury. **Hamilton Grange National Memorial** (Map 9, C6; daily 9am–5pm; free; ☏212/666-1640), at 287 Convent Ave, at 142nd St, may soon be moved to a site in nearby St Nicholas Park. For now, the Federal-style mansion sits uncomfortably between the fiercely Romanesque St Luke's Church and an apartment building.

The northernmost part of Manhattan Island, **Washington Heights**, offers only a couple of stop-offs. The **Hispanic Society of America**, on Audubon Terrace between 155th and 156th streets (Map 9, B4; Tues–Sat 10am–4.30pm, Sun 1–4pm; free; ☏212/926-2234), contains one of the largest collections of Hispanic art outside Spain, with works by Spanish masters such as Goya, El Greco and Velázquez, and more than 6000 decorative works of art.

The **Morris–Jumel Mansion**, at 65 Jumel Terrace, between 160th Street and Edgecombe Avenue (Map 9, C3; Wed–Sun 10am–4pm; $3, $2 students and seniors;

☎212/923-8008), is another uptown surprise. Cornered in its garden, the mansion, with its proud Georgian outlines faced with a later Federal portico, somehow survived the destruction all around.

THE CLOISTERS

Tues–Sun; March–Oct 9.30am–5.15pm; Nov–Feb 9.30am–4.45pm; suggested donation $10, students $5, including same-day admission to the Metropolitan Museum; ☎212/923-3700. #A to 190th St–Ft Washington Ave.

The Cloisters, the Metropolitan Museum's collection of medieval art, is housed in a beautiful ersatz monastery in Fort Tryon Park. Unequivocally, this is a must, and if you're game for riding up on the subway you'll find an additional reward in the park itself, the stone-walled promenade overlooking the Hudson and English-style garden making for a sweepingly romantic spot.

Starting from the entrance hall and working counter-clockwise, the collection is laid out in roughly chronological order. First off is the simplicity of the **Romanesque Hall**, featuring French remnants such as an arched, limestone doorway dating to 1150 and a thirteenth-century portal from a monastery in Burgundy. The frescoed Spanish **Fuentidueña Chapel** is dominated by a huge, domed twelfth-century apse from Segovia that immediately induces a reverential hush. Hall and chapel form a corner on one of the prettiest of the five cloisters here, **St Guilhelm**, ringed by strong Corinthian-style columns topped by busily carved capitals with floral designs from thirteenth-century Southern France.

The highlight of the collection, however, are the **Unicorn Tapestries** (*c.*1500, Netherlands), which are brilliantly alive with color, observation and Christian symbolism, more so now than ever, as all seven were recently repaired, restored and rehung in a refurbished gallery with new lighting.

The outer boroughs

Manhattan is a hard act to follow, and the four outer boroughs – **Brooklyn**, **Queens**, **the Bronx** and **Staten Island** – inevitably pale in comparison. But while they lack the glamour of Manhattan, and life in them, essentially residential, is less obviously dynamic, they all offer uniquely unexpected and refreshing perspectives on the city.

Most visitors never set foot off Manhattan, but if you have more than a few days there's much out here to be recommended. In Brooklyn, there's salubrious **Brooklyn Heights** and beautiful **Prospect Park**, along with the evocatively run-down, carnivalesque seaside resort of **Coney Island**. Queens features the bustling Greek community of **Astoria** and **Flushing Meadows**, a vast park that played host to the 1939 and 1964 World's Fairs. The Bronx has in recent years begun to conquer its reputation as a vast danger zone; the notorious **South Bronx** – whose highlight is **Yankee Stadium** – has been largely rehabilitated, and the borough contains one of the country's best zoos and several historic private estates. And while a trip on the **Staten Island ferry** affords a grand view of New York Harbor as well as the downtown skyline, there is little on the island itself to detain most visitors from the immediate return voyage to Manhattan.

SUBWAYS AND BUSES

Be warned that the outer boroughs are much larger than Manhattan, and to get to some of the highlights you'll have to take various subways and buses in succession. It can be a long haul, but you'll grow to appreciate the MTA's ability to connect vastly separated areas. Make sure you're familiarized with the transit system by studying "City transportation" (see p.6), before you start. Taxi cabs can be taken to and from any borough, though remember they are harder to find the farther you are from Manhattan.

Brooklyn

Brooklyn's most visited and most attractive neighborhood is **Brooklyn Heights**, whose tree-lined streets seem a world away from the bustle of Manhattan. More specific reasons to leave Manhattan island are the **Brooklyn Museum of Art** and the **Brooklyn Botanical Gardens**, a half-dozen more subways stops to the east. There's also Frederick Law Olmsted and Calvert Vaux's **Prospect Park**, which for many is an improvement on their more famous bit of landscaping in Manhattan, Central Park. Aficionados of seedy seaside resorts will love **Coney Island**.

THE BROOKLYN BRIDGE

If you are going to **Brooklyn Heights**, begin by walking over the **Brooklyn Bridge** – it's less than a mile across and may hold the best views of Manhattan that you will get. The walkway begins on Centre Street right in front of the Municipal Building (see p.38) and ends in Brooklyn at the

BROOKLYN

Cadman Plaza East staircase.

Walk down the stairs and bear right, following the path through the park at Cadman Plaza. If you cross onto Middagh Street, you'll soon be in the heart of Brooklyn Heights; follow Cadman Plaza West down the hill to Old Fulton Street, and you'll find yourself in the Fulton Ferry District.

BROOKLYN HEIGHTS

Brooklyn Heights, Brooklyn's original city and maybe the most coveted section in the borough, is one of New York City's most stately neighborhoods, composed of brownstone houses along narrow streets that reveal the occasional cobblestoned mews.

Walking up the hill from Old Fulton Street, you can take Everett or Henry streets into the oldest part of Brooklyn Heights proper. It's easy and enjoyable to wander these streets lined with a plethora of Federal-style brick buildings; 24 Middagh St (on the corner of Willow) is an unassuming but perfectly preserved wooden house dating to 1824, the neighborhood's oldest. Two blocks east, on Orange Street between Hicks and Henry, you'll see the simple **Plymouth Church of the Pilgrims**, the one-time preaching base of **Henry Ward Beecher**, abolitionist and campaigner for women's rights.

Retrace your steps one block and follow Henry Street to the corner of Pierrepont, where the **Herman Behr House**, a chunky Romanesque Revival mansion, has been, successively, a hotel, brothel, Franciscan monastery (it was the brothers who added the horrific canopy) and, currently, private apartments. Further down Pierrepont, look in if you can on the **Brooklyn Unitarian Church** – originally known as the Church of the Savior – which is notable for its exquisite neo-Gothic interior.

The Promenade

Walk west on any of the streets between Clark and Remsen and you'll reach the **Promenade** (aka "the Esplanade"), a boardwalk with one of the most spectacular – and renowned – views in all of New York. It's hard to take your eyes off the skyline, the water, the Brooklyn Bridge and the Statue of Liberty in the distance, but do turn around and notice between the trees the monstrous homes set back modestly from the walkway.

Housed in an abandoned 1930s subway station at Schermerhorn Street and Boerum Place, the **New York Transit Museum** (Tues–Fri 10am–4pm, Sat & Sun noon–5pm; $3, children $1.50; ☎718/243-3060, ⓦwww.mta.nyc.ny.us/museum) offers more than 100 years worth of transportation history and memorabilia. Some of the better items are the antique turnstiles and more than twenty restored subway cars and buses dating back to the turn of the nineteenth century. At the time of writing, the museum is closed for renovation and is due to reopen in 2003.

THE BROOKLYN ACADEMY OF MUSIC

30 Lafayette Ave, between Ashland Place and St Felix St; ☎718/636-4100, ⓦwww.bam.org. Take the #Q, #1, #2, #3, #4 or #5 train to Atlantic Ave or the #M, #N, #R or #W train to Pacific Ave.

The **Brooklyn Academy of Music** (BAM to its fans, who come from all over the city) is the oldest performing arts center in America (1859) and one of the borough's most hyped institutions. Located on the edge of Fort Greene, an up-and-coming neighborhood dominated by brownstones, it has played host over the years to a glittering – and innovative – array of artists, from Charles Dickens to Booker T. Washington to Sergei Rachmaninoff to Philip Glass. BAM's new four-screen, state-of-the-art cinema fea-

BROOKLYN

tures art films and the occasional new release.

PROSPECT PARK DISTRICT AND AROUND

Brooklyn really asserts itself – architecturally, at any rate – in the area surrounding **Prospect Park**. A cab ride from downtown Manhattan (about $10) or the #1 or #2 train to Grand Army Plaza is well worth the price to see some excellent urban planning and a lovely green space in the middle of it all.

Grand Army Plaza

Laid out in the late nineteenth century, Central Park architects Robert Law Olmsted and Calvert Vaux designed **Grand Army Plaza** as a dramatic approach to their newly completed Prospect Park. The triumphal **Soldiers and Sailors' Memorial Arch**, which you can climb during spring and autumn (weekends only), was designed in 1892 by John Duncan in tribute to the triumph of the north in the Civil War.

Inside the arch are bas reliefs, including one of Abraham Lincoln by Thomas Eakins and one of General Ulysses S. Grant by William O'Donovan, both installed in 1895. **The Victory Quadriga** (1898), a fiery sculpture atop the arch designed by Frederick William MacMonnies, depicts a rider, chariot, four horses and two heralds.

Prospect Park

Energized by their success with Central Park, Olmsted and Vaux landscaped Prospect Park (℡718/965-8951, Ⓦwww.prospectpark.org) in the early 1890s, completing it just as the finishing touches were being put to Grand Army Plaza outside. The park itself is 526 acres, with a sixty-acre lake on the east side, a ninety-acre open meadow on the

BROOKLYN

west side, and completely surrounded by a 3.5-mile two-lane road, which is primarily reserved for runners, cyclists, rollerbladers and the like.

The Prospect Park Zoo (Nov–March 10am–4.30pm; April–Oct Mon–Fri 10am–5pm, Sat & Sun 10am–5.30pm; $2.50, $1.25 seniors, under 12 50¢) is not a bad place to while away the time, with its richly restored carousel. The park's highlight, however, is the ninety-acre **Long Meadow**, which cuts through the center of the park. On warm weekends you can find soccer and volleyball matches, families hosting grand picnics and couples reading or romantically entwined.

Brooklyn Museum of Art

200 Eastern Parkway. Wed–Fri 10am–5pm, Sat & Sun 11am–6pm, first Sat of every month 11am–11pm; $6, $3 students; ℡718/638-5000, ⊛www.brooklynart.org. #1 or #2 to Eastern Parkway-Brooklyn Museum.

The second-largest art museum in New York City, the **Brooklyn Museum of Art** seems doomed to stand in the shadow of the Met. A trip through the museum, one of the largest US art museums, with 1.5 million objects in its collection and **five floors of exhibits**, requires considerable selectivity. The permanent collection includes Egyptian, Classical and Ancient Middle Eastern Art; Arts of Africa, the Pacific and the Americas; Decorative Arts; Costumes and Textiles; Painting, Sculpture, Prints, Drawings and Photography; and 28 evocative **period rooms**, ranging from an early American farmhouse to a nineteenth-century Moorish castle.

Look in on the **American and European Painting and Sculpture galleries** on the top story, which progress from eighteenth-century portraits – including one of George Washington by **Gilbert Stuart** – and bucolic paintings by members of the **Hudson River School** to works by **Winslow Homer** and **John Singer Sargent** to pieces by **Charles Sheeler** and **Georgia O'Keefe**. A handful of paintings by European artists – **Degas**, **Cezanne**, **Toulouse-Lautrec**, **Monet** and **Dufy**, among others – are also displayed, although nothing here approaches their best work. You will also find a large collection of **Rodin** sculptures. The museum's gift shop sells genuine ethnic items from around the world at reasonable prices.

Brooklyn Botanical Gardens

1000 Washington Ave. April–Sept Tues–Fri 8am–6pm, Sat & Sun 10am–6pm; Oct–March Tues–Fri 8am–4.30pm, Sat & Sun 10am–4.30pm; $3, free Tues & Sat before noon; ☎718/623-7200, ⓦwww.bbg.org. #1 or #2 to Eastern Parkway-Brooklyn Museum.

One of the most enticing park spaces in the city, the **Brooklyn Botanical Gardens**, just south of the Brooklyn Museum, is smaller and more immediately likeable than its more celebrated rival in the Bronx, and makes for a relaxing place to unwind after a couple of hours in the museum next door. Some 12,000 plants from around the world occupy 52 acres of manicured terrain. Sumptuous, but not overplanted, it offers a Rose Garden, Japanese Garden, a Shakespeare Garden (laid out with plants mentioned in the Bard's plays), the Celebrity Path (a winding walk studded with leaf-shaped plaques that honor Brooklyn's famous), and some delightful lawns draped with weeping willows and beds of flowering shrubs. A conservatory houses, among other things, the country's largest collection of bonsai, and a gift shop stocks a wide array of exotic plants, bulbs and seeds.

CONEY ISLAND

Accessible to anyone for the price of a subway ride, the beachfront amusement spot of **Coney Island** has long

BROOKLYN

given working-class New Yorkers the kind of holiday they just couldn't get otherwise. It brings to mind old black-and-white photos from the earlier part of the nineteenth century. Find out for yourself by taking the subway to Stillwell Avenue (last stop on the #F, #M, #Q or #W train). These days, the music blares louder than it once did, the language of choice on the boardwalk is Spanish or Russian as often as English, and the rides look a bit worse for the wear.

The beach can be overwhelmingly crowded on hot days, and it's never the cleanest place in or out of the water. But show up for the annual **Mermaid Parade** on the first Saturday of summer and you'll get caught up in the fun of what's got to be one of the oddest – certainly glitziest – small-town festivals in the country, where paraders dress in King Neptune and mermaid attire.

The amusement area comprises several parks, none of which offers a deal that makes a lot of sense – unless you have kids (nearly all the children's rides are in Deno's Wonder Wheel Park) or plan on riding one ride more than four times. Still, the 75-year-old **Wonder Wheel** ($3, plus a free children's ticket to the New York Aquarium, see below) is a must. After 75 years, it's still the tallest Ferris wheel in the world, and the *only* one on which two-thirds of the cars slide on serpentine tracks, shifting position as the wheel makes its slow circle twice around. The rickety **Cyclone** rollercoaster ($4, $3 for a repeat ride) is another landmark, but if you're used to slick modern loop-coaster rides, be forewarned: this low-tech wooden coaster is not for the faint of heart.

Further down the boardwalk, halfway to Brighton Beach is the seashell-shaped **New York Aquarium** (Mon–Fri 10am–5pm, Sat & Sun 10am–5.30pm; $9.75; ☎718/265-FISH). It is worth a visit if you have the time, especially the dolphin shows or during the seals' feeding hours.

BRIGHTON BEACH

East along the boardwalk from Coney Island, at Brooklyn's southernmost end, lies **Brighton Beach**, once an affluent seaside resort complete with a racetrack, casino and major hotel. Today, the largely residential neighborhood is often referred to as "Little Odessa" (the film of the same name was set here), and is home to the country's largest community of Russian émigrés, who arrived in the 1970s following a relaxation of emigration restrictions on Soviet citizens entering the US.

The main attractions of Brighton Beach are the restaurants, which really heat up each evening, becoming a near-parody of a rowdy Russian night out with lots of food, loud live music, lots of glass-clinking and free-flowing chilled vodka. Guests dress to the nines, and the dancing girls will have you feeling like you've landed in a foreign Vegas. The most popular and accessible spots are *National*, *Ocean* and *Odessa*, all on Brighton Beach Avenue at 273, 1029, and 1113, respectively.

WILLIAMSBURG

Williamsburg, easily accessed by the Bedford Street stop on the #L train, is a self-consciously hip pocket in North Brooklyn largely populated by artists and various scenesters. Many dilapidated buildings along N 6th Street have been put to creative use and the face of the neighborhood changes daily. Indeed, with easy access to Manhattan and excellent waterfront views, it's not hard to see why this area has exploded.

Williamsburg also boasts more than a dozen **contemporary art galleries** ranging in ambience from ultraprofessional to makeshift, and run by an international coterie of artists; the most sophisticated is Pierogi 2000, 177 N 9th St

BROOKLYN

(☎718/599-2144, ⊛www.pierogi2000.com).

You can tour the **Brooklyn Brewery**, 79 N 11th St (☎718/486-7422, ⊛www.brooklynbrewery.com), or hang out in their tasting room (Fri 6–10pm). Around 1900 there were nearly fifty breweries in Brooklyn, and this is the first successful one in the borough since Schaefer and Rheingold closed in 1976.

For other things to do in Williamsburg, look west toward the water and let the old Pfizer smokestack lead you to **Grand Ferry Park**, one of the few waterfront parks left in Brooklyn and where you'll find a great view of the Williamsburg Bridge.

Queens

Of New York City's four outer boroughs, its largest, **Queens** is probably the least visited by outsiders – not counting when they arrive in New York via Queens' airports: La Guardia or John F. Kennedy International. Unlike Brooklyn or the Bronx, Queens has no hyped drawing card to pull visitors in. However, the individuality of its neighborhoods, a leftover from the fact it was never its own city before being incorporated into New York in 1898, just a county of separate towns and villages, is reason enough to warrant exploring the borough.

While here, you can travel from Greek **Astoria** through Irish **Woodside** to Indian and South American **Jackson Heights** and finally Asian **Flushing**, which can feel as suburban as Long Island some days and as exotic as Hong Kong on others. You'll find a few underrated museums and no shortage of delicious ethnic foods – just follow the #7

MOMAQNS

From summer 2002 through 2005, Queens will be the home of the Museum of Modern Art, while its new facility is being constructed in Manhattan. **MoMaQNS**, 45-20 33rd St at Queens Boulevard (℡212/708-9400) can be reached by the #7 train to 33rd St stop and will offer exhibitions and educational programs, along with a café and design shop. Highlights include a special installation of the museum's permanent collection (see p.90). Call ahead for scheduling.

train, which chugs through most of the borough; Turkish breads, Romanian sausage, Indonesian noodles, Tibetan pork, Argentinean steak, vegetarian Indian, Cantonese dim sum, and some of the best Texas barbecue in the city await.

ASTORIA

Astoria is known for two things: filmmaking and the fact that it has the largest single concentration of Greeks outside Greece itself (or so it claims). Until the movie industry moved out to the West Coast in the early 1930s, Astoria was the cinematic capital of the world, and Paramount had its studios here until the lure of Hollywood's reliable weather left Astoria empty and disused. That's how it remained until recently, when Hollywood's stranglehold on the industry weakened and interest – in New York in general and Astoria in particular – was renewed. After a major renovation, the **Kaufman-Astoria Studios** (34-12 36th St; call ℡718/392-5600, ⓦwww.kaufmanastoria.com) have reopened.

More film history can be found in the old Paramount complex. Here, the **American Museum of the Moving Image**, 35th Avenue at 36th Street (Tues–Fri noon–5pm, Sat & Sun 11am–6pm; $8.50; ℡718/784-0077,

QUEENS

159

@www.ammi.org), houses a stellar collection of over 1000 objects, from posters to stills to sets and equipment both from Astoria's golden age and more recent times. On weekends, the AMMI has matinée showings of classic and occasionally cult films.

Meanwhile, **Greek Astoria** stretches from Ditmars Boulevard in the north down to Broadway, and from 31st Street across to Steinway Street. Between 80,000 and 100,000 Greeks live here (together with a smaller community of Italians and an influx of Eastern Europeans, Bangladeshis and Latin Americans), evidenced by the large number of **restaurants** and **patisseries**.

SHEA STADIUM AND FLUSHING MEADOW PARK

Take #7 train to Willets Point for **Shea Stadium** (Roosevelt Avenue off Grand Central Parkway; ☎718/507-8499), home of the New York Mets. The Beatles famously played here in 1965 as did the Rolling Stones in 1989; but concerts out here are very rare. Baseball games, on the other hand, are frequent between April and October, and the Mets have a solid and loyal fan base. See Chapter 34, "Sports and outdoor activities," for ticket details.

From Shea, you'll easily find your way to Flushing Meadow Park. The **New York Hall of Science**, 46th Avenue and 111th Street (hours vary, so call ahead; $7.50, $5 under 17; ☎718/699-0005, @www.nyhallsci.org), is a concrete and stained-glass structure retained from the 1964 World's Fair (you'll see the best remaining structures deeper within the park). This is an interactive science museum kids will love; it's fun but can be exhausting for adults. The adjacent **Wildlife Center** (once the zoo) features exclusively North American animals. But the main reason to come here is to see the **Unisphere** and the **Queens Museum of Art** (see opposite).

The **Unisphere** is a 140-foot-high, stainless steel globe that weighs 380 tons – probably the main reason why it never left its place in the park following the 1964 World's Fair. It was finally declared a landmark, to the delight of the borough, and it's now lit at night – you may have seen it when you came in from the airport. Carefully designed pathways connect lawns, small pools and two lakes. On a summer day, the park is swarming with kids on bikes and rollerblades; you can rent a bicycle yourself, or even a boat.

Queens Museum of Art

Tues–Fri 10am–5pm, Sat & Sun noon–5pm; suggested donation $5; ℡718/592-9700, ℗www.queensmuse.org . #7 to 111th St.

Housed in a 1939 World's Fair building which served briefly as the first home of the United Nations, the **Queens Museum** has been open since 1972. The must-see here is the **Panorama of the City of New York**, which was also built for the 1964 World's Fair. With a one-inch model equal to one hundred feet of city, the Panorama (and its 835,000 buildings, plus bridges, piers, rivers and airports) is the world's largest architectural model.

The Bronx

The city's northernmost borough, **The Bronx**, was for a long time believed to be its toughest and most notoriously crime-ridden district – and presented as such in films like *Fort Apache, the Bronx* and books like *Bonfire of the Vanities*, even after urban renewal was underway. Indeed, there was no other part of the city about which people were so ready to roll out their most gruesome horror stories. Nowadays its poorer reaches still suffer from severe urban deprivation, but almost all of the borough has undergone a successful recent transformation.

THE SOUTH BRONX AND YANKEE STADIUM

A trip to the borough on the elevated #4 train affords a good general view of the **South Bronx**, if you haven't got time to go visiting individual neighborhoods – and there's not much reason to do so in any case. The area consists of the segment of the Bronx south of Fordham Road, yet most visitors come here to visit **Yankee Stadium** (first stop on the #B and #D subways after leaving Manhattan, and the third such stop on the #4), home to the New York Yankees baseball team. You can go on the Babe Ruth Tour, which includes history, monument park, clubhouse, press-box and dugout (Mon–Fri 10am–4pm, Sat 10am–noon, Sun noon only; $10, $5 children and seniors; ☏718/579-4531, ⓦwww.yankees.com).

CENTRAL BRONX AND BELMONT

Few tourists come up this way, a shame, because where real Italian flavor is concerned, **Belmont** makes Little Italy look like Disneyland. **Arthur Avenue** is the neighborhood's main thoroughfare, a mixture of tenements and clapboard houses that is home to one of the largest segments of New York's Italian community – and the most authentic. Although there has been a small influx of other ethnic groups – most notably Haitians, Mexicans and Albanian Yugoslavs (who love Italian food) – the staunch Italian community is still the dominant force.

There's no better part of the Bronx if you want to eat, particularly if you're on your way to the zoo. Choose restaurants on Arthur Avenue with care: swanky *Mario's* at no. 2342 (supposedly where the scene in *The Godfather* in which Al Pacino shot the double-crossing policeman was filmed) is popular but pricey. Recommended spots include *Pasquale Rigoletto* and *Emilia's* restaurants at nos. 2311 and 2331, respectively.

The Bronx Zoo

Mon–Fri 10am–5pm, Sat & Sun 10am–5.30pm; $9, $5 for seniors and kids, free on Wed, rides and some exhibits are an additional charge; ☎718/367-1010, ⊚www.wcs.org. #2 or #5 train to Pelham Parkway.

Accessible either by its main gate on Fordham Road or by a second entrance on Bronx Park South, **Bronx Zoo/Wildlife Conservation Park** is probably the only reason many New Yorkers from outside the borough ever visit the Bronx. Opened in 1899 and centered around a cluster of original buildings, this is arguably America's greatest zoo, certainly its largest urban one, and also one of the first to realize that animals both looked and felt better out in the open. This humane environment has been artfully achieved through a variety of simulated natural habitats. Visit in summer to appreciate it at its best; in winter, a surprising number of the animals are kept in indoor enclosures without viewing areas.

New York Botanical Gardens

Tues–Sun 10am–6pm; $3, $2 seniors and students, 3–12 $1, free on Wed, parking $5; ☎718/817-8700, ⊚www.nybg.org. #B or #D train to Bedford Park Blvd.

Across the road from the zoo's main entrance is the back turnstile of the **New York Botanical Gardens**, incorporated in 1891, which in their southernmost reaches are as wild as anything you're likely to see upstate. Its scientific

THE BRONX

facilities include a museum, library, herbarium, and a research laboratory. Further north near the main entrance are more cultivated stretches. The **Enid A. Haupt Conservatory**, a landmark, turn-of-the-nineteenth-century crystal palace, showcases jungle and desert ecosystems, a palm court and a fern forest, among other seasonal displays.

The Poe Cottage

Grand Concourse and E Kingsbridge Rd. Sat 10am–4pm, Sun 1–5pm, otherwise by appointment only; $2; ☎718/881-8900. #D or #4 train to Kingsbridge Rd or the Bx9 bus up Fordham Rd.

Located in Poe Park, the **Edgar Allan Poe Cottage** was built in 1812. This tiny, white-clapboard anachronism in the midst of a working-class Hispanic neighborhood was Edgar Allan Poe's rural home for the last three years of his life, from 1846 to 1849, though it was only moved here recently when threatened with demolition. Poe was rarely happy in the cottage, but he did manage to write the short, touching poem "Annabel Lee" and the better known "The Bells."

Museum of Bronx History

3266 Bainbridge Ave. Sat 10am–4pm, Sun 1–5pm, otherwise by appointment only; $2; ☎718/881-8900. #D to 205th St-Bainbridge Ave, or #4 to Kingsbridge Rd.

Housed a fieldstone farmhouse built in 1758, the **Museum of Bronx History** is more notable for its historic building than for its exhibitions of Bronx-related artifacts from the pre-Colonial era to the Depression. Considering how much the Bronx has changed – there was still plenty of farm country left only fifty years ago – the old photographs and lithographs can be fascinating.

THE BRONX

NORTH BRONX

The **North Bronx** is the topmost fringe of New York City, and if anyone actually makes it up here it's to see the luminary-filled **Woodlawn Cemetery**. Accessible from Jerome Avenue at Bainbridge (last stop, Woodlawn, on the #4), this is a prime example of how New Yorkers in the 1850s took in the air. For many years, Woodlawn has been a celebrity cemetery, and boasts a number of tombs and mausolea that are memorable mainly for their garishness. It's a huge place, but there are some monuments that stand out: F.W. Woolworth has himself an Egyptian palace guarded by sphinxes, while Jay Gould, not most people's favorite businessman when he was alive, takes it easy in a Greek-style temple. Pick up a guide from the office at the entrance to locate the many larger-than-life individuals buried here: they include Herman Melville, Irving Berlin, George M. Cohan, Fiorello LaGuardia, Robert Moses, Miles Davis, and Duke Ellington, among others.

STATEN ISLAND FERRY

The bargain that still can't be beaten, even more so now that the fare has been eliminated, is the free Staten Island ferry (☎718/390-5253), which leaves from its own terminal in lower Manhattan's Battery Park. It's a commuter boat, so avoid crowded rush hours if you can; at other times, grab a spot at the back (going out) and watch the skyline shrink away. Departures are every 15–20 minutes at rush hours, every thirty minutes midday and evenings, and every hour late at night – weekend services are less frequent.

THE BRONX

LISTINGS

LISTINGS

Accommodation

Accommodation in New York definitely eats up the lion's share of a traveler's budget. Many **hotels** in the city charge somewhere in the neighborhood of $150–200 a night, not to mention the **taxes** tacked on to that, and some go well beyond that price. With some planning, it is possible to get a decent-sized clean room for $150 or less, but in truth it's far easier to hunt splurges than bargains. Make your **reservations** as far ahead as possible; most hotels cite "supply and demand" as the main influence on their room rate. Don't even think of calling a day before during Christmas and summer when you're likely to find everything (and we mean this) full.

Bear in mind all-included flight and hotel package vacations. Booking services – see box, p.176 – reserve rooms at discount prices and usually for no extra charge. Also, you might try booking through hotel's websites for the occasional special deal.

The best advice regarding discounts is simply to **ask** – discounts may also be available in the form of **promotional specials** or **corporate rates**. The **internet** is worth a try: ⓦwww.nycvisit.com has listed specials (which come with a list of restrictions, and require that you pay with an American Express card). Furthermore, several consolidator-type sites are available (try ⓦwww.hotres.com, ⓦwww.travelscape.com, or ⓦwww.hoteldiscounts.com).

For full hotel listings and prices, consult the New York Convention and Visitors Bureau **leaflet**, *Hotels in New York City*, available from one of their offices.

HOSTELS AND YMCAs

Hostels and **YMCAs** are just about the only option for cash-strapped backpackers in New York, with dorm beds going for as little as $25 a night. YMCAs are better if you want privacy because they have private single and double rooms, though they tend to have a more institutional feel than the more relaxed hostels. For a comprehensive listing of hostels in New York and across North America, obtain *The Hostel Handbook* for $4 plus shipping by phoning ☏212/926-7030 or emailing ✉infohostel@aol.com. Or, you can visit the Internet Guide to Hosteling at ⓦwww.hostelhandbook.com. The following is a small selection of the best hostels and Ys:

Blue Rabbit International House

Map 9, C5. 730 St Nicholas Ave (at 146th St), NY 10031 ☏1-800/6-HOSTEL or 212/491-3892, ✉bluerabbit@hostelhandbook.com.
This Harlem hostel charges $25 for dorms, with a limited number of double rooms, available only on a first-come, first-served basis, for $30 per person per night (plus $10 deposit), maybe the cheapest doubles in the city. Has kitchens, and bed linen is included in the price.

Central Park Hostel

Map 8, E3. 19 W 103rd St (near Central Park West), NY 10025 ☏212/678-0491, ☏678-0453, ✉info@CentralParkHostel.com.
New Upper West Side hostel has dorm beds for four, six or eight people ($26–36), and some private two-bed rooms in a five-story renovated walk-up. All rooms share clean bathrooms, and lockers

are available (bring a padlock). Payment in cash or travelers' checks only; you must have a foreign passport or international student ID.

Chelsea Center Hostel

Map 6, E5. 313 W 29th St (near 8th Ave), NY 10001 ☏212/643-0214, ℱ473-3945, ⓦwww.chelseacenter hostel.com.

Reputable, clean, safe and friendly, the *Chelsea Center Hostel* has beds for $30 with breakfast and clean sheets and blankets included. Well situated for Midtown West, Chelsea and the West Village (the hostel also has a second location in the East Village). Book well in advance in high season. Office hours are 8.30am to 11pm, there's no curfew; cash only.

Chelsea International Hostel

Map 6, F7. 251 W 20th St, NY 10011 ☏212/647-0010, ℱ727-7289, ⓦwww.chelseahostel.com.

Situated in the heart of Chelsea, this is the closest hostel to downtown. Beds (130 in all) are $27 a night, including tax, and the rooms, which sleep four or six, are small with bathrooms in the hall (though larger rooms for six at the back of the hostel have bathrooms). Private rooms for two are $65 a night. Accommodation is rudimentary, but the location is the hostel's main attraction. Desk open 8am–9pm, and there are security guards and sign-in at night. Passport required.

Hosteling International – New York

Map 8, C3. 891 Amsterdam Ave (at 103rd St), NY 10025 ☏212/932-2300, ℱ932-1600, ⓦwww.hinewyork.org.

This historic Upper West Side building has 480 dormitory-style beds for $29–35 for IYHA members (on-the-spot membership is $25 for US citizens or $18 for those with a foreign address); $3 extra for nonmembers per night. Though the place is large, it may be heavily booked; reserve at least 24 hours in advance (at least a

HOSTELS AND YMCAS

week in the summer). Open
24 hours.

Jazz on the Park

Map 8, E2. 36 W 106th St (at
Central Park W), NY 10025
☎212/932-1600, ℉932-1700,
⊛www.jazzhostel.com.
This groovy bunkhouse, just
a stone's throw from the park,
boasts a TV-gameroom,
rooftop barbecues and the
Java Joint Café. The rooms,
sleeping between two and
fourteen, are clean, bright
and air-conditioned. Beds
cost between $30 and $35 a
night (including tax, linen
and a light breakfast); a two-
bed room is $88.
Reservations essential
June–Oct and over Christmas
and New Year's (when rates
are a little higher).

Vanderbilt YMCA

Map 7, J8. 224 E 47th St
(between 2nd and 3rd aves), NY
10017 ☎212/756-9600.
Smaller and quieter than most
of the hostels above, and
neatly placed in midtown,
just five-minutes' walk from
Grand Central Station.
Inexpensive restaurant,
swimming pool, gym and
laundromat. Singles start at
$70, doubles at $85.

Westside YMCA

Map 7, E4. 5 W 63rd St, NY
10023 ☎212/875-4173
or 875-4273.
A wonderfully situated Y
next to Central Park and
Lincoln Center with single
rooms for $70/$110 per night
(with or without bath),
doubles for $80/$120, and
free use of two pools, saunas,
gym and sports facilities. All
rooms air-conditioned.

BED AND BREAKFAST

Choosing a **bed and breakfast** can be a good way of staying right in the center of Manhattan at a reasonably affordable price. All rooms – except for a few which we've found off the beaten track (listed on p.175) – are let out via the following official agencies and they all recommend making your reservations as far in advance as possible, especially for the cheapest rooms. In cases where landlords/ladies prefer that visitors reserve in advance rather than show up on their doorsteps, we have omitted addresses.

B&B AGENCIES

Affordable New York City

Map 5, E2. 21 E 10th St, NY 10003 ☎212/533-4001, ⓕ387-8732, ⓦwww. affordablenewyorkcity.com. Established network of 120 properties (B&Bs and apartments) around the city, with detailed descriptions. B&B accommodations from $85 (shared bath) and $100 (private), unhosted studios $140–175 and one-bedrooms $175–225. Cash or travelers' checks only; three-night minimum. Very customer-oriented and personable.

Bed and Breakfast Network of New York

Map 5, B4. 130 Barrow St, NY 10014 ☎1-800/900-8134 or 212/645-8134, Mon–Fri 8am–6pm. Growing network with hosted singles for $80–100, doubles $110–150; prices for unhosted accommodation run from $130 to luxury multibedded apartments for $400. Weekly and monthly rates also available. For an assured booking write at least a month in advance; make short-notice reservations by phone.

City Lights Bed & Breakfast

PO Box 20355, Cherokee Station, NY 10021 ⓣ212/737-7049, ⓕ535-2755, ⓔreservations @citylightsbandb.com.

More than 400 carefully screened B&Bs (and short-term apartment rentals) on its books, with many of the hosts involved in theater and the arts. Hosted singles run $90–125, doubles $95–135. Unhosted accommodation costs $135 to $300 per night depending on whether it's a studio or four-bedroom apartment. Minimum stay two nights, reserve well in advance.

CitySonnet.com

Village Station, PO Box 347, NY 10014 ⓣ212/614-3034, ⓕ425/920-2384, ⓦwww.CitySonnet.com. Small, personalized B&B/short-term apartment agency with accommodations all over the city, but specializing in downtown and the West Village. Singles start at $80; doubles $100–155; unhosted flats start at $140.

Colby International

139 Round Hey, Liverpool L28 1RG, England ⓣ0151/220 5848, ⓦwww.colbyintl.com.

If you want guaranteed B&B accommodation, Colby International is without doubt your best bet – and they can fix up accommodation from the UK. Excellent-value double rooms start at $95 a night, singles are $80, and apartments range from $125–300, depending on size and location: book as far ahead as possible in high season.

Gamut Realty Group

Map 7, L1. 301 E 78th St, NY 10021 ⓣ212/879-4229 or 1-800/437-8353, ⓕ517-5356, ⓦwww.GamutNYC.com. Fully automated agency that can fax or email sample listings of available rooms and apartments for nightly or longer-term stays. Unhosted studio apartments for $120–150, and one-bedroom apartments for $165 and up. Has accommodation all over Manhattan, some in luxury buildings or artists' lofts.

B&B PROPERTIES

Bed & Breakfast on the Park

☎718/499-6115, ⓕ499-1385, ⓦwww.bbnyc.com.

A handsome 1892 Park Slope limestone townhouse with views over Prospect Park, with eight double rooms $125–300 a night (two-night minimum).

Chelsea Brownstone

☎212/206-9237, ⓕ388-9954.

Conveniently situated on a safe, quiet street in Chelsea, this well-maintained, family-run brownstone contains a number of private, self-contained apartments (recently upgraded) starting at $130 for studios and $150 for one-bedrooms, per night (with good discounts for stays of more than a week), each with its own TV, phone, bathroom and fully equipped kitchen. Best to book well in advance by phone.

Inn at Irving Place

Map 6, K9. 56 Irving Place, NY 10003 ☎1-800/685-1447 or 212/533-4600, ⓕ533-4611, ⓦwww.innatirving.com.

It costs $295–500 a night for one of the twenty rooms – each named after a famous architect, designer or actor – in this handsome pair of 1834 brownstones, which must rank as one of the most exclusive guesthouses in the city. The *Inn* offers five-course high teas, along with free access to a local gym.

New York Bed and Breakfast

Map 9, E8. 134 W 119th St (at Lenox Ave), NY 10026 ☎212/666-0559, ⓕ663-5000.

This lovely old brownstone just in the heart of Harlem features nice double rooms for $65 a night for two people.

HOTELS

Most of New York's **hotels** tend to be in midtown Manhattan, which is fine if you want to be close to theaters and the main tourist sights (and large clusters of tourists), but it's hardly the makings of a restful vacation. If you're going to be spending a lot of time in the West Village or SoHo, you might want to try one of the handful of downtown or Chelsea hotels. Or the Upper West or East Side will do if your taste runs more to Central Park, the museums or Lincoln Center.

Taxes will add 13.25 percent to your bill (state tax 8.25 percent, city tax five percent), and there is also a $2 per night "occupancy tax." This will add about $15 to a $100 room.

HOTEL BOOKING SERVICES

Accommodations Express
☎1-800/444-7666, ℻609/525-0111,
🌐www.accommodationsexpress.com.

CRS
☎407/740-6442 or 1-800/950-0232, ℻407/740-8222,
🌐www.reservation-services.com.

Express Reservations
(weekdays only) ☎1-800/356-1123 or 303/440-8481,
℻303/440-0166,🌐www.expressreservations.com.

Hotel Reservations Network
☎1-800/964-6835, 🌐www.hoteldiscount.com.

Meegan's Services
☎1-800/441-1115 or 718/995-9292, ℻718/995-4439.

The Room Exchange
450 7th Ave, NY 10123 ☎1-800/846-7000, ℻212/760-1013.

HOTEL PRICE CODES

The code in the following listings refers to the price of a hotel's cheapest double room throughout most of the year and includes all taxes. Where there's a significant seasonal variation, the high-season rate is usually given. Where prices are based on a per-person rate, however, they are given in dollars.

1 under $100		**5** $200–250	
2 $100–130		**6** $250–300	
3 $130–160		**7** $300–350	
4 $160–200		**8** over $350	

At the more upmarket hotels, tipping is expected: unless you firmly refuse, a bellhop will grab your bags when you check in and expect up to $5 to carry them to your room. For housekeeping, figure $2 minimum per day for cheaper hotels, more for the nicer establishments.

BELOW 14TH STREET

----

60 Thompson
Map 5, E7. 60 Thompson St (between Spring and Broome sts), NY 10012 ⊤212/431-0400, ⓕ431-0200, ⓦwww.60thompson.com. With excellent proximity to SoHo's chic restaurants and vibrant galleries, the handsome *60 Thompson* offers 100 modern guestrooms and suites. It further indulges visitors with a rooftop garden and in-house DVD library. Upstairs rooms look out over SoHo's rooftops. **8**

Larchmont
Map 5, E2. 27 W 11th St (between 5th and 6th aves), NY 10011 ⊤212/989-9333, ⓦwww.larchmonthotel.com.

Budget hotel in the heart of the West Village, on a beautiful tree-lined street, just off Fifth Ave. Hotels are a rarity in this residential area, so this is a real find. Rooms are small but nicely decorated and clean, and all have TV, air conditioners, phones and washbasins. Small kitchens and bathrooms with showers are on each corridor. Prices include continental breakfast. Very small singles as low as ❶, doubles at ❷.

The Mercer

Map 5, F6. 147 Mercer (at Prince St) ☎1-888/918-6060 or 212/966-6060, ⓕ965-3838, ⓦwww.themercer.com.
The last word in discreet "boutique" chic. Rooms are stylish with simple furnishings, high ceilings, walk-in closets and oversized bathrooms. The occasional celebrity will share your sofa in the smart lobby, and trendy *Mercer Kitchen* provides your room service 24 hours. All this in the heart of SoHo. ❽

Soho Grand

Map 5, E8. 310 W Broadway (at Grand St), NY 10013 ☎1-800/965-3000 or 212/965-3000, ⓕ965-3200, ⓦwww.sohogrand.com.
Great location at the edge of SoHo, and many guests exude the attitude that comes with the territory: rock stars, models, actors and the like. Still, the staff is surprisingly helpful, the rooms are stylishly appointed, if a bit small, with classic New York photographs from a local gallery and an optional goldfish (ask and you shall receive). The hotel also boasts an elegant bar, restaurant and fitness center. ❽

Tribeca Grand

Map 4, D2. 2 6th Ave (between White and Walker sts), NY 10013 ☎1-877/519-6600 or 212/519-6600, ⓕ965-3244, ⓦwww.tribecagrand.com.
Unlabeled, and hidden by a brick facade like a brand-new train station, the *Tribeca Grand* is close to *Soho Grand* in location and spirit. Once inside, the Church Lounge, one of the more striking

hotel public spaces, beckons with a warm orange glow. The rooms are stylish yet understated, though each bathroom boasts a phone and built-in TV. Off-season weekends can be as low as ❺; for most weekdays, count on rates in the ❽ bracket.

Washington Square

Map 5, D3. 103 Waverly Place, NY 10011 ☎212/777-9515 or 1-800/222-0418, Ⓕ979-8373, Ⓦwww.washington squarehotel.com.
An ideal location: bang in the heart of the West Village, just off Washington Square Park, and a stone's throw from the NYU campus. The rooms are more than adequate and some have views over the park. Continental breakfast and use of the exercise room are included in the price. Book two months in advance for the summer. ❹

CHELSEA AND THE WEST SIDE: W 14TH TO 34TH STREETS

Chelsea Hotel

Map 6, F7. 222 W 23rd St (between 7th and 8th aves), NY 10011 ☎212/243-3700, Ⓕ675-5531, Ⓦwww.hotelchelsea.com.
One of New York's most noted landmarks, both for its ageing neo-Gothic building and, more importantly, its long list of alumni, from Dylan Thomas to Bob Dylan (see p.73 for a fuller cast). If you check into the *Chelsea* you may find yourself staying in somebody's apartment, surrounded by their belongings. Ask instead for a renovated room with polished wood floors, log-burning fireplaces, and plenty of space to cram a few extra friends into. ❹ for a double room, ❼ for a suite.

Chelsea Lodge

Map 6, D7. 318 W 20th St, NY 10011 ☎212/243-4499, Ⓕ243-7852, Ⓦwww.chelsealodge.com.
The plaid-papered "lodge"

rooms (with sink and shower – the shared toilet is down the hall) are a little small for two, but the few deluxe rooms (❹) are a great value and have new full bathrooms. There's also a choice of four one-room suites (❺) that can sleep four (there's a pull-out bed) and have a kitchenette (and two have access to a small patio/garden).

Chelsea Savoy Hotel
Map 6, F7. 204 W 23rd St, NY 10011 ☎212/929-9353, ℱ741-6309.
A few doors away from the *Chelsea Hotel*, the *Savoy* has none of its neighbor's funky charm but its rooms, though small, are clean and nicely decorated and the staff is helpful. Try to avoid rooms facing the main drags outside. ❸

Herald Square
Map 6, H4. 19 W 31st St (between 5th Ave and Broadway), NY 10001 ☎1-800-727-1888 or 212/279-4017, ℱ643-9208, ⓦwww.heraldsquarehotel.com.
The original home of *Life*

magazine, *Herald Square* still features Philip Martiny's golden sculptured cherub *Winged Life* over the doorway of this Beaux-Arts building. Inside it's meticulously clean, but without much in the way of extras, and somewhat soulless. ❸; triples and quads ❹. Very small single rooms go for as low as $76 a night with shared bathroom.

Hotel Pennsylvania
Map 6, F4. 401 7th Ave, NY 10001 ☎1-800/223-8585 or 212/736-5000, ℱ502-8712, ⓦwww.hotelpenn.com.
Standing right across from Madison Square Garden, this hotel offers every possible convenience in its 1705 rooms, though you can't help thinking it once looked better. ❹, dropping to ❸ in summer.

Stanford
Map 6, H4. 43 W 32nd St (between Broadway and 5th Ave), NY 10001 ☎1-800/365-1114 or 212/563-1500, ℱ629-0043, ⓦwww.hotelstanford .citysearch.com.

Rooms are a tad small, but attractive and very quiet, and the hallways are well lit, if a little narrow. The *Stanford* offers free continental breakfast and valet laundry, a cocktail lounge and good Korean cuisine (in the very relaxing surroundings of the *Gam Mee Ok* restaurant), and the efficient and friendly staff would be welcome in hotels twice this price. **❹**

Wolcott

Map 6, H4. 4 W 31st St (between 5th Ave and Broadway), NY 10001 ☎212/268-2900, ⓦwww.wolcott.com. A surprisingly relaxing budget hotel, with a gilded, ornate Louis XVI-style lobby full of mirrors and lion reliefs (even the ceiling is lavish). The rooms, while much more staid, are more than adequate, all with (somewhat old-fashioned) bathrooms. **❸**

UNION SQUARE TO MURRAY HILL: E 14TH TO 42ND STREETS

Carlton Arms

Map 6, K6. 160 E 25th St (between 3rd and Lexington aves), NY 10010 ☎212/679-0680. One of the city's latest Bohemian hangouts, with eclectic interior decor by would-be artists, very few comforts, and a clientele made up of Europeans, down-at-the-heel artists and long-staying guests. Discount rates available for students and foreign travelers, with an extra ten-percent discount if you pay for seven nights in advance. Singles with bath can be as low as $75 plus tax. Reserve well in advance for summer. **❷**

Doral Park

Map 6, J2. 70 Park Ave (at 38th St), NY 10016 ☎1-800/223-6725 or 212/687-7050, ⓕ808-9029, ⓦwww.doralparkavenue.com. A multimillion-dollar

HOTELS

●

restoration has turned the *Doral Park* into one of the snazziest deluxe hotels, with re-creations of classical friezes and frescoes and original designs for lighting and furnishings. Rooms are in shades of turquoise/green and orange (it's not as bad as it sounds). Service is excellent. ❻, promotional rates ❹.

Gershwin Hotel

Map 6, I5. 7 E 27th St, NY 10016 ☎212/545-8000, ℻684-5546, ⓦwww.gershwinhotel.com.

A young person's hotel just off Fifth Ave in the Flatiron district that also functions as a hostel. The 110 private double rooms with bathrooms cost about $169 a night (plus tax); weekends are $15 extra. Imaginatively decorated with a Pop Art theme, the *Gershwin* has an astroturfed rooftop (where parties are held on the weekend), a small bar, a well-priced restaurant and a friendly staff. Try to book well in advance. ❹

Library

Map 6, I1. 299 Madison Ave (at 41st St), NY 10022 ☎1-877/793-READ or 212/983-4500, ℻204-5401, ⓦwww.libraryhotel.com.

Each floor is devoted to one of the ten major categories of the Dewey Decimal System, and each room's artwork and books reflect a different pursuit within that group. Only those with a serious sense of purpose could design sixty unique rooms and handpick more than 6000 books for the place, and the dedication shows in other ways, notably in the lovely Poet's Garden on the roof. ❼

The Metro

Map 6, H3. 45 W 35th St, NY 10001 ☎1-800/356-3870 or 212/947-2500, ℻279-1310, ⓦwww.hotelmetronyc.com.

A very stylish hotel – it's Art Deco sensible, with old Hollywood posters on the walls, a delightful rooftop terrace, spacious communal areas, clean rooms and free continental breakfast. A few more extras (like a fitness room, and the highly recommended *Metro Grill* restaurant on the first floor) than normally expected in this category. ❺; summer specials ❹.

Murray Hill Inn

Map 6, K5. 143 E 30th St (between Lexington and 3rd aves), NY 10016 ☎1-888/996-6376 or 212/683-6900, ⓕ545-0103, ⓦwww.murrayhillinn.com.

It's easy to see why young travelers and backpackers line the *Inn's* narrow halls. Although the rooms are smallish, they are air-conditioned and all have telephone, cable TV, and sink; some also have private bathrooms. With a friendly staff and a residential locale that offers a breather from the bustle. Rates per room: singles $75, doubles $95 (shared bath), $125 (private), additional costs if more than two in a room. They also have weekly rates for single rooms. ❶

Roger Williams

Map 6, I4. 131 Madison Ave (at 31st St), NY 10016

☎1-888/448-7788 or 212/448-7000, ⓕ448-7007, ⓦwww.rogerwilliamshotel.com

At some point during its $2 million "boutique" renovation, this hotel made a turn onto Madison and its prices shot up exponentially. Still, Rafael Vinoly's mellow, Scandinavian/Japanese fusion rooms with Aveda bath gels and fluted zinc pillars in the lobby make it well worth the extra bucks. European breakfast, and 24-hour espresso/cappuccino bar. ❻; Sept through Dec ❼.

Seventeen

Map 6, L8. 225 E 17th St (between 2nd and 3rd aves), NY 10003 ☎212/475-2845, ⓕ677-8178, ⓦwww.hotel17.citysearch.com.

Budget accommodation as you'd expect it to look: rudimentary bedrooms, and bathrooms on the corridors that have seen better days. But *Seventeen* is clean and friendly, and it can't be beaten either for location – it's on a pleasant, tree-lined street and very handy if you want to spend your time in the East

HOTELS

Village, only a few blocks away. Singles ❶, doubles ❷

Thirty Thirty

Map 6, I4. 30 E 30th St, NY 10016 ☎1-800/804-4480 or 212/689-1900, ⓦwww.stayinny.com. Small welcoming budget hotel, with a few small but welcome design touches, like the framed black-and-white scenes of old New York in the rooms. ❸

Thirty-One

Map 6, J4. 120 E 31st St (between Lexington and Park aves), NY 10016 ☎212/685-3060, ⓕ532-1232, ⓦwww.hotel31.com. A new hotel in Murray Hill brought to you by the folks who own *Seventeen* (see overleaf). The rooms are clean and the street is quiet and pleasant. ❶ (shared bathroom) or ❸ (private bathroom).

W Union Square

Map 6, J9. 201 Park Ave (at Union Square), NY 10003 ☎1-877/W-HOTELS or 212/253-9119, ⓕ253-9229, ⓦwww.whotels.com. Located in the former Guardian Life Building, this is really the only upscale hotel in the area, and boasts Todd English's *Olives* restaurant as well as a bar scene that lasts from after work to after hours. The artificial green grass and corkscrewing bamboo in the lobby is just a prelude to the rooms with deep purple accents, which are called "Wonderful," "Spectacular" or "Mega"; all will set you back. ❽

MIDTOWN WEST: W 34TH TO 59TH STREETS

Algonquin

Map 7, G9. 59 W 44th St (between 5th and 6th aves), NY 10036 ☎1-800/555-8000 or 212/840-6800, ⓦwww.camberleyhotels.com. New York's classic literary hangout for the past century, as created by Dorothy Parker and her associates and perpetuated by the likes of Noel Coward, George

Bernard Shaw, and Irving Berlin. The cabaret in the *Oak Room* perpetuates the air of hushed sophistication. Some decor remains little changed, but the rooms, bathrooms and lobby were handsomely refurbished in 1998. From ⑤

Ameritania Hotel 54

Map 7, E7. 230 W 54th St (at Broadway), NY 10019 ℡1-800/922-0330 or 212/247-5000, ⓦwww.nychotels.com. The well-furnished rooms come with marble bathroom, cable TV and CD player; and there's a bar/restaurant off the high-tech, Neoclassical lobby. $5 off their basic rates if you mention *Rough Guides*. ⑥, with July and Aug specials at ③.

Broadway Inn

Map 7, E8. 264 W 46th St, NY 10036 ℡1-800/826-6300 or 212/997-9200, ⓕ768-2807, ⓦwww.broadwayinn.com. Cozy, reasonably priced bed-and-breakfast hotel in the heart of the theater district on the corner of charmless Eighth Ave, but a skip away

from Times Square and Restaurant Row. Guests get a twenty-percent discount at the restaurant downstairs. An excellent staff makes up for the lack of an elevator. ④

Casablanca

Map 7, F9. 147 W 43rd St (between 6th and 7th aves), NY 10036 ℡1-888/9-CASABLANCA, ⓦwww.casablancahotel.com. Moorish tiles, ceiling fans and, of course, *Rick's Cafe* are all here in this unusual, thoughtful and understated theme hotel. While the feeling is Morocco in the 1940s, the features (dataports for laptops, VCRs) are all up-to-date, and bottled water and Belgian chocolates appear at turndown. ⑥

Essex House

Map 7, F5. 160 Central Park S (between 6th and 7th aves), NY 10019 ℡1-800/WESTIN-1 or 212/247-0300, ⓕ315-1839, ⓦwww.westin.com. A beautiful hotel for a special occasion, *Essex House* was restored by its previous Japanese owners to its

HOTELS

original Art Deco splendor. The best rooms have spectacular Central Park views. Despite the excellent service and marble lobby, the atmosphere is not at all formal or hushed. ⑧, dropping to ⑥ on weekends.

Gorham

Map 7, F6. 136 W 55th St (between 6th and 7th aves), NY 10019 ☏1-800/735-0710 or 212/245-1800, ℱ582-8832, ⓦwww.gorhamhotel.com. Cosmopolitan midtown hotel renovated to reflect the style of its original opening in 1929. Handy for Central Park and the Museum of Modern Art. All the rather generous rooms have convenient self-service kitchens; suites have whirlpool baths. Doubles ⑥, with occasional promotional specials at ⑤.

Helmsley Windsor

Map 7, F6. 100 W 58th St (between 6th and 7th aves), NY 10019 ☏1-800/221-4982 or 212/265-2100, ℱ315-0371, ⓦwww.helmsleyhotels.com. Enjoy coffee on the house each morning in the richly decorated, wood-paneled lobby. Like other Helmsley hotels, the *Windsor* has a pleasantly old-fashioned air, with plenty of useful extras in the rooms. Central Park is a block north. ⑤; summer weekends at ④.

Le Parker Meridien

Map 7, F6. 118 W 57th St (between 6th and 7th aves), NY 10019 ☏212/245-5000, ℱ247-4698, ⓦwww.parkermeridien.com. Five years and $60 million transformed the famous *Parker Meridien*. The mood has been lightened – the breakfast-only *Norma's* restaurant has fun with its many inventive options, room numbers (and doorbells) emit a cobalt glow, and classic cartoons play in the elevators. With a huge fitness center, a rare rooftop swimming pool, and 24-hour room service, this is hard to pass up, with weekends at ⑤. Weekday pricing is at ⑦.

Mansfield

Map 7, H9. 12 W 44th St, NY 10036 ☏1-877/847-4444 or

212/944-6050, Ⓕ764-4477,
Ⓦwww.mansfieldhotel.com.
One of the loveliest hotels in
the city, with its recessed
floor spotlighting, copper-
domed salon, clubby library
and nightly jazz welcoming
guests from behind the front
desk. There's a charming,
slightly quirky feel about the
place – an echo, perhaps, of
its turn-of-the-nineteenth-
century role as a pad for New
York's most eligible bachelors.
With the European breakfast
and all-day cappuccino, a
great deal at Ⓢ.

Mayfair

Map 7, E8. 242 W 49th St
(between Broadway and 8th
Ave), NY 10019
Ⓣ1-800/556-2932
or 212/586-0300, Ⓕ307-5226,
Ⓦwww.mayfairnewyork.com.
This new, nonsmoking,
"boutique"-style hotel, across
the street from the St
Malachay Actor's Chapel, has
beautifully decorated rooms,
its own restaurant and a
charming "old-world" feel,
emphasized by the historic
photographs on loan from the
Museum of the City of New

York that are everywhere on
display. Ⓢ, with summer rates
at Ⓢ.

Paramount

Map 7, E8. 235 W 46th St
(between Broadway and 8th
Ave), NY 10036
Ⓣ212/764-5500,
Ⓦwww.ianschragerhotels.com.
Popular with a pop and
media crowd that comes to
enjoy the theatrical public
space (blue-lit staircase strewn
with tea candles, gift shop as
concession stand) designed by
Philippe Starck. The branch
of *Dean and DeLuca* off the
lobby, the *Whiskey Bar* and
the *Coco Pazzo Teatro*
restaurant are all busy and
fun. Ⓢ, with some rates as
low as Ⓢ.

Plaza

Map 7, H5. 768 5th Ave (at
Central Park S), NY 10019
Ⓣ1-800/527-472
or 212/759-3000, Ⓕ546-5234.
Ⓦwww.fairmonthotels.com.
The last word in New York
luxury, at least by reputation,
and worth the money for the
fine old pseudo-French
chateau building if nothing

HOTELS

●

187

else. Doubles start at $365 and run to $15,000 (no kidding) for a specialty suite, and that's before taxes. A place to stay if someone else is paying. ❽

Royalton

Map 7, G9. 44 W 44th St (between 5th and 6th aves), NY 10036 ☎1-800/635-9013 or 212/869-4400, ℻869-8965, ⓦwww.ianschragerhotels.com. The *Royalton* attempts to capture the market for the discerning style-conscious, with white-draped chairs and candle-filled interiors designed by Philippe Starck. It has tried to become the new *Algonquin*, and is as much a power-lunch venue for NYC's media and publishing set as a place to stay. ❼, with discounts sometimes available at ❻.

The Time

Map 7, E7. 224 W 49th St, NY 10019 ☎1-877/TIME-NYC or 246-5252, ℻245-2305, ⓦwww.thetimeny.com. The waist-level clock in the lobby and the hallways bedecked with Roman numerals remind you to spend your time in New York wisely. Designer Adam Tihany created a hip hotel that may see a Clinton one day or a rap impressario the next. Small-to-medium-size rooms are tricked out with the latest accoutrements (dual-line phones, ergonomic workstation, in-room fax) and a minibar. ❺

Warwick

Map 7, G7. 65 W 54th St (at 6th Ave), NY 10019 ☎1-800/223-4099 or 247-2700,ⓦwww.warwick hotels.com. Stars of the 1950s and 1960s – including Cary Grant, the Beatles, Elvis Presley and JFK – stayed here as a matter of course. Although the hotel has lost its showbiz cachet, it's a pleasant place, from the elegant lobby to the *Ciao Europa* restaurant. ❽; summer specials at ❺.

Wellington

Map 7, F6. 871 7th Ave (at 55th St), NY 10019 ☎1-800/652-1212 or 212/247-3900, ℻581-1719,

ⓦwww.wellingtonhotel.com.
The gleaming, mirror-clad lobby is the result of fresh renovations, and similar attention has been paid to the rooms. Some have kitchenettes, and family rooms offer two bathrooms. Close to Carnegie Hall and Lincoln Center, the hotel's a good value for this stretch of town. ❹

Westpark
Map 7, E5. 6 Columbus Circle (off 8th Ave), NY 10019 ⓣ1-866/WESTPARK or 212/445-0200, ⓕ246-3131, ⓦwww.westparkhotel.com.
The best rooms look out over Columbus Circle and the southwestern corner of Central Park. The staff is somewhat reserved but helpful, and it's a great deal for the area, with Lincoln Center and the park nearly right outside the door, and a daily continental breakfast buffet. Reserving on the internet will save a few bucks from the call-in rates. ❹

MIDTOWN EAST AND UPPER EAST SIDE: E 42ND TO 96TH STREETS

Box Tree
Map 7, J8. 250 E 49th St (between 2nd and 3rd aves), NY 10017 ⓣ212/758-8320, ⓕ308-3899, ⓦwww.theboxtree.com.
Thirteen elegant rooms and suites fill two adjoining eighteenth-century townhouses and make one of New York's more eccentric lodgings. The Egyptian-, Chinese- and Japanese-style rooms have fur throws on the beds, great lighting, and ornaments and decoration everywhere. A credit of up to $100 toward the hotel bill is offered to weekend diners in the excellent *Box Tree Restaurant*. ❻; weekend rates are $100 more expensive.

Drake
Map 7, I6. 440 Park Ave (at 56th St), NY 10022 ⓣ212/421-0900.
A first-class hotel with a bustling cocktail bar and

HOTELS

superb seafood restaurant (*Quantum 56*), a spa and gym. This was once an apartment building, so the rooms are large (and the suites are super large and expensive), and a bit more stylish than most others of the same level. ⑦, with weekends closer to ⑤.

Lyden House

Map 7, K7. 320 E 53rd St (between 1st and 2nd aves), NY 10022 ☏212/888-6070.
Even the smallest suites in this exclusive hotel on Sutton Place are apartment-sized by New York standards and most could sleep four (second two adults at $20 plus tax per person per night). All suites have eat-in kitchens and a maid to do the dishes. ⑥; off-season rates can drop to ⑤ if available.

Mark

Map 7, I1. 25 E 77th St (at Madison Ave), NY 10021 ☏212/744-4300, ⑭744-2749.
A hotel that really lives up to its claims of sophistication and elegance. A redesign has kitted the lobby out with Biedermeier furniture and sleek Italian lighting. In the guestrooms, restaurant and invitingly dark *Mark's Bar*, there's a similar emphasis on the best of everything. ⑦

Pickwick Arms

Map 7, J6. 230 E 51st St, NY 10022 ☏212/355-0300, ⓦwww.pickwickarms.com.
A pleasant budget hotel and, for the price, one of the best deals you'll get on the East Side. All 400 rooms are air-conditioned, with cable TV, direct-dial phones and room service. The open-air roof deck with stunning views and café are added attractions. A single room with a shared bathroom is $75. ③

Roger Smith

Map 7, J8. 501 Lexington Ave (at 47th St), NY 10017 ☏1-800/445-0277 or 212/755-1400, ⑭319-9130.
One of the best midtown hotels with very helpful service, individually decorated rooms, a great restaurant, and artworks and sculpture on display. Breakfast is included in the price, along with VCRs in most rooms

HOTELS

●

and 2000 videos available from the hotel's library. Popular with bands and guests who like the artsy ambience. ❻; summer rates drop to ❹.

San Carlos

Map 7, J8. 150 E 50th St (between Lexington and 3rd aves), NY 10022 ☏1-800/722-2012 or 212/755-1800, ℻688-9778, ⓦwww.sancarloshotel.com. Well situated near plenty of bars and restaurants; most of the large rooms have fully equipped kitchenettes. A useful standby when everything else is booked. ❺; summer rates can drop to ❹.

W

Map 7, J8. 541 Lexington Ave (between 49th and 50th sts), NY 10022 ☏212/755-1200, ℻319-8344. ⓦwww.whotels.com. If the crowd hanging out in the *Whiskey Blue* bar, dining at *Heartbeat* or just posing in the Living Room (that's the feel of the lobby, and its name, too) are anything to go by, the *W* might well be the hippest dosshouse in town.

Clean, stylish rooms and other perks: Egyptian cotton on the feather beds, business services, gym and spa. ❽ – though weekend specials are available.

Waldorf-Astoria

Map 7, I8. 301 Park Ave at E 50th St, NY 10022 ☏1-800/WALDORF or 212/355-3000, ℻872-7272, ⓦwww.waldorf.com. One of the great names in New York hotels, and restored to its 1930s glory, making it a great place to stay if you can afford it or someone else is paying. ❽; promotional rates can drop to ❺.

THE UPPER WEST SIDE: ABOVE 59TH STREET
- - - - - - - - - - - - - - - - - - - -

Lucerne

Map 8, C9. 201 W 79th St (at Amsterdam Ave), NY 10024 ☏1-800/492-8122 or 212/875-1000, ℻721-1179, ⓦwww.newyorkhotel.com. This beautifully restored 1904 brownstone, with its extravagantly Baroque red

HOTELS

191

terra-cotta entrance, charming rooms, and friendly, helpful staff is a block from the American Museum of Natural History and close to the liveliest restaurant stretch of Columbus Ave. ❺, with summer rates ❹.

Malibu Studios

Map 8, B3. 2688 Broadway (at W 103rd St), NY 10025 Ⓣ212/222-2954, outside the city 1-800/647-2227, Ⓕ678-6842, Ⓦwww.malibuhotelnyc.com. Excellent-value budget accommodation, within walking distance of plenty of restaurants and nightlife. Prices, all before taxes, range from $79 for a single room with shared facilities to $149 for a double with private bathroom. Also triples and quads. Mention the *Rough Guides* and pay for three nights or more upfront and get a ten-percent discount on any room. Credit cards not accepted. ❶

Mayflower

Map 7, E5. 15 Central Park W (at 61st St), NY 10023-7709, Ⓣ1-800/223-4164 or 212/265-0060, Ⓕ265-0227, Ⓦwww.mayflowerhotel.com. A slightly down-at-the-heel but comfortable hotel a few steps from Central Park and Lincoln Center. It's so close to the latter that performers and musicians are often seen in the hotel's very good *Conservatory Café*. ❻, with occasional promotional rates.

Riverside Tower

Map 8, B9. 80 Riverside Drive (at W 80th St), NY 10024 Ⓣ1-800/724-3136 or 212/877-5200, Ⓕ873-1400. Although the hallways are plain as can be and rooms – all with small refrigerators – are ultrabasic, it's the location in this exclusive and safe neighborhood, flanked by one of the city's most beautiful parks and with (on upper floors) stunning views of the Hudson River, that sets this budget hotel apart from the others. Quads work out at around $35 per person, per night. For a few dollars more than the double, get the two-room suite for two people. ❷

Cafés, snacks and light meals

New York's **cafés and bakeries** run the gamut of its population's ethnic and cultural influences. They can be found in every neighborhood, with the usual French, Italian and American favorites probably most visible. The city also has a number of **coffeehouses and tearooms**, which outside of the obvious also might offer fruit juices, pastries, light snacks and, on occasion, full meals. Most places more suitable for sit-down dinners we've listed in Chapter 26, "Restaurants"; what follows is a neighborhood by neighborhood guide to where to get stuff fast, usually quite cheap, and always delicious.

CHINATOWN, LITTLE ITALY AND THE LOWER EAST SIDE

Café Gitane
Map 5, H6. 242 Mott St (between Prince and Houston sts) ☎212/334-9552.

Sunny little café serving coffee and creative light lunch fare.

Caffè Roma

Map 5, H7. 385 Broome St (between Mulberry and Mott sts) ☎212/226-8413.

Old Little Italy *pasticceria*, ideal for a drawn-out coffee and pastry. Try the homemade Italian cookies, exceptionally good cannoli (plain or dipped), or gelato at the counter in back.

Ceci-Cela

Map 5, H7. 55 Spring St (at Mulberry St) ☎212/274-9179.

Tiny French *patisserie* with a stand-up counter and bench out front for coffee and delectable baked goods. The croissants and palmiers are divine.

Chinatown Ice Cream Factory

Map 4, G2. 65 Bayard St (between Mott and Elizabeth sts) ☎212/608-4170.

An essential stop after sampling one of the restaurants nearby, but the wondrously unusual flavors make it good anytime. Specialties include green tea, ginger, almond cookies and lychee ice cream.

Ferrara's

Map 4, G1. 195 Grand St (between Mott and Mulberry sts) ☎212/226-6150.

The best-known and most traditional of the Little Italy coffeehouses, this landmark has been around since 1892. Try the cheesecake, cannoli or *granite* (Italian ices) in summer.

Grilled Cheese

Map 5, K6. 168 Ludlow St (between Houston and Stanton sts) ☎212/982-6600.

Great salads and grilled cheese sandwiches; very tiny dining space.

Kossar's

Map 4, I1. 367 Grand St (at Essex St) ☎212/473-4810.

Jewish baker whose bialys may be the best in New York.

Kwong Wah Cake Company

Map 4, F2. 234 Canal St (at Lafayette St) ☎212/925-3614.

You can't get more authentically Chinese than this cake establishment on teeming Canal St.

Saint's Alp Teahouse
Map 4, G2. 51 Mott St (between Canal and Bayard sts) ⊤212/766-9889.
Great stopoff in Chinatown's heart if you don't want the full restaurant experience, with hot green tea, Chinese fruit drinks and shakes (many with tapioca pearls at the bottom of the cup), and a good choice of snacks – try the vegetable dumplings or preserved eggs.

Yonah Schimmel's
Map 5, J5. 137 E Houston St (between Forsyth and Eldridge sts) ⊤212/477-2858.
Knishes, baked fresh on the premises, and wonderful bagels. Unpretentious and patronized by a mixture of wrinkled old men wisecracking in Yiddish and young uptowners slumming it while they wade through the Sunday papers.

Check out the "Food and drink" section in Chapter 32, "Shops and markets," for more quick food ideas; many shops have ready-to-go sandwiches and the like ideal for snacking.

SOHO AND TRIBECA

Balthazar Bakery
Map 5, G7. 80 Spring St (between Crosby St and Broadway) ⊤212/965-1414.
Next door to the celebrated *Balthazar* brasserie, this bakery has wonderful breads and pastries both simple and ornate, without the attitude.

Bassett Café
Map 4, D3. 123 W Broadway (at Duane St) ⊤212/349-1662.
Salads, light bites and an assortment of sides in spare but pleasant surroundings.

Bouley Bakery Cafe
Map 4, D3. 120 W Broadway (between Duane and Reade sts) ⊤212/964-2525.

SOHO AND TRIBECA

Wunderkind David Bouley's latest, a tiny bakery-restaurant with truly great breads and baked goods, as well as reasonably priced light food. Make sure to turn right once through the door, or you'll end up in the *tres* expensive restaurant.

Hampton Chutney

Map 5, G6. 68 Prince (at Crosby St) ☎212/226-9996. The American sandwich takes a detour through Indian breads and ingredients. Out of the ordinary, and quite good.

Snack

Map 5, E6. 105 Thompson (between Prince and Spring sts) ☎212/925-1040. Some fresh Greek food and mezzes will only set you back about $10 at lunch. Be prepared to wait for a table at this thimble-sized space.

Yaffa Tea Room

Map 4, C3. 19 Harrison St (at Greenwich St) ☎212/966-0577. Hidden in an unassuming corner of TriBeCa next to the *Yaffa Bar*, this restaurant serves Mediterranean-style dinners, good brunch and a cozy high tea (reservations required).

WEST VILLAGE

A Salt and Battery

Map 5, C2. 112 Greenwich Ave ☎212/691-2713. Run by the Brits from *Tea and Sympathy* next door, and an authentic enough affair, with decent battered cod and plaice, great chips and mushy peas. However, it may be the most expensive chippie in the

world, with a fish supper costing you a good twenty bucks.

Café Le Figaro

Map 5, D5. 184 Bleecker St (at MacDougal St) ☎212/677-1100. Former Beat hangout during the 1950s now ersatz Left Bank, serving cappuccino and pastries. If you want to watch weekend tourists flooding West Village streets, this is a good place to do it.

Caffè Dante

Map 5, D5. 79 MacDougal St (between Bleecker and Houston sts) ☏212/982-5275.
A morning stop-off for many locals since 1915. Good cappuccino, double espresso and caffè alfredo with ice cream. Often jammed with NYU students and teachers.

Caffè Reggio

Map 5, D4. 119 MacDougal St (between Bleecker and 3rd sts) ☏212/475-9557.
One of the first Village coffeehouses, dating back to the 1920s, always crowded and with tables outside for people- or tourist-watching in warm weather.

Elixir

Map 5, A3. 523 Hudson St (between 10th and Charles sts) ☏212/352-9952; also in TriBeCa, 95 W Broadway (between Reade and Chambers sts) ☏212/233-6171.
Casual, friendly joint where you can order juices, smoothies, seasonal elixirs, or just park yourself and think healthy.

Magnolia Bakery

Map 5, A3. 401 Bleecker St (at 11th St) ☏212/462-2572.
Like you've died and gone to cake heaven: huge slabs of moist crumbly cake, that homemade smell in the air, and staff frosting cakes while you watch. In addition to chocolate, vanilla, hummingbird (a mix of carrots, pineapple, coconut and nuts) and red velvet, there's banana pudding with wafer cookies and cupcakes.

Peanut Butter and Company

Map 5, E4. 240 Sullivan St (at W 3rd) ☏212/677-3995.
This establishment serves up peanut butter, on sandwiches and otherwise, in ways you never imagined.

Tea and Sympathy

Map 5, C2. 108 Greenwich Ave (between 12th and 13th sts) ☏212/807-8329.
Self-consciously British

WEST VILLAGE

tearoom, serving an afternoon high tea full of traditional British staples like jam roly-poly and treacle pud, along with shepherd's pie and scones. Perfect for British tourists feeling homesick.

EAST VILLAGE

B & H Dairy

Map 5, I3. 127 2nd Ave (between 7th St and St Mark's Place) ℡212/505-8065.
This tiny luncheonette serves homemade soup, challah and latkes. You can also create your own juice combination to stay or go. Good veggie choice.

Caffè Della Pace

Map 5, I3. 48 E 7th St (at 2nd Ave) ℡212/529-8024.
Dark and cozy East Village café with decent food and a great selection of coffees and desserts, especially the tiramisu.

Village Delight

Map 5, B4. 323 Bleecker St (between Christopher and Grove sts) ℡212/633-9275.
Healthy-sized sandwiches of whole turkey or roast beef (made daily), with an assortment of Middle Eastern side dishes.

Damask Falafel

Map 5, K4. 89 Ave A (between 5th and 6th sts) ℡212/673-5016.
One of the better Middle Eastern snack providers in the area.

Moishe's

Map 5, I3. 115 2nd Ave (between 7th St and St Mark's Place) ℡212/505-8555.
Good prune danishes, excellent *humentashen*, seeded rye and other kosher treats.

Pomme Frites

Map 5, I3. 123 2nd Ave (between 7th and 8th sts) ℡212/674-1234.
Arguably the best fries in the

city, with Belgian-style gooey toppings available.

Veniero's
Map 5, J2. 342 E 11th St (between 1st and 2nd aves) ☎212/674-4415. An institution since 1894, *Veniero's* sells wonderful pastries and has an expanded seating area in the back. Desserts and decor are fabulously over-the-top. The ricotta cheesecake and homemade gelati are great in the summer.

BAGELS

Theories abound as to the origin of the modern bagel. Most likely, it is a derivative of the pretzel, with the word bagel coming from the German *beigen*, "to bend," and the famous hole made them easy to carry on a long stick to hawk on street corners. Whatever their birthplace, these are a New York institution. Most traditionally enjoyed with cream cheese and lox (smoked salmon), though of course they can be topped with anything you like. A list of some of the better bagel purveyors is below. (If you prefer bialys, a drier flatter bagel without a hole, head straight to *Kossar's*, p.194.)

Bagel Buffet 406 6th Ave (between 8th and 9th sts) ☎212/477-0448
Bagels on the Square 7 Carmine St (between Bleecker St and 6th Ave) ☎212/691-3041
Columbia Hot Bagels 2836 Broadway (between 110th and 111th sts) ☎212/222-3200

Ess-A-Bagel 359 1st Ave (at E 21st St) ☎212/260-2252
H & H Bagels 2239 Broadway (at W 80th St) ☎212/595-8000
Yonah Schimmel's 137 E Houston St (between Forsyth and Eldridge sts) ☎212/477-2858

EAST VILLAGE

CHELSEA

Amy's Bread
Map 6, D9. 75 9th Ave (between 15th and 16th sts) ☏212/462-4338.
You can find Amy's Bread in fine stores citywide – but it's freshest here; they make great cakes, too.

Big Cup
Map 6, E7. 228 8th Ave (between 21st and 22nd sts) ☏212/206-0059.
Popular coffee shop with fresh muffins and (big) hot cups of joe. Comfortable couches and chairs make it the perfect place to read the papers and relax into your day.

F&B
Map 6, F7. 269 W 23rd St (between 7th and 8th aves) ☏646/486-4441.
Unusual premise and a chic (for a slender storefront) execution: all manner of franks (vegetarian too) and beignets (awesome with apricot dip), with fries of course. Humorous menu, and classy cheap joint. Eat-in or take-out.

News Bar
Map 6, H8. 2 W 19th St (between 5th and 6th aves) ☏212/255-3996.
Tiny minimalist café with equally great selections of pastries and periodicals. Draws photographer and model types as well as regular people, making it good for people-watching.

Wild Lily Tea Room
Map 6, H7. 511 W 22nd St (between 5th and 6th aves) ☏212/691-2258.
Convenient for a gallery tour of west Chelsea, the shop has over forty different brews, and strange-sounding but delicious tea sandwiches.

UNION SQUARE, GRAMERCY PARK, MURRAY HILL

Chez Laurence

Map 6, I2. 245 Madison Ave (at 38th St) ☎212/683-0284. Well-placed, friendly little *patisserie* that makes cheap breakfasts and decent, inexpensive lunches – and good coffee at any time of the day. Closed Sun.

City Bakery

Map 6, I8. 22 E 17th St (between Broadway and 5th Ave) ☎212/366-1414. Minimalist bakery that uses fresh Greenmarket ingredients from around the corner.

Serves reasonable soups and light lunch fare, but above all masterfully delicate tartlets, creamy hot chocolate, and *crème brûlée*. Closed Sun.

Eisenberg's Sandwich Shop

Map 6, I7. 174 5th Ave (between 22nd and 23rd sts) ☎212/675-5096. This narrow little restaurant is a Flatiron institution. A tuna sandwich and some matzoh ball soup will cure what ails you.

MIDTOWN WEST

Brasserie Centrale

Map 7, F7. 1700 Broadway (at W 53rd St) ☎212/757-2233. A rare midtown place where you can linger over coffee, freshly baked treats or a full meal. The menu offers a range of burgers, soups, salads, pastas and average French-tinged brasserie

standards (stick with the simpler items on the menu). Large outdoor seating area. Open 24 hours.

Cupcake Café

Map 6, D2. 522 9th Ave (at W 39th St) ☎212/465-1530. A delightful little joint, offering decent soup and sandwiches at bargain prices, and great cakes, cupcakes and pies. Anything with fruit is a must.

Poseidon Bakery

Map 7, D9. 629 9th Ave (between 44th and 45th sts) ☎212/757-6173.
Decadent baklava and other sweet Greek pastries, strudels and cookies, as well as spinach and meat pies. Known for the hand-rolled phyllo dough that it makes on the premises and supplies to many restaurants in the city. Closed Sun and Mon.

Schlotzsky's

Map 7, G6. 1380 6th Ave (at 56th St) ☎212/247-2867.
Reliably tasty sandwiches on specialty bread, or mini-pizzas with sourdough crust.

Soup Kitchen International

Map 7, E6. 259A W 55th St (off 8th Ave) ☎212/757-7730.
The real-life counterpart of Jerry Seinfeld's friend the Soup Nazi, with rich soups highly priced but worth it. Closed in summer.

MIDTOWN EAST

Little Pie Company

Map 6, J1. Grand Central Station (Lower Food Concourse), no phone.
True to its name, the *Little Pie Company* serves three-berry pies that are to die for, while the peach-raspberry, available in summer, has been known to provoke rioting. If it's just you, pick up a five-inch personal pie.

Shoebox Cafe

Map 6, J1. Grand Central Station (Lower Food Concourse) ☎212/986-5959.
Instead of taking the train to the deep South, just stop here, with authentic fried chicken and bourbon and pecan country ham available.

UPPER WEST SIDE AND MORNINGSIDE HEIGHTS

Café Lalo
Map 8, C8. 201 W 83rd St (between Amsterdam and Broadway) ☎212/496-6031. The spirit of Paris, complete with cramped tables and inconsistent service. Try the "shirred" eggs (made fluffy with a cappuccino machine) with all sorts of herbs and add-ins, or the wonderful Belgian waffles. Great desserts.

Café Mozart
Map 7, E3. 154 W 70th St (between Central Park W and Columbus Ave) ☎212/595-9797. This faded old Viennese coffeehouse serves rich tortes and apple strudel.

Caffè la Fortuna
Map 7, E2. 69 W 71st St (between Central Park W and Columbus Ave) ☎212/724-5846. The atmosphere is dark, comfy and inviting. You can sip a coffee all day long in the shade of their peaceful

garden, and their Italian pastries are heavenly.

Edgar's Café
Map 8, B8. 255 W 84th St (between West End Ave and Broadway) ☎212/496-6126. A pleasant coffeehouse with good (though expensive) desserts and light snacks, great hot cider in the winter, and well-brewed coffees and teas all the time.

Gray's Papaya
Map 7, C2. 2090 Broadway (at W 72nd St) ☎212/799-0243. Order two all-beef franks and a papaya juice for a true New York experience. No ambience, no seats, just good cheap grub.

Hungarian Pastry Shop
Map 8, C1. 1030 Amsterdam Ave (between 110th and 111th sts) ☎212/866-4230. This simple, no-frills coffeehouse is a favorite with Columbia University students and faculty alike. You sip your espresso and read all day

if you like; the only problem is choosing amongst the

pastries, cookies and cakes, all made on the premises.

UPPER EAST SIDE

Les Friandises
Map 7, J3. 922 Lexington Ave (between 70th and 71st sts) ☏212/988-1616.
A paradise of French pastries on the Upper East Side. Wonderful croissants and brioches and a sublime tarte tatin.

Payard Patisserie & Bistro
Map 7, J2. 1032 Lexington Ave (between 72nd and 73rd sts) ☏212/717-5252.
This is real Parisian pastry – buttery, creamy and over the top. Cookies, cakes, and *crème brûlée* made to the exacting standards of the kitchen staffs of local millionaires.

Serendipity 3
Map 7, J5. 225 E 60th St (between 2nd and 3rd aves) ☏212/838-3531.
Long-established eatery and ice-cream parlor adorned with Tiffany lamps. The frozen hot chocolate, a trademarked and copyrighted recipe, is out of this world, and the wealth of ice-cream offerings are a real treat too.

Wildgreen Cafe
Map 8, J7. 1555 3rd Ave (at E 88th St) ☏212/828-7656.
A small-town feel adds to the draw of this shop "where natural foods become gourmet." It's justly known for its muffins, salads, wraps, and juices.

HARLEM AND THE OUTER BOROUGHS

Athens

32-01 30th Ave, Astoria,
Queens ☏718/626-2164.
The Greekest of cafés, with
spinach pies and specialty
desserts.

Bedouin Tent

405 Atlantic Ave, Brooklyn
☏718/852-5555.
Fresh, delicious Middle
Eastern pita sandwiches,
salads, and pitzas; convenient
to Brooklyn Heights and
Cobble Hill.

Bruno Bakery

602 Lorimer St (between
Skillman Ave and Conselyea
St), Williamsburg, Brooklyn
☏718/349-6524.
Relaxing Italian bakery, open
daily 9am–7pm.

Nathan's Famous

Surf and Stillwell aves, Coney
Island, Brooklyn ☏718/266-
3161.
The original hot-dog stand –
crowded, greasy, and totally
irresistible.

Wilson's Bakery and Restaurant

Map 9, C4. 1980 Amsterdam
Ave (at W 158th St) ☏212/923-
9821.
Luscious Southern specialties,
like sweet potato pie and
peach cobbler, but much
more than desserts – try the
chicken and waffle
combination.

Restaurants

ew York is a rich port city that can get the best foodstuffs from anywhere in the world, and, as a major immigration gateway, it attracts chefs who know how to cook the world's cuisines properly, even exceptionally. As you stroll through the streets of New York, heavenly odors seem to emanate from every corner; it's not hard to work up an appetite.

Outside of **American** and **continental cuisines** (more or less including New American, which can either dazzle with its inventive fusions or fail miserably and pretentiously), be prepared to confront a startling variety of **ethnic food**. In New York, none has had so dominant an effect as **Jewish food**, to the extent that many Jewish specialties – bagels, pastrami, lox and cream cheese – are now considered archetypal New York. Others retain more specific identities. **Chinese** food includes the familiar Cantonese, as well as spicier Szechuan and Hunan dishes – most restaurants specialize in one or the other. **Japanese** food is widely available and very good; other Asian cuisines include **Indian** and a broad sprinkling of **Thai**, **Korean**, **Vietnamese** and **Indonesian** restaurants.

Italian cooking is widespread and not terribly expensive, and typically a fairly safe bet. **French** restaurants tend to be pricier, although there are an increasing number of bistros and brasseries turning out authentic and reliable French nosh for attractive prices. Somewhat similar in spirit are **Belgian** brasseries and steak frites joints, a surprising number of which opened in the last half-decade (and many of which subsequently closed).

There is also a whole range of **Eastern European** restaurants – Russian, Ukrainian, Polish and Hungarian – that serve well-priced, filling fare. **Caribbean**, **Central** and **South American** restaurants are on the rise in New York, and often offer a good deal and a large, satisfying and often spicy meal. Other places include weird hybrids like Chinese-Peruvian, Japanese-Brazilian, and any number of **vegetarian** and **wholefood** eateries to cater to any taste or fad.

As for where you'll be going for these foods, we've divided our selections below by **neighborhood** (and then cuisine), and have given very brief descriptions for what you might expect to find in those areas. For the most part you won't have to walk very far to find a good place in almost any district, but many of the ones listed here are worth a trip on the subway or in a cab.

Note that most restaurants open at lunchtime, which is often a good opportunity to sample fine food at nearly half the cost of dinner; also, dim sum in Chinatown makes for a memorable lunch experience.

FINANCIAL DISTRICT AND CITY HALL AREA

The culinary focal point of lower Manhattan is the Fulton Fish Market, so not surprisingly many of the restaurants in the area serve seafood. Unfortunately, with few exceptions, most overcharge the power-broker lunch regulars for relatively unimpressive fare. The area revolves around trading hours, so many restaurants close early, and are closed or have reduced hours on weekends.

AMERICAN AND CONTINENTAL

Bridge Café

Map 4, G5. 279 Water St (at Dover St) ☏212/227-3344. They say there's been a bar here since 1794, but this place looks very up-to-the-minute. The good crabcakes come from the local fish market, and there are plenty of upscale beers with which to wash them down. The rare eighteenth-century frame house, painted red with black trim, is well worth a look. Entrees are priced between $15–25.

Hudson River Club

Map 4, C5. 4 World Financial Center, 250 Vesey St, Upper Level (at West St) ☏212/786-1500. Worth the $70 or so per head for the view over the harbor to the Statue of Liberty. The food is American, with special emphasis on cooking from New York State's Hudson River Valley. Start with the seafood martini (shrimp, lobster and lump crabmeat with a citron aioli) or just go straight for the apricot-glazed halibut entree.

ITALIAN

Carmine's Bar and Grill

Map 4, G5. 140 Beekman St (at Front St) ☏212/962-8606. In business since 1903, this place specializes in Northern Italian-style seafood and exudes a comfortable if run-down ambience. Try a glass of the house wine and a bowl of linguini in clam sauce for lunch.

CHINATOWN AND LITTLE ITALY

If authentic Chinese, Thai and Vietnamese food is what you're after, best head for the busy streets of **Chinatown**. Mulberry Street is **Little Italy**'s main drag, and though often crowded with tourists, the carnival atmosphere can make dinner and coffee a worthwhile excursion.

ASIAN

Canton
Map 4, H2. 45 Division St at the Manhattan Bridge (between Bowery and Market sts) ☎212/226-4441.
Fairly upscale compared to other Chinatown restaurants in terms of decor, style and service, but only marginally more expensive. Seafood is the specialty here; bring your own booze. Closed Mon and Tues.

Joe's Shanghai
Map 4, G3. 9 Pell St (between Bowery and Mott sts) ☎212/233-8888.
Probably Chinatown's most famous restaurant, this place is always packed, with good reason. Start with the soup dumplings and work through some seafood dishes for the main course; communal tables.

New York Noodletown
Map 4, G2. 28 Bowery (at Bayard St) ☎212/349-0923.
Despite the name, noodles aren't the real draw at this down-to-earth eatery – the soft-shell crabs are crisp, salty, and delicious. Good roast meats (try the baby pig) and soups too.

Sweet 'n' Tart Restaurant
Map 4, G2. 20 Mott St (at Canal St) ☎212/964-0380.
The place for shark's-fin soup and other Hong Kong–style seafood delicacies, as well as superb dim sum. Very popular, so expect to wait. The older establishment, with a more limited menu, is located just up the street at 76 Mott St.

Thailand Restaurant

Map 4, G2. 106 Bayard St (at Baxter St) ☏212/349-3132.
The well-priced Thai food is eaten at long communal tables here. The whole-fish dishes, crispy and spicy, are standouts.

Vietnam

Map 4, G3. 11–13 Doyers St (between Bowery and Pell sts) ☏212/693-0725.
This hard-to-find underground eatery doesn't offer much in the way of decor, but the inexpensive Vietnamese fare is among the city's best; you can't go wrong with the ginger whole fish, caramel pork, or sauteed watercress.

ITALIAN

La Luna

Map 5, H9. 112 Mulberry St (between Canal and Hester sts) ☏212/226-8657.
One of Little Italy's longest established and best value choices. The attitude of the waiters is gruff, and the food only middling – but the atmosphere is fun and it's a popular joint, packing in a crowd.

Lombardi's

Map 5, H7. 32 Spring St (between Mott and Mulberry sts) ☏212/941-7994.
Arguably some of the best pizza in town, including an amazing clam pie; no slices though. Ask for roasted garlic on the side.

Vincent's Clam Bar

Map 5, H8. 119 Mott St (at Hester St) ☏212/226-8133.
A Little Italy mainstay that serves fresh, cheap and spicy seafood dishes – clams, mussels and squid.

THE LOWER EAST SIDE

In spots, the **Lower East Side** seems like a throwback to early immigrant sweatshop days; at others it's a place where the city's hipsters hang out. Either way, it's still the best place to get a pickle.

AMERICAN AND CONTINENTAL

----

71 Clinton Fresh Food

Map 5, L6. 71 Clinton St (at Rivington St) ☎212/614-6960. Popular with foodies and hipsters alike, this cozy spot serves some of the best food in the city. Either the beer-braised short ribs or sea bass crusted with edamame will send you for a loop; start with the potato torte or salmon-avocado tartare.

Lansky Lounge & Grill

Map 5, K7. 104 Norfolk St (between Delancey and Rivington sts) ☎212/677-9489. With a hidden, back-alleyway entrance, this former speakeasy was once a haunt of gangster Meyer Lansky. With a bone-in ribeye that's fit for a king and a lounge that hops late at night, this hotspot has

all the makings of a sinful evening.

JEWISH AND EASTERN EUROPEAN

Katz's Deli

Map 5, K5. 205 E Houston St (between Essex and Ludlow sts) ☎212/254-2246. Cafeteria-style or sit down and be served. The overstuffed pastrami or corned beef sandwiches, doused with mustard and with a side pile of pickles, should keep you going for about a week. Also famous for their egg creams; open seven days a week. Don't lose your meal ticket or they'll charge you an arm and a leg.

Sammy's Roumanian Restaurant

Map 5, I7. 157 Chrystie St

(between Delancey and Rivington sts) ☏212/673-0330. The food, at around $25 or so for a full meal, is undeniably good, but most people come for the raucous live music.

TRIBECA

Still one of New York's trendiest neighborhoods, here you often pay for the vista rather than the victuals. Yet who can argue with sitting outside at a sidewalk café and feeling like you've traveled (rather cheaply) to Europe? Even so, there are appropriately divine meals, and occasional deals, to be had in **TriBeCa** – and the people-watching is not bad either.

AMERICAN AND CONTINENTAL

Bubby's

Map 4, C2. 120 Hudson St (between Franklin and N Moore sts) ☏212/219-0666.
A relaxed TriBeCa restaurant serving homely health-conscious American food. Great scones, mashed potatoes, rosemary chicken and soups. A good, moderately priced brunch spot, too – the trout and eggs is a killer.

Odeon

Map 4, D3. 145 W Broadway (at Thomas St) ☏212/233-0507.
Odeon has shown surprising staying power, perhaps because the eclectic food choices are actually pretty good and the people-watching still can't be beat. Entrees go for around $15–20 and, on the whole, are worth it.

TriBeCa Grill

Map 4, C2. 375 Greenwich St (at Franklin St) ☏212/941-3900.
Some people come for a glimpse of the owner, Robert de Niro, when they should really be concentrating on the fine American cooking with Asian and Italian accents at

around $30 a main course. The setting is nice too; an airy, brick-walled eating area around a central Tiffany bar. Worth the money as a treat, despite the trendy scene and gawking tourists.

ASIAN

Nobu

Map 4, C2. 105 Hudson St (at Franklin St) ☎212/219-0500. Robert De Niro's best-known New York restaurant, whose lavish woodland decor complements really superlative Japanese cuisine, especially sushi, at the ultra-high prices you would expect. If you can't get a reservation, try *Next Door Nobu,* located just next door.

FRENCH AND BELGIAN

Bouley

Map 4, D3. 165 Duane St (between Greenwich and Hudson sts) ☎212/608-3852. One of New York's best French restaurants, serving modern French food made from the freshest ingredients. Popular with city celebrities, but costs for the magnificent meals can be softened by opting for the prix-fixe lunch and dinner options. (For details on next-door *Bouley Bakery* see p.195).

Capsouto Frères

Map 4, B1. 451 Washington St (at Watts St) ☎212/966-4900. Tucked away in a discreet corner of TriBeCa is this wonderful, if pricey, French bistro with a lofty feel. Dinner entrees are about $14–24. Try the duck with ginger and cassis, and don't miss the dessert soufflés.

MEXICAN

El Teddy's

Map 4, D2. 219 W Broadway (between Franklin and White sts) ☎212/941-7070. Eccentrically decorated restaurant that serves creative Mexican food, like goat cheese quesadillas, and the best margaritas in town. Try the fried tortillas wrapped

TRIBECA

around spicy chicken for starters. Entrees ($15–19) feel a bit pricey for what you get.

SoHo

Some of the city's trendiest – and most celebrated – restaurants can be found in **SoHo**, covering a wide array of cuisines. And while they tend toward the expensive, the people-watching can be good fun.

ASIAN

Blue Ribbon Sushi
Map 5, D6. 119 Sullivan St (between Prince and Spring sts) ☏212/343-0404.
Widely considered one of the best sushi restaurants in New York, the lines for a table can be long and it doesn't allow reservations. Our advice: have some cold sake and relax – the kitchen is open until 2am.

Rice
Map 5, H7. 227 Mott St (between Prince and Spring sts) ☏212/226-5775.
Small, inexpensive pan-Asian spot, where you mix-and-match various rices (black, sticky, etc) with interesting meat choices (lemongrass chicken, beef salad and the like).

FRENCH AND BELGIAN

Alison on Dominick
Map 5, C7. 38 Dominick St (between Hudson and Varick sts) ☏212/727-1188.
About as tucked away and romantic as you can get in the middle of a huge city, with great Southwestern French food that is served with a creative, light touch. Very expensive, but worth it for a special occasion with the one you love.

Balthazar
Map 5, G7. 80 Spring St (between Crosby St and

Broadway) ☎212/965-1414.
The tastefully ornate Parisian
decor and nonstop beautiful
people keep your eyes busy
until the food arrives; then all
you can do is savor the fresh
oysters and mussels, the
exquisite pastries and
everything in between.
Worth the money and
attitude.

L'Ecole

Map 5, F8. 462 Broadway (at
Grand St) ☎212/219-3300.
Students of the French
Culinary Institute serve up
affordable French delights –

and they rarely fail. The
three-course prix-fixe dinner
costs $29.95 per person; book
in advance. Closed Sun.

Raoul's

Map 5, E6. 180 Prince St
(between Sullivan and
Thompson sts) ☎212/966-3518.
French bistro seemingly lifted
from Paris. The food,
especially the steak *au poivre*
and crayfish risotto, plus
service are wonderful – as
you'd expect at the high
prices you'll find here.
Reservations recommended.
Closed Aug.

WEST VILLAGE

The **West Village** offers a decent array of discreet, upscale
spots in its angled streets, and is probably the most popular
neighborhood of all for langorous weekend brunches.

AMERICAN AND
CONTINENTAL
- - - - - - - - - - - - - - - - - - - -

Corner Bistro

Map 5, A2. 331 W 4th St (at
Jane St) ☎212/242-9502.
Down-home pub with
cavernous cubicles, paper

plates and maybe the best
burger and fries ($6.50) in
town. Longstanding haunt of
West Village literary and artsy
types, a mix of locals and die-
hard fans line up nightly, but
don't be discouraged, the line
moves faster than it looks.

WEST VILLAGE

Grange Hall

Map 5, B4. 50 Commerce St (at Barrow St) ☎212/924-5246. Tucked away in one of the most beautiful West Village corners, this Depression era-designed eatery is a hit for dinner, brunch and drinks. Cranberry porkchops and potato pancakes are recommended. Entrees $11–17.

The Pink Teacup

Map 5, B4. 42 Grove St (between Bleecker and Bedford sts) ☎212/807-6755. Longstanding Southern soulfood institution in the heart of the Village, with good smothered pork chops, cornbread and the like. Brunch too, but no credit cards.

ASIAN

Little Basil

Map 5, D3. 39 Greenwich Ave ☎212/645-8965. Such Thai staples as green and red curries, Pad Thai and the like are served along with pan-Asian dishes like crispy duck, in a comfortably casual environment.

Tomoe Sushi

Map 5, E5. 172 Thompson St (between Bleecker and Houston sts) ☎212/777-9346. While the nightly lines might look daunting, the wait is worth it for some of the best sushi in Manhattan. If they have soft-shell crab, get it rolled.

Yama

Map 5, C5. 40 Carmine St ☎212/989-9330. This intimate yet bustling Japanese restaurant features great sushi, great everything. Try the wasabi shumai dumplings.

CARIBBEAN, CENTRAL AND SOUTH AMERICAN

Caribe

Map 5, A3. 117 Perry St (between Hudson and Greenwich sts) ☎212/255-9191. A funky Caribbean restaurant filled with leafy jungle decor and blasted with reggae

WEST VILLAGE

216

music. Jerk chicken, washed down with wild tropical cocktails, makes it the place for a fun night out. Entrees around $9–16.

FRENCH AND BELGIAN

Café de Bruxelles

Map 6, E9. 118 Greenwich Ave (at 13th St) ☎212/206-1830. Very authentic and popular Belgian restaurant in the West Village. Try the *waterzooi*, a rich and creamy chicken stew, or mussels served everyway you like.

Chez Brigitte

Map 5, B2. 77 Greenwich Ave (between Bank St and 7th Ave) ☎212/929-6736. Only a dozen people fit in this tiny restaurant, which serves stews, all-day roast meat dinners for under $10, and other bargains from a simple menu.

Markt

Map 6, D9. 401 W 14th St ☎212/727-3314. Very large and very noisy

brasserie, serving decent Belgian standards – mussels, *waterzooi*, and of course frites – along with one of the city's best choice of Belgian ales. Not the place for a quiet tête-à-tête.

Paris Commune

Map 5, A3. 411 Bleecker St (between 11th and Bank sts) ☎212/929-0509. Romantic West Village bistro with reliable French home cooking and a fireplace. Memorable French toast and wild mushroom ravioli at moderate prices. Long lines for brunch.

ITALIAN

Arturo's Pizza

Map 5, E5. 106 W Houston St (at Thompson St) ☎212/475-9828. Coal-oven pizzas, no slices, that rival some of the best pies in town. While-you-eat entertainment often includes live jazz, and there are a couple outdoor tables on busy Houston St.

WEST VILLAGE

217

Babbo

Map 5, D3. 110 Waverly Place (between 6th Ave and MacDougal St) ☎212/777-0303. This eatery offers delicious, creative Italian dishes – beef cheek ravioli and various takes on scrapple garner much of the praise – attentive service and an interesting selection of wine; it's quite popular, so reserve in advance. Expect to pay at least $50 or so a head.

John's Pizzeria

Map 5, C4. 278 Bleecker St (between 6th and 7th aves) ☎212/243-1680. No slices, no takeaways. A full-service restaurant that serves some of the city's best and most popular pizza, with a crust that is thin and coal-charred. Be prepared to wait in line. Uptown branches at 408 E 64th St (between 1st and York aves) ☎212/935-2895 and 48 W 65th St (between Columbus Ave and Central Park W) ☎212/721-7001.

Lupa

Map 5, E5. 170 Thompson St (between Bleecker and Houston sts) ☎212/982-5089. A fine, moderately priced trattoria, serving hearty, rustic Italian specialties such as *osso buco*, *saltimbocca* and gnocchi with fennel sausage. Hint: go before 6.30pm and you'll have no problem getting a table.

SPANISH

Sevilla

Map 5, B3. 62 Charles St (at 4th St) ☎212/929-3189. Wonderful Village old-timer that is still a favorite neighborhood haunt. Dark, fragrant (from garlic) restaurant with good, moderately priced food. Terrific paella and large pitchers of strong sangria.

Spain

Map 5, B1. 113 W 13th St (between 7th and 8th aves) ☎212/929-9580. Modest prices (entrees are $9–18) and large portions are the prime attractions of this cozy Spanish restaurant. Casual atmosphere and tacky decor in the larger back dining room – this neighborhood place has been here forever. Order the paella and split it with a friend.

EAST VILLAGE

It seems a new upscale Italian restaurant, sushi bar, or chic café opens every day in the **East Village**. By contrast the homely Indian restaurants on E 6th Street and Ukrainian spots just a bit north will fill you up for very little.

AMERICAN AND CONTINENTAL

- - - - - - - - - - - - - - - - - - - -

Gotham Bar & Grill

Map 5, F2. 12 E 12th St (between 5th Ave and University Place) ☎212/620-4020. This restaurant serves marvelous American fare in an airy, trendy setting. Generally reckoned to be one of the city's best restaurants, and it's worth a drink at the bar to see the beautiful people walk in.

Miracle Grill

Map 5, J3. 112 1st Ave (between 6th and 7th sts) ☎212/254-2353. Moderately priced Southwestern specialties (the catfish tacos are excellent) with interesting taste combinations and an attractive garden out back. Save room for the vanilla bean flan.

Prune

Map 5, I5. 54 E 1st St (between 1st and 2nd aves) ☎212/677-6221. The star addition to what has become the East Village's most popular restaurant row, *Prune*'s rustic country fare (rabbit, capon, bacon-wrapped pork chop) comes with some surprises (a rye omelette here, a deviled egg there). Slightly confusing menu, as appetizers, entrees and side dishes aren't designated as such, but the pricing (not cheap) will clue you in. Closed Mon.

ASIAN

Bond Street

Map 5, G5. 6 Bond St (between Broadway and Lafayette) ☎212/777-2500.
Very hip, super-suave, multileveled Japanese restaurant (with happening bar on first floor). The sushi is amazing, the miso-glazed sea bass exquisite, and steak a treat. Fairly pricey.

Dok Suni's

Map 5, J3. 119 1st Ave (between 7th St and St Mark's Place) ☎212/477-9506.
This dimly lit, somewhat cramped East Village restaurant has fast become a favorite for Korean home cooking like *bibimbop*, seafood pancake, or kim chee rice; moderately priced.

Shabu Tatsu

Map 5, I2. 216 E 10th St (between 1st and 2nd aves) ☎212/477-2972.
This place offers great and moderately priced Korean barbecue. Choose a combination of meat or seafood platters, and have them cooked right at your table.

Takahachi

Map 5, K4. 85 Ave A (between 5th and 6th sts) ☎212/505-6524.
Superior sushi, the best in the neighborhood, at affordable prices. For dinner you'll probably have to wait – they don't take reservations.

CARIBBEAN, CENTRAL AND SOUTH AMERICAN

Boca Chica

Map 5, J5. 13 1st Ave (at 1st St) ☎212/473-0108.
This is real South American stuff, piled high and washed down with black beer and fancy, fruity drinks. It gets crowded, especially late and on weekends, and the music is loud, so come in a party mood and bring your dancing shoes. Inexpensive.

EAST VILLAGE

Casa Adela

Map 5, M4. 66 Ave C (between 4th and 5th sts) ☎212/473-1882.

Slightly off the beaten path, this neighborhood is a great spot to taste true Puerto Rican food. Try the *mofungo* (fried plantains mixed with pork and garlic) or the roast pork. All entrees $6.50–8. Cash only.

GREEK AND MIDDLE EASTERN

Khyber Pass

Map 5, I3. 34 St Mark's Place (between 2nd and 3rd aves) ☎212/473-0989.

Afghan food, which, if you're unfamiliar, is filling and has plenty to offer vegetarians (pulses, rice and eggplant are frequent ingredients). The lamb dishes are tasty. Excellent value for around $10.

INDIAN

Gandhi

Map 5, J3. 345 E 6th St (between 1st and 2nd aves) ☎212/614-9718.

One of the best and least expensive of the E 6th St Indian restaurants – also one of the more spacious, with two shared dining areas. Try the lamb *muglai* and the light, fluffy *poori* bread.

ITALIAN

Frank

Map 5, I4. 88 2nd Ave (between 5th and 6th sts) ☎212/420-0202.

This tiny, neighborhood favorite serves basic, traditional Italian dishes at communal tables. It's packed every night with hungry locals looking for the closest thing to a home-cooked meal at a very reasonable price.

Il Buco

Map 5, H5. 47 Bond St (between Lafayette and the Bowery) ☎212/533-1932.

While leaning more toward Italian, this cash-only eatery boasts French and Spanish flairs as well. Once an antique store and sometimes eatery, *Il*

EAST VILLAGE

221

Buco now serves food full-time. In fact, the food is amazing.

JEWISH AND EASTERN EUROPEAN

B & H Dairy
Map 5, I3. 127 2nd Ave (between 7th St and St Mark's Place) ☎212/505-8065.
Good veggie choice, this tiny luncheonette serves homemade soup, challah and latkes. You can also create your own juice combination to stay or go.

Second Avenue Deli
Map 5, I2. 156 2nd Ave (between 9th and 10th sts) ☎212/677-0606.
An East Village institution, serving up marvelous burgers, hearty pastrami sandwiches, matzoh ball soup, and other deli goodies in ebullient, snap-happy style – and not nearly as cheap as you'd think. The star plaques in the sidewalk out front commemorate this area's Yiddish theater days.

Veselka
Map 5, I3. 144 2nd Ave (at 9th St) ☎212/228-9682.
East Village institution that offers fine homemade hot borscht (and cold in summer), latkes, pierogies, and great burgers and fries. Open 24 hours.

SPANISH

Xunta
Map 5, J2. 174 1st Ave (between 10th and 11th St) ☎212/614-0620.
This electric East Village gem buzzes with hordes of young faces perched on rum barrels downing pitchers of sangria and choosing from the dizzying tapas menu – try the mussels in fresh tomato sauce, shrimp with garlic, and the mushrooms in brandy. You can eat (and drink) very well for around $20.

VEGETARIAN

Anjelica Kitchen
Map 5, I2. 300 E 12th St (between 1st and 2nd aves)

EAST VILLAGE

☎212/228-2909.
Vegetarian macrobiotic restaurant with various daily specials for a decent price.

Patronized by a colorful downtown crowd and considered by many to be the best veggie food in NYC.

CHELSEA

Retro diners, Cuban-Chinese greasy spoons along Eighth Avenue, increasingly trendy restaurants, and cute brunch spots characterize **Chelsea**. Perhaps the best and most reasonably priced offerings are to be had in the area's Central American establishments, though there is also a mosaic of international cuisines – Thai, Austrian, Mexican, Italian and traditional American.

AMERICAN AND CONTINENTAL

- - - - - - - - - - - - - - - - - - - -

Cafeteria
Map 6, F8. 119 7th Ave (at 17th St) ☎212/414-1717.
Don't let the name fool you: while *Cafeteria* is open 24 hours and has great chicken fried steak, meatloaf and macaroni and cheese, this place is anything but a trucker's dream. Modern, plastic-designed and always packed with beautiful diners.

Empire Diner
Map 6, C7. 210 10th Ave

(between 22nd and 23rd sts)
☎212/243-2736.
With its gleaming chrome-ribbed Art Deco interior, this is one of Manhattan's original diners, still open 24 hours and still serving up plates of simple (if not much better than average) American food such as burgers and grilled cheese sandwiches.

The Old Homestead
Map 6, D9. 56 9th Ave (between 14th and 15th sts) ☎212/242-9040.
Steak. Period. But really gorgeous steak, served in an almost comically old-fashioned

CHELSEA

●

walnut dining room by waiters in black vests. Huge portions, but expensive.

CARIBBEAN, CENTRAL AND SOUTH AMERICAN

Cuba Libre

Map 6, E7. 200 8th Ave (between 20th and 21st sts) ☎212/206-0038.

Tapas, mojitos and hip-swinging music make this airy, reasonably priced eatery a Chelsea favorite with the predominately gay crowd.

Negril

Map 6, D7. 362 W 23rd St (off 9th Ave) ☎212/807-6411.

An enormous aquarium and colorful decor add to the pleasure of eating at this Jamaican restaurant. Spicy jerk chicken or goat, stews and other dishes keep 'em coming, as do the reasonable prices (around $10–12 for an entree).

ITALIAN

Bottino

Map 6, C6. 246 10th Ave (between 25th and 26th sts) ☎212/206-6766.

One of Chelsea's most popular restaurants, *Bottino* attracts the in-crowd looking for some honest Italian food served in a very downtown atmosphere. The homemade leek tortolloni (winter months only) is truly tantalizing.

Frank's

Map 6, C9. 85 10th Ave (at 15th St) ☎212/243-1349.

Long-established Italian-American steakhouse, with pasta and other Italian dishes from $10 up. The casual atmosphere provides a real taste of old New York.

CHELSEA

UNION SQUARE

The area around **Union Square**, known variously as the Flatiron district and Park Avenue South, has experienced an increase in fancyish spots – though whether that will remain in the wake of the dot-com fall is hard to say (NY's Silicon Alley is/was right along here).

AMERICAN AND CONTINENTAL

Alva

Map 6, I7. 36 E 22nd St (between Broadway and Park Ave S) ☎212/228-4399. Mirrors and photos of Thomas Alva Edison cover the walls in this eclectic continental restaurant. Specialties include grilled duck, double garlic roast chicken and soft-shell crabs. It's expensive, but the weekday pre-theater prix-fixe dinner (served 5.30–7pm; three courses and a glass of wine for about $30) is good value.

Union Square Café

Map 6, H8. 21 E 16th St (between 5th Ave and Union Square W) ☎212/243-4020. Choice California-style dining with a classy but comfortable downtown atmosphere. No one does salmon like they do. Not at all cheap – prices average $100 for two – but the creative menu is a real treat. Don't miss it if you have the bucks.

FRENCH AND BELGIAN

L'Express

Map 6, J7. 249 Park Ave S (at 20th St) ☎212/254-5858. A good, airy bistro with the usual food at somewhat reasonable prices, but with two important points of distinction: the waiters are actually friendly, and it's open 24 hours – by far the classiest all-night place in the neighborhood.

UNION SQUARE

●

225

Steak Frites
Map 6, H8. 9 E 16th St
(between Union Square W and
5th Ave) ☎212/463-7101.
With its classic European feel,
Steak Frites offers an upscale
ambience as well as good
service. As the name suggests,
great steak and frites, for
around $25.

GERMAN

Rolf's
Map 6, K7. 281 3rd Ave (at
22nd St) ☎212/473-8718.
A nice, dark, chintz-
decorated Old World feeling
dominates this East Side
institution. Schnitzel and
sauerbraten are always good
but somehow taste better at
the generous bar buffet,
commencing around 5pm all
through the week.

GRAMERCY PARK, MURRAY HILL AND THE GARMENT DISTRICT

While not the best neighborhoods for dining in NYC,
Gramercy Park, **Murray Hill** and the **Garment District**
are picking up the pace. The area around Lexington Avenue
in the upper 20s is a good place to sample cheap and filling
Indian fare. It's also a fantastic place to find a number of
crowded sushi bars and small French bistros.

AMERICAN AND CONTINENTAL

El Rio Grande
Map 6, K2. 160 E 38th St
(between Lexington and 3rd
aves) ☎212/867-0922.
Long-established Murray Hill
Tex-Mex place with a
gimmick: you can eat
Mexican or, if you prefer,
Texan, by simply crossing the
"border" and walking
through the kitchen.
Personable and fun – and the
margaritas are earth
shattering.

Verbena

Map 6, K8. 54 Irving Place
(between 17th and 18th sts)
☏212/260-5454.
This simple and elegant
restaurant serves a seasonal
menu of creative (and pricey)
New American food. Don't
miss the *crème brulée* with
lemon verbena, the herb for
which the restaurant was
named. Try to get seated in
the garden, and reserve in
advance.

ASIAN

- - - - - - - - - - - - - - - - - - - -

Choshi

Map 6, K8. 77 Irving Place (at
19th St) ☏212/420-1419.
Reasonably priced Gramercy
Japanese serving first-rate
fresh sushi. The $22 dinner
prix-fixe menu is a good deal,
including drinks, soup,
appetizer, main dish (even
sushi) and dessert.

Hangawi

Map 6, I4. 12 E 32nd St
(between 5th and Madison
aves) ☏212/213-0077.

An elegant vegetarian and
vegan-safe Korean restaurant.
The autumn rolls are a great
starter. A little pricey, but
quite good.

FRENCH AND
BELGIAN

- - - - - - - - - - - - - - - - - - - -

Les Halles

Map 6, J5. 411 Park Ave S
(between 28th and 29th sts)
☏212/679-4111.
Noisy, bustling bistro with
carcasses dangling in a
butcher's shop in the front.
Very pseudo Rive Gauche,
serving rabbit, steak frites and
other staples. Entrees range
$15–25. Not recommended
for veggies.

Park Bistro

Map 6, J5. 414 Park Ave S
(between 28th and 29th sts)
☏212/689-1360.
This friendly bistro is sister to
Les Halles and similar in
prices and style, though a
little less hectic.

MIDTOWN WEST

While the majority of Manhattan's best dining occurs downtown, some manifold good meals await you in **Midtown West**, a neighborhood whose restaurants encompass Greek, South American, Japanese, African, French and everything in between. Restaurant Row (W 46th St between Eighth and Ninth avenues), is a frequent stopover for theatergoers seeking a late-night meal, though Ninth Avenue offers cheaper and generally better alternatives.

AMERICAN AND CONTINENTAL

Aquavit
Map 7, H7. 13 W 54th St (between 5th and 6th aves) ☎212/307-7311.
Superb Scandinavian food – pickled herrings, salmon, even reindeer – in a lovely atrium restaurant with a mock waterfall cascading down one of the walls. A real treat, and priced accordingly; reserve well ahead.

Hamburger Harry's
Map 7, F9. 145 W 45th St (between Broadway and 6th Ave) ☎212/840-0566.
Handy diner just off Times Square; some claim its burgers are the best in town.

Joe Allen's
Map 7, E8. 326 W 46th St (between 8th and 9th aves) ☎212/581-6464.
Tried and true formula of checkered tablecloths, old-fashioned barroom feel, and reliable American food at moderate prices. The calf's liver with spinach and potatoes has been on the menu for years. Popular pre-theater spot, so reserve well in advance unless you can arrive after 8pm.

Stage Deli
Map 7, F7. 834 7th Ave (between 53rd and 54th sts) ☎212/245-7850.
Another reliable all-night standby, and longtime rival to the *Carnegie Deli*, p.232. More genuine New York

attitude and big overstuffed sandwiches but it's not at all cheap.

West Bank Café

Map 7, D9. 407 W 42nd St (at 9th Ave) ☏212/695-6909. Some French, some American, all delicious and not as expensive as you'd think – pastas and entrees range from $11 to $20. Very popular with theater people before and especially after a performance.

ASIAN

China Grill

Map 7, H7. 52 W 53rd St (between 5th and 6th aves) ☏212/333-7788. An eclectic, slightly pretentious see-and-be-seen pan-Asian eatery that always seems to be busy. Fun destination whether you're seeking lunch, dinner or drinks.

Ollie's Noodle Shop

Map 7, E9. 190 W 44th St (between Broadway and 8th Ave) ☏212/921-5988; also 2315 Broadway (at 84th St) ☏212/362-3111; 2957 Broadway (at 116th St) ☏212/932-3300. Good Chinese restaurant that serves marvelous noodles, barbecued meats and spare ribs. Not, however, a place to linger. Very cheap, very crowded and very noisy. Also very popular pre-theater place, so don't be alarmed if there are long lines – but due to the rushed service, they move fast.

CARIBBEAN, CENTRAL AND SOUTH AMERICAN

Cabana Carioca

Map 7, F9. 123 W 45th St (between 6th Ave and Broadway) ☏212/581-8088. Animated restaurant decorated with colorful murals. A great place to try out Brazilian-Portuguese specialties, like *feijoada* (black bean and pork stew), washed down with fiery *caipirinhas*. Portions large enough for two make it reasonably inexpensive.

MIDTOWN WEST

El Papasito

Map 7, D7. 370 W 52nd St (at 9th Ave) ☎212/265-2225.
Inexpensive and tasty Dominican fare, this small eatery offers excellent pork *chicharrones* (fried on the bone), *asopado* (thick garlic rice soup) and for dessert try the flan, which will melt in your mouth.

Victor's Café 52

Map 7, E7. 236 W 52nd St (between Broadway and 8th Ave) ☎212/586-7714.
A well-established hangout, serving real Cuban food at moderate prices. Great black bean soup and sangria.

FRENCH AND BELGIAN

Chez Napoleon

Map 7, E8. 365 W 50th St (between 8th and 9th aves) ☎212/265-6980.
Owing to this neighborhood's proximity to the docks, it became a hangout for French soldiers during World War II, leading to the creation of several highly authentic Gallic eateries here in the 1940s and 1950s. This is one of them, and it lives up to its reputation. A friendly, family-run bistro; bring a wad to enjoy the tradition, though.

Hourglass Tavern

Map 7, E8. 373 W 46th St (between 8th and 9th aves) ☎212/265-2060.
Tiny midtown French restaurant, which serves an excellent-value, two-course prix-fixe menu for between $12.75 and $15.75. The gimmick is the hourglass above each table, the emptying of which means you're supposed to leave and make way for someone else. In reality they seem to last more than an hour, and they only enforce it if there's a line. Cash only.

Le Madeleine

Map 7, D9. 403 W 43rd St (between 9th and 10th aves) ☎212/246-2993.
Pretty midtown French bistro with good service, above-average food (including some knockout desserts) and moderate to expensive prices.

Get a seat in the outdoor garden if you can. Usually crowded pre-theater.

GREEK AND MIDDLE EASTERN

Afghanistan Kebab House

Map 7, F8. 155 W 46th St (between 6th and 7th aves) ℡212/768-3875; 1345 2nd Ave (between 70th and 71st sts) ℡212/517-2776.

Inexpensive lamb, chicken and seafood kebabs, served with a variety of side dishes. Complete dinners for under $15.

Lotfi's Couscous

Map 7, D8. 358 W 46th St (between 8th and 9th aves) ℡212/582-5850.

Moderately priced Moroccan hidden away on the second floor. Lots of spicy dishes, vegetarian options and inexpensive salads. Closed in Aug.

ITALIAN

Julian's

Map 7, D7. 802 9th Ave (between 53rd and 54th sts) ℡212/262-4800.

Light and inventive Mediterranean fare in a bright, pleasing room and clever dining garden tucked in an alley. Whether you want sandwiches or scaloppine, this is a safe bet in the Hell's Kitchen area.

Trattoria dell'Arte

Map 7, F6. 900 7th Ave (between 56th and 57th sts) ℡212/245-9800.

Unusually nice restaurant for this rather tame stretch of midtown, with a lovely airy interior, excellent service and good food. Great, wafer-thin crispy pizzas, decent and imaginative pasta dishes for around $20 and a mouth-watering antipasto bar – all eagerly patronized by an elegant out-to-be-seen crowd. Best to reserve.

MIDTOWN WEST

JEWISH AND EASTERN EUROPEAN

Carnegie Deli

Map 7, F6. 854 7th Ave (between 54th and 55th sts) ☎212/757-2245.

This place is known for the size of its sandwiches – by popular consent the most generously stuffed in the city, and a full meal in themselves. The chicken noodle soup is good, too. Not cheap, however, and the waiters are among New York's rudest.

Russian Tea Room

Map 7, F6. 150 W 57th St (between 6th and 7th aves) ☎212/265-0947.

One of New York's favorite places to hobnob with the glitterati. Rates are perhaps not as high as in the city's top dining spots, and it's easier to get a table (though unless you're a celeb you may get relegated to the second floor dining room). The wonderfully garish interior makes eating here a real occasion, too. Stick to the old favorites – blinis, borscht and chicken Kiev.

MIDTOWN EAST

Catering mostly to lunchtime office-going crowds that swarm the sidewalks on weekdays, **Midtown East** overflows with restaurants, most of them on the pricey side. You probably won't want to make it the focal point of too many culinary excursions but, that said, there are a few timeworn favorites in the neighborhood.

AMERICAN AND CONTINENTAL

Four Seasons

Map 7, I7. 99 E 52nd St (between Park and Lexington aves) ☎212/754-9494.

Housed in Mies van der Rohe's Seagram Building, this is one of the city's most noted restaurants, not least for the decor, which includes murals by Picasso, sculptures by Richard Lippold and interior design by Philip Johnson. The food isn't at all bad either, and there's a relatively inexpensive pre-theater menu – $55 – if you want to try it. Somewhat stuffier than the other top restaurants.

Lipstick Café

Map 7, J7. 885 3rd Ave (at 54th St) ⓣ212/486-8664. Unlike most restaurants in the neighborhood, this one serves up delectable lunchtime food at affordable prices. It features tasty homemade soups, salads and delicious baked goods. Closed weekends.

Oyster Bar

Map 7, I9. Lower level, Grand Central Terminal (at 42nd St and Park Ave) ⓣ212/490-6650. Atmospheric turn-of-the-nineteenth-century place located down in the vaulted dungeons of Grand Central station, where midtown execs and others break for lunch. The oyster appetizers are particularly good, while seafood entrees go for a minimum of $25 per dish. If you're hard up, just saddle up to the bar for a bowl of excellent clam chowder, or great creamy bowls of pan-roasted oysters or clams.

Rosen's Delicatessen

Map 7, H7. 23 E 51st St (between 5th and Madison aves) ⓣ212/541-8320. Enormous Art Deco restaurant, renowned for its pastrami and corned beef, and handily situated for those suffering from midtown shopping fatigue. Good breakfasts too.

Smith and Wollensky

Map 7, J8. 797 3rd Ave (at 49th St) ⓣ212/753-1530. Clubby atmosphere in a grand setting, where waiters – many of whom have worked here for twenty years or more – serve you the primest cuts of beef imaginable. Quite pricey – you'll pay at least $33 a steak – but worth the splurge. Go basic with the sides and wines.

ASIAN

Hatsuhana

Map 7, H8. 17 E 48th St (between 5th and Madison aves) ☎212/355-3345; 237 Park Ave (at 46th St) ☎212/661-3400.

Every sushi lover's favorite sushi restaurant now has two branches. Not at all cheap, so try to get there for the prix-fixe lunch.

FRENCH

Lutèce

Map 7, J8. 249 E 50th St (between 2nd and 3rd aves) ☎212/752-2225.

Still rated one of the best restaurants in the country, and a favorite of many well-to-do New Yorkers. The classic French food is top-notch, the service elegant and understated. What's surprising is how low-key and completely unpretentious it is, though you do need big bucks and reservations in advance. Worth every penny.

ITALIAN

Luna Piena

Map 7, J7. 243 E 53rd St (between 2nd and 3rd aves) ☎212/308-8882.

One of the better local Italians in a neighborhood of many mediocre restaurants. The food is good, the service is friendly, and there's a nice enclosed garden for warm summer evenings.

UPPER WEST SIDE

Restaurants on the **Upper West Side** offer a wide array of ethnic and price choices (particularly if you avoid the over-priced Lincoln Center area). There are lots of generous burger joints, Chinese restaurants, friendly coffee shops, and delectable, if a bit pricey, brunch spots, so you'll never be at a loss for good meals.

UPPER WEST SIDE

AMERICAN AND CONTINENTAL

Big Nick's

Map 7, C1. 2175 Broadway (between 76th and 77th sts) ☎212/362-9238.
If you want a hamburger or pizza on the Upper West Side, this is a fun, New York kind of place. In his crowded, chaotic little wooden-table restaurant, Big Nick has been serving them up all night long to locals for 20-plus years.

Boat Basin Café

Map 7, A1. 79th St at the Hudson River (access through Riverside Park) ☎212/496-5542.
An outdoor restaurant, open May through Sept, with informal tables covered in red-and-white checked cloths, some under a sheltering overhang. The food is standard, but inexpensive considering the prime location – burgers with fries ($7.75), hot dogs, sandwiches and some more serious entrees like grilled salmon ($14.50).

Boathouse Café

Map 7, G2. Central Park Lake (E 72nd St entrance) ☎212/517-2233.
Peaceful retreat from a hard day's trudging around the Fifth Avenue museums. You get great views of the famous Central Park skyline and decent American/continental cuisine, but at very steep prices. Closed from Oct to March.

Dock's Oyster Bar

Map 8, B6. 2427 Broadway (between 89th and 90th sts) ☎212/724-5588; also 633 3rd Ave (at 40th St) ☎212/986-8080.
Some of the best seafood in town at this popular uptown restaurant, with a raw bar, great mussels and a wide variety of high-quality fresh fish. The Upper West Side is the original and tends to have the homier atmosphere – though both can be noisy and service can be slow. Reservations recommended on weekends.

Tom's Restaurant

Map 8, B1. 2880 Broadway (at

112th St) ☎212/864-6137.
Cheap, greasy-spoon fare.
This is the Tom's of *Seinfeld*
fame, usually filled with
students from Columbia and
tourists. Great breakfast deals
– a large meal for under $6.

ASIAN

Hunan Park
Map 7, D3. 235 Columbus Ave
(between 70th and 71st sts)
☎212/724-4411.
Some of the best Chinese
food on the Upper West Side
is served here, in a large,
crowded room, with typically
quick service and moderate
prices. Try the spicy noodles
in sesame sauce and the
dumplings. A good, less-
expensive option within a
few blocks of Lincoln Center.

Jaya
Map 8, C8. 494 Amsterdam
Ave (at 84th St)
☎212/769-9585.
A good standby in this part of
town if you're craving
Malaysian or Indonesian food
– neither a cuisine you find
that often in Manhattan.

Reasonably priced, too.

CARIBBEAN, CENTRAL AND SOUTH AMERICAN

Café con Leche
Map 8, C9. 424 Amsterdam
Ave (at 80th St)
☎212/595-7000.
Great neighborhood
Dominican that serves
fantastic roast pork, rice and
beans, and some of the
hottest chili sauce you've ever
tasted. Cheap and very
cheerful.

Calle Ocho
Map 8, D8. 446 Columbus Ave
(between 81st and 82nd sts)
☎212/873-5025.
Very tasty Latino fare, such as
ceviches and *chimchuri* steak
with yucca fries, is served in
an immaculately designed and
a hopping bar, whose mojitos
are as potent as any in the
city.

La Caridad
Map 7, C1. 2199 Broadway (at
78th St) ☎212/874-2780.
This is something of an

Upper West Side institution, a tacky, no-frills eatery that doles out plentiful and cheap Cuban-Chinese food to hungry diners (the Cuban is better than the Chinese). Bring your own beer, and expect to wait in line.

FRENCH AND BELGIAN

Café Luxembourg

Map 7, C3. 200 W 70th St (between Amsterdam and West End aves) ☎212/873-7411. Trendy Lincoln Center area bistro that packs in (literally) a self-consciously hip crowd to enjoy its first-rate contemporary French food. Not too pricey – two people can eat for $60 or so.

Jean Georges

Map 7, E5. Trump International Hotel, 1 Central Park West (between 60th and 61st sts) ☎212/299-3900. This is French at its finest, crafted by star chef Jean-Georges Vongerichten. Definitely the place for a special occasion when you

don't mind dropping a pretty penny. For the more money conscious, the front-room, *Nougatine* has a prix-fixe summer brunch for $20. But whatever you do, don't miss the rhubarb tart for dessert.

INDIAN

Mughlai

Map 7, D3. 320 Columbus Ave (at 75th St) ☎212/724-6363. Uptown, upscale Indian with prices about the going rate for this strip: $11–16 an entree. The food, though, is surprisingly good.

ITALIAN

Gennaro

Map 8, C6. 665 Amsterdam Ave (between 92nd and 93rd sts) ☎212/665-5348. A tiny outpost of truly great Italian food, with room only for about fifty people (and thus perpetual lines to get in). Standouts include a warm potato, mushroom and goat cheese tart (incredible) and braised lamb shank in red

UPPER WEST SIDE

wine. The desserts are also worth the wait. Moderate prices – open for dinner only.

JEWISH AND EASTERN EUROPEAN

Barney Greengrass
Map 8, C7. 541 Amsterdam Ave (between 86th and 87th sts) ☎212/724-4707.
A West Side deli and restaurant that's been around since time began. The smoked salmon section is a particular treat. Cheese blintzes are tasty too.

Fine & Schapiro
Map 7, D2. 138 W 72nd St (between Broadway and Columbus Ave) ☎212/877-2721.
Longstanding Jewish deli that's open for lunch and dinner and serves delicious old-fashioned kosher fare – an experience that's getting harder to find in New York. Great chicken soup.

UPPER EAST SIDE

Upper East Side restaurants cater mostly to a discriminating mixture of well-heeled clientele and young professionals from Wall Street; many of the best French and Italian restaurants call this neighborhood home. For a change of pace, try a wurst and some strudel at one of Yorkville's old-world German luncheonettes.

AMERICAN AND CONTINENTAL

E.A.T.
Map 8, I9. 1064 Madison Ave (between 80th and 81st sts) ☎212/772-0022.
Expensive and crowded but with excellent food (celebrated restaurateur and gourmet grocer Eli Zabar is the owner, so that's no surprise) – especially the soups and breads, and the ficelles and Parmesan toast.

Post House

Map 7, H4. 26 E 63rd St
☎212/935-2888.
Classic American food in an
elegant and comfortable,
typically Upper East Side
setting. It's reasonably
unpretentious for the area,
and does very good steaks
and chops, though not all that
cheaply.

Rathbones

Map 8, K7. 1702 2nd Ave
(between 88th and 89th sts)
☎212/369-7361.
Take a window seat to watch
the stars arrive at celeb
hotspot *Elaine's* (across the
street), and eat for a fraction
of the price. Steaks and fish
for around $15 – and a wide
choice of beers.

ASIAN

Pig Heaven

Map 8, K9. 1540 2nd Ave
(between 80th and 81st sts)
☎212/744-4333.
Good-value Chinese
restaurant decorated with
images of pigs, serving lean
and meaty spare ribs, among

other things. In case you
hadn't guessed, the accent is
on pork.

Wu Liang Ye

Map 8, K7. 215 E 86th St
(between 2nd and 3rd aves)
☎212/534-8899.
Excellent, authentic Szechuan
food. The menu here features
dishes you've never seen
before, and if you like spicy
food, you will not be
disappointed. Perhaps one of
the best Chinese restaurants
in the whole city.

FRENCH AND BELGIAN

Le Refuge

Map 8, J8. 166 E 82nd St
(between Lexington and 3rd
aves) ☎212/861-4505.
Quiet, intimate and
deliberately romantic old-
style French restaurant
situated in an old city
brownstone. The bouillabaisse
and other seafood dishes are
delectable. Expensive but
worth it; save for special
occasions. Closed Sun during
the summer.

UPPER EAST SIDE

Mme Romaine de Lyon

Map 7, I5. 29 E 61st St (between Madison and Park aves) ☎212/758-2422.
The best place for omelettes: they've got 350 on the lunch menu, and dinner features an expanded non-omelette menu (though honestly, why bother? Eggs are the thing here).

Payard Patisserie & Bistro

Map 7, J2. 1032 Lexington Ave (between 72nd and 73rd sts) ☎212/717-5252.
This is real Parisian pastry – buttery, creamy and over the top. Cookies, cakes, and *crème brulée* made to the exacting standards of the kitchen staffs of local millionaires.

INDIAN

Dawat

Map 7, J6. 210 E 58th St (between 2nd and 3rd aves) ☎212/355-7555.
One of the most elegant gourmet Indian restaurants in the city. Try the Cornish game hen with green chili or the leg of lamb. A bit pricey – entrees average about $17. For an extra charge, Beverly will give you a tarot card reading.

ITALIAN

Caffe Buon Gusto

Map 7, J1. 243 E 77th St (between 2nd and 3rd aves) ☎212/535-6884.
This stretch of the Upper East Side has plenty of cool, Italian joints: what *Buon Gusto* lacks in style it makes up for in taste and low prices. The vodka sauce is excellent.

Contrapunto

Map 7, J5. 200–206 E 60th St (at 3rd Ave) ☎212/751-8616.
More than twenty fresh pastas daily at this friendly, reasonably priced neighborhood Italian restaurant.

UPPER EAST SIDE

JEWISH AND EASTERN EUROPEAN

Heidelburg

Map 8, K7. 1648 2nd Ave (between 85th and 86th sts) ☎212/628-2332.

The atmosphere here is mittel-European kitsch, with gingerbread trim and waitresses in Alpine goatherd costumes. But the food is the real deal, featuring excellent liver dumpling soup, Bauernfruestuck omelettes,

and pancakes (both sweet and potato). And they serve *weissbeer* the right way, too – in giant, boot-shaped glasses.

Mocca Hungarian

Map 8, K8. 1588 2nd Ave (between 82nd and 83rd sts) ☎212/734-6470.

Yorkville restaurant serving hearty portions of Hungarian comfort food – schnitzel, cherry soup, goulash and chicken paprikash, among others. Moderately priced, but be sure to come hungry.

UPPER MANHATTAN: MORNINGSIDE HEIGHTS, HARLEM AND ABOVE

Cheap Cuban, African, Caribbean and the best soulfood restaurants in the city abound in and around **Harlem**; even institutions like *Sylvia's*, touristy and crowded as it may be, remain reasonably priced.

AFRICAN

Zula

Map 9, C8. 1260 Amsterdam Ave (at 122nd St) ☎212/663-1670.

High-quality and inexpensive ($8 up) Ethiopian food that's popular with the folk from Columbia University. Spicy chicken, beef and lamb dishes mainly, though a few veggie plates too.

AMERICAN AND CONTINENTAL

Amy Ruth's

Map 9, D9. 113 W 116th St. (between Lenox and 7th aves) ☏212/280-8779.

Surprisingly cheap, considering its enormous portions, this new soulfood spot draws Harlemites and visitors with its outstanding fried chicken and ribs. The desserts are excellent, too.

Sylvia's Restaurant

Map 9, D8. 328 Lenox Ave (between 126th and 127th sts) ☏212/996-0660.

The most well-known Southern soulfood restaurant in Harlem – so famous that Sylvia herself even has her own package food line. While some find the barbecue sauce too tangy, the fried chicken is exceptional at $16.95 and the garlic-mashed potatoes and candied yams are justly celebrated. Also famous for the Sunday Gospel brunch but be prepared for a thirty-minute wait.

BROOKLYN

In **Brooklyn**, lower Atlantic Avenue offers some of the city's best Middle Eastern food, Brighton Beach features the most authentic Russian food in NYC, and Park Slope, Carroll Gardens, Cobble Hill and Fort Greene all have burgeoning restaurant rows.

Al Di Là

248 5th Ave (at Carroll St), Park Slope ☏718/783-4565.

Venetian country cooking at its finest at this husband-and-wife-run eatery. Standouts include beet ravioli, grilled sardines, *saltimbocca* and salt-baked striped bass. Invariably crowded.

Banania

241 Smith St (at Douglass St), Cobble Hill ☏718/237-9100.

BROOKLYN

French bistro serving brunch and dinner for quite reasonable prices; steaks and fish dishes, like pan-roasted cod, stand out. Average price for entrees is $14; cash only.

Diner

85 Broadway (at Berry St), Williamsburg ☎718/486-3077.
Located in a refurbished dining car under the Williamsburg Bridge, this local favorite dishes out a superb array of food that includes fantastic burgers, French standards and a wealth of daily specials. Kitchen open nightly to 2am.

Grimaldi's Pizza

19 Old Fulton St (between Water and Front sts), Brooklyn Heights ☎718/858-4300.
Delicious, thin and crispy pies that bring even Manhattanites across the water – cheap and crowded.

Heights Café

84 Montague St (at Hicks St), Brooklyn Heights ☎718/625-5555.
Near the Esplanade overlooking the East River and the Manhattan skyline, this mainstay offers a great environment for a drink and appetizers at the bar or a decent-priced American eclectic meal at one of the sidewalk tables.

Junior's

386 Flatbush Ave (at DeKalb Ave), downtown Brooklyn ☎718/852-5257.
Open 24-hours in a sea of lights that makes it worthy of Vegas, *Junior's* offers everything you can imagine from chopped liver sandwiches to ribs and meatloaf. Whatever you do, save room for the cheesecake, which many consider to be NYC's finest.

Moroccan Star

205 Atlantic Ave (between Court and Clinton sts), downtown Brooklyn ☎718/643-0800.
Perhaps New York's best Moroccan restaurant, offering wonderful tajines and couscous with lamb. The chef once worked at the *Four Seasons*, and the quality of his cooking remains

BROOKLYN

●

undiminished. Entrees are generally around $9.

Peter Luger's Steak House

178 Broadway (at Driggs Ave), Williamsburg ☏718/387-7400.
Catering to carnivores since 1873, *Peter Luger's* may just be the city's finest steakhouse. The service is surly and the decor plain, but the porterhouse steak – the only cut served – is divine. Cash only; expect to pay at least $60 per head.

Primorski

282 Brighton Beach Ave (between 2nd and 3rd sts), Brighton Beach ☏718/891-3111.
Perhaps the best of Brighton Beach's Russian hangouts, serving up a huge menu of authentic Russian dishes, including blintzes and stuffed cabbage, at absurdly cheap prices. Live music in the evening.

QUEENS

The most ethnically diverse of all the boroughs, **Queens** holds the city's largest Greek, South American, Slavic and Asian communities, thus some of the best examples of that type of food.

Elias Corner

24-02 31st St (at 24th Ave), Astoria ☏718/932-1510.
Pay close attention to the seafood on display as you enter, for *Elias Corner* does not have menus and the staff is not always forthcoming. This informal Astoria institution, with open-air seating when weather permits, serves some of the best and freshest fish as well as a myriad of salads.

Jade Palace

136-14 38th Ave, Flushing ☏718/353-3366.

Fantastic and very inexpensive dim sum. The *har gow* (shrimp dumplings) and taro cakes are a great place to start.

Pastrami King
124-24 Queens Blvd (at 82nd Ave), Kew Gardens ☎718/263-1717.
The home-smoked pastrami and corned beef are better than any you'll find in Manhattan. Closed Sat.

Uncle George's
33-19 Broadway (at 34th St), Astoria ☎718/626-0593.
This 24–hour joint serves excellent and ultracheap authentic Greek food, including some of the top Greek BBQ and *spanakopita* in the city.

THE BRONX

In the **Bronx**, Belmont is one of the best places in the city to eat authentic Italian cuisine.

The Crab Shanty
361 City Island Ave (at Tier St), City Island ☎718/885-1810.
While the decor is cheesy to say the least, the fried clams and Cajun fried fish specials at this City Island favorite are worth the trip.

Dominick's
2335 Arthur Ave (at 187th St), Belmont ☎718/733-2807.
All you could hope for in a neighborhood Italian: great, rowdy atmosphere, communal family-style seating, wonderful food and low(ish) prices. As there are no menus, pay close attention to your waiter. Stuffed baby squid, veal parmigiana and chicken *scarpariello* are standouts.

Mister Taco
2255 White Plain Rd, Central Bronx ☎718/882-3821.
Makes for a great snack or

THE BRONX

meal after walking around the nearby Bronx Botanical Garden. The tamales are the call here. No English spoken.

Sam's

596-598 Grand Concourse, South Bronx ☎718/665-5341. Located just a hop away from Yankee Stadium, *Sam's* makes for a tasty, cheap pre-game meal. Stay with the chicken, jerked or fried.

Drinking

You can't walk a block along most Manhattan avenues (and many of the side streets) without passing one or two bars. The **bar scene** in New York City is a varied one, with a broader range of places to drink than in most American cities, and prices to suit most pockets. Bars generally open from mid-morning (around 10am) to the early hours – 4am at the latest, when they have to close by law. Bar kitchens usually stop operating around midnight or a little before.

The best spots are below 14th Street, where the **West Village** takes in a wide range of taste, budget and purpose, and equally good hunting grounds can be found in the **East Village**, **NoLita**, **SoHo** and the more western reaches of the **Lower East Side**. There's a decent choice of **midtown** bars, though bars here tend to be geared to an after-hours office crowd and (with a few notable exceptions) can consequently be pricey and rather dull. The **Upper West Side** has a small array of bars, some interesting, although most tend to cater to more of a clean-cut and dully yuppie crowd; and the bars of **Harlem**, while not numerous, offer some of the city's most affordable jazz in a relaxed environment.

While most visitors to New York may not have time or occasion to check out the bar scenes in the outer boroughs, those that venture to **Williamsburg**, **Park Slope**, **Brooklyn Heights** and **Fort Greene** in Brooklyn or to **Astoria** in Queens will find both some of the hippest and also most neighborly spots around.

Predominantly gay bars are gathered together
in "Gay and lesbian New York," Chapter 30.

Whether you wind up sipping a martini in a swank lounge or a downing a pint in a seedy dive, you'll be expected to tip; figure about a buck a drink. Remember too that the legal **drinking age** is 21.

FINANCIAL DISTRICT AND SOUTH STREET SEAPORT

Jeremy's Alehouse
Map 4, H5. 254 Front St (at Dover St) ☎212/964-3537.
An earthy bar near the South Street Seaport, housed in an old garage, *Jeremy's* also happens to serve some of the city's best calamari and clams.

North Star Pub
Map 4, G6. 93 South St (at Fulton St) ☎212/509-6757.
Pseudo-British alehouse where you can wash down your bangers 'n' mash with a pint of Newcastle Brown Ale – or choose from some 80 single malt Scotch whiskies. Fairly small, the *North Star* is very popular with Wall Street types and visiting Limeys.

TRIBECA

Grace
Map 4, D2. 114 Franklin St (between Church St and West Broadway) ☎212/343-4200. An excellent cocktail and olives spot teeming with old-school class – there's a 40ft mahogany bar. Top-notch drink selection for a twenty-something clientele.

Knitting Factory Tap Bar
Map 4, E3. 74 Leonard St (between Church St and Broadway) ☎212/219-3006. Street-level bar and cozy downstairs taproom with eighteen draft microbrews and free live music – usually some revolutionary form of jazz – from 11pm. (For details on the jazz venue upstairs, see "Live music and clubs," p.270.)

Liquor Store Bar
Map 4, D2. 225 W Broadway (at White St) ☎212/226-7121. Homely little wood-paneled pub with sidewalk seating that feels like it's been around since colonial times. A welcome respite from the trendy local scene.

No Moore
Map 4, D2. 234 W Broadway (at White St) ☎212/925-2901. Sprawling, friendly lounge with live music at weekends (some weeknights too). No food, but, oddly, you can order in or bring your own dinner.

SOHO AND NOLITA

Ear Inn
Map 5, B7. 326 Spring St (between Washington and Greenwich sts) ☎212/226-9060. "Ear" as in "Bar" with half the neon "B" chipped off. Be that as it may, this cozy pub, a stone's throw from the Hudson River, has a good mix of beers on tap, serves basic, reasonably priced, American food and claims to

TRIBECA • SOHO AND NOLITA

be the second oldest bar in the city.

Fanelli

Map 5, F7. 94 Prince St (at Mercer St) ☎212/226-9412. Established in 1872, *Fanelli* is one of the city's oldest bars, relaxed and informal and a favorite of the not-too-hip after-work crowd. The food is simple American fare: burgers, salads and such.

Pravda

Map 5, G6. 281 Lafayette St (between Houston and Prince sts) ☎212/334-5015. Very tasteful, pseudo-exclusive bar, maybe a little too grandiose for most tastes. There's nothing Communist about the place – think caviar and cocktails, all washed down with champagne.

Sweet and Vicious

Map 5, I7. 5 Spring St (between Bowery and Elizabeth sts) ☎212/334-7915. A neighborhood favorite, it's the epitome of rustic chic with its exposed brick and wood, replete with antique chandeliers. The atmosphere makes it seem all cozy, as does the back garden.

Toad Hall

Map 5, E8. 57 Grand St (between W Broadway and Wooster St) ☎212/431-8145. With a pool table, good service and excellent bar snacks, this stylish alehouse is a little less hip, more of a local hangout than *Lucky Strike* next door.

LOWER EAST SIDE AND CHINATOWN

Double Happiness

Map 5, H7. 174 Mott St (at Broome) ☎212/941-1282. Low ceilings, dark lighting and lots of nooks and crannies make this Asian-theme bar an intimate place to be. If the decor doesn't seduce you, one of the house specialties – a green tea martini – should soon loosen you up.

Idlewild

Map 5, I5. 145 Houston St (between 1st and 2nd aves) ☏212/477-5005.
Hugely popular super-sleek bar themed on all things airplane – a 1967 747 to be exact – and the owners have done everything to make the experience as authentic as possible. Beware the cocktails – you know what they say about alcohol at a high altitude.

Max Fish

Map 5, K6. 178 Ludlow St (between Houston and Stanton sts) ☏212/529-3959.
Visiting indie rock bands come here in droves, lured by the unpretentious but arty vibe and the jukebox which, quite simply, rocks any other party out of town.

Orchard Bar

Map 5, J6. 200 Orchard St (between Houston and Stanton sts) ☏212/673-5350.
A Lower East Side stalwart that features walls lined with glass display cases, filled with nature and neon lights; cozy recesses to whisper in and some of the nicest bar staff in town.

Swim

Map 5, J6. 146 Orchard St (between Rivington and Stanton sts) ☏212/673-0799.
Sleek two-floor bar that packs in a hip and rich crowd with its strong DJ listings, its strong drinks and maybe a bite of sushi or two.

Many bars have happy hours, typically
5–7pm, when drinks might be two for one,
or some bar food is available for free.

WEST VILLAGE

Blind Tiger Ale House

Map 5, A4 . 518 Hudson St (at 10th St) ☏212/675-3848.

You could easily leave here with things looking a bit foggy after you choose from the 24 beers on tap and eclectic bottled selection. Come on Sun between 1pm and 6pm for the free brunch of bagels and cream cheese with complimentary newspapers.

Cedar Tavern
Map 5, F2. 82 University Place (between 11th and 12th sts) ⊤212/741-9754.
The original *Cedar Tavern*, situated just a block away, was a legendary Beat and artists' meeting point in the1950s. The new version, a homey bar with food, reasonably priced drinks, and occasional poetry readings, retains the bohemian feel, though. All year round you can eat under the stars in their covered roof garden.

Chumley's
Map 5, B4. 86 Bedford St (between Grove and Barrow sts) ⊤212/675-4449.
It's not easy to find this former speakeasy, owing to its unmarked entrance, but it's worth the effort – offering up a good choice of beers and food, both reasonably priced.

Best arrive before 8pm if you want to eat at one of the battered tables.

Hogs & Heifers
Map 6, C9. 859 Washington St (at 13th St) ⊤212/929-0655.
Hogs as in the burly motorcycles parked outside; heifers as in, well, ladies. Though officially there's no more bar dancing (Julia Roberts was famously photographed doing so here), those bold enough to venture into this rough-and-tumble meat-packing district joint can still drink to excess.

Kava Lounge
Map 5, A2. 605 Hudson St (at 12th St) ⊤212/989-7504.
Maori-style murals grace the walls of this charming, intimate and truly original Village bar, which serves mainly Australian and New Zealand wines – as well as smoothies – to a fairly moneyed crowd.

Kettle of Fish
Map 5, D3. 59 Christopher St (at 6th Ave) ⊤212/414-2278.
A refreshing dive that houses

the locals and old-timers in the area looking for a cheap drink in a laid-back atmosphere.

White Horse Tavern

Map 5, A3. 567 Hudson St (at 11th St) ☎212/243-9260.

Greenwich Village institution where Dylan Thomas drank his last before being carted off to hospital with alcoholic poisoning. The beer and food are cheap and palatable here, and outside seating is available in the summer.

EAST VILLAGE

7B

Map 5, L3. 108 Ave B (at 7th St) ☎212/473-8840.

Quintessential East Village hangout with an extremely mixed crowd that has often been used as a sleazy set in films and commercials – recall the bar brawls in *Crocodile Dundee*. It features deliberately mental bartenders, strong, cheap booze and one of best punk jukeboxes in the Village.

Baraza

Map 5, M3. 133 Ave C (between 8th and 9th sts) ☎212/539-0811.

Quirky yet welcoming, this gem of a bar plays great music, serves great drinks and

is the jewel in the crown of the Loisaida.

Bowery Bar

Map 5, H4. 40 E 4th St (at Bowery) ☎212/475-2220.

Once the place to see and be seen, the *Bowery Bar* still pulls in a high volume of celebrities and beautiful people – as well as commoners – who come to sip cocktails or share a bottle of wine in the serene, fairy-lit garden.

Decibel

Map 5, I3. 240 E 9th (between 2nd and 3rd aves) ☎212/979-2733.

Great, beautifully decorated underground sake bar with a

rocking atmosphere (and good tunes). The inevitable wait for a wooden table will be worth it, guaranteed.

KGB

Map 5, H4. 85 E 4th St (between 2nd Ave and Bowery) ☎212/505-3360.

A lovely dark bar on the second floor, which claims to have been the HQ of the Ukrainian Communist party. The Eastern European edge remains, making it popular with off-off Broadway theater crowds and wannabe Beats.

Lakeside Lounge

Map 5, L2. 162 Ave B (between 10th and 11th sts) ☎212/529-8463.

Opened by a local DJ and a record producer who have stocked the jukebox with old rock, country and R&B. A down-home hangout, with live music four nights a week.

McSorley's

Map 5, H3. 15 E 7th St (between 2nd and 3rd aves) ☎212/473-9148.

New York City's longest-established watering hole, so

it claims, and a male-only bar until a 1969 lawsuit. These days it retains a saloon look, with mostly an out-of-towner crowd. There's no trouble deciding what to drink – you can have McSorley's ale, and you can have it dark or light.

OpenAir

Map 5, J3. 121 St Mark's Place (between 1st Ave and Ave A) ☎212/979-1459.

A little newcomer that is the antithesis of St Marks: beautifully designed, it somehow divides itself into a chill-out lounge, an eerie middle space lit by flickering flat screens and a front bar, all imbued with the same well-spun tunes from the DJ.

St Dymphna's

Map 5, J3. 118 St Mark's Place (between 1st Ave and Ave A) ☎212/254-6636.

With a tempting menu and perhaps the city's best Guinness, this snug and tasteful (no fake-shamrocks here) Irish watering hole is, understandably, a favorite among young East Villagers.

EAST VILLAGE

BARS WITH FOOD

Though you're more likely to go to a restaurant for a meal (see Chapter 26), plenty of bars offer limited, or even full, menus, mostly along the lines of burgers and the like; look out especially for:

Cedar Tavern p.252

Citron 47 p.256

Ear Inn p.249

Half King p.256

Jeremy's Ale House p.248

Old Town Bar p.255

St Dymphna's p.254

White Horse Tavern p.253

UNION SQUARE, GRAMERCY PARK, MURRAY HILL AND MIDTOWN EAST

Cibar

Map 6, K8. 56 Irving Place (between 17th and 18th sts) ☏212/460-5656.
Innovative cocktails, elegant decor and a sweet garden make this cozy hotel bar a local hotspot.

No Idea

Map 6, J7. 30 E 20th St (between Broadway and Park Ave S) ☏212/777-0100.
Bizarre palace of inebriation has something for most barflies – from $4.50 pints of mixed drinks, to a pool room, TV sports and even a drink-for-free-if-your-name's-on-the-wall night.

Old Town Bar and Restaurant

Map 6, J8. 45 E 18th St (between Broadway and Park Ave S) ☏212/529-6732.
One of the oldest and still one of the very best bars in the city, although it can get packed, especially when the

suits from the Flatiron district get off work to enjoy its excellent, if standard, menu of chili, burgers and the like. It was regularly featured on the old *David Letterman Show*.

P.J. Clarke's

Map 7, J6. 915 3rd Ave (between 55th and 56th sts) ℡212/759-1650.
One of the city's most famous watering holes, this is a spit-and-sawdust alehouse with a not-so-cheap restaurant out the back. You may recognize it as the setting of the film *The Lost Weekend*.

Pete's Tavern

Map 6, K8. 129 E 18th St (at Irving Place) ℡212/473-7676.
Former speakeasy that claims to be the oldest bar in New York – opened in 1864 – though these days it inevitably trades on its history, which included such illustrious patrons as John F Kennedy Jr and O'Henry, who allegedly wrote *The Gift of the Magi* in his regular booth here.

CHELSEA, GARMENT DISTRICT AND MIDTOWN WEST

Citron 47

Map 7, D8. 401 W 47th St (between 9th and 10th aves) ℡212/397-4747.
Charming hybrid of a French bistro, hip bar and New England farmhouse situated in gentrified Hell's Kitchen. Great place to knock a few back.

The Collins Bar

Map 7, E8. 735 8th Ave (between 46th and 47th sts) ℡212/541-4206.
Sleek, stylish bar has choice sports photos along one side, original art works along the other – not to mention perhaps the most eclectic juke in the city.

Half King

Map 6, B7. 505 W 23rd St (between 10th and 11th aves) ℡212/462-4300.

Media bar on the far west side that is run by *Perfect Storm* author Sebastian Junger and some other literary types, and is a pleasant, warm place, kind of like an antique living room.

Jimmy's Corner

Map 7, F9. 140 W 44th St (between Broadway and 6th Ave) ☏212/221-9510.

The walls of this long, narrow corridor of a bar, owned by ex-fighter/trainer Jimmy Glenn, are a virtual Boxing Hall of Fame. You'd be hard pressed to find a more characterful dive anywhere in the city – or a better jazz/R&B jukebox.

Park

Map 6, C8. 118 10th Ave (between 17th and 18th sts) ☏212/352-3313.

It's easy to get lost in this vast warren of rooms filled with fireplaces, geodes and even a Canadian redwood in the middle of the floor. The garden is a treat though, and the servers are the best dressed in New York.

Rudy's Bar and Grill

Map 7, D9. 627 9th Ave (between 44th and 45th sts) ☏212/974-9169.

One of New York's cheapest, friendliest and liveliest dive bars, a favorite with local actors and musicians. *Rudy's* offers free hot dogs and a backyard that's great in the summer.

Russian Vodka Room

Map 7, F7. 265 W 52nd St (between Broadway and 7th Ave) ☏212/307-5835.

They have several different kinds of vodka, as you might expect, and a lot of Russian and Eastern European expatriates.

St Andrews

Map 7, F9. 120 W 44th St (between 6th Ave and Broadway) ☏212/840-8413.

A friendly Scottish bar that is a welcome addition to midtown, with a huge collection of draft beers and the city's largest selection of single malts.

UPPER WEST SIDE

Dead Poet

Map 8, C9. 450 Amsterdam Ave (between 81st and 82nd sts) ☎212/595-5670.
You'll be waxing poetical and then dropping down dead if you stay for the duration of this sweet little bar's happy hour: it lasts from 8am to 8pm and offers draft beer at $3 a pint. There's a backroom with armchairs, books and even a pool table, too, so you can both exercise and educate yourself while you drink.

Potion Lounge

Map 8, D9. 370 Columbus Ave (between 78th and 79th sts)

☎212/721-4386.
A little more expensive than most of the bars around here, *Potion* is also a little better thought out. A bubble motif reigns throughout, from the windows to the futuristic bar to the house "potions" that will intoxicate you for a mere $10 a pop.

Smoke

Map 8, B2. 2751 Broadway (at 105th St) ☎212/864-6662.
Seductively mellow jazz lounge – a real find in this neighborhood. Live music most nights. $8 cover at the weekend.

UPPER EAST SIDE

American Trash

Map 7, L1. 1471 1st Ave (between 76th and 77th sts) ☎212/988-9008.
Self-styled "professional drinking establishment" has a friendly barstaff, a pool table, a sing-a-long jukebox and a

happy hour dedicated to getting you there.

The Cocktail Room

Map 7, K2. 334 E 73rd St (between 1st and 2nd aves) ☎212/988-6100.
Fancy-schmanzy bar, with

couches, dim lighting and a modish 1960s' theme. Popular with singles, and groups who go to lounge on the couches in the back, this neighborhood anomaly throbs on weekends.

Metropolitan Museum of Art

Map 8, H8. 1000 5th Ave (at 82nd St) ☎212/535-7710.
It's hard to imagine a more romantic spot to sip a glass of wine, whether it's up on the Cantor Roof Garden (open only in warm weather, see p.121) enjoying one of the very best views in the city or on the Great Hall Balcony listening to live chamber

music (Fri and Sat 5–8pm).

Phoenix Park

Map 7, J3. 206 E 67th (between 2nd and 3rd aves) ☎212/717-8181.
Nothing special about this Irish pub, except it's sociable, has a jukebox, TVs and a pool table – and there's very little else happening in this part of town.

Subway Inn

Map 7, J5. 143 E 60th St (at Lexington Ave) ☎212/223-8929.
Downscale neighborhood dive bar across the street from Bloomingdale's. A great spot for a late-afternoon beer.

HARLEM

Lenox Lounge

Map 9, D8. 288 Lenox Ave (between 124th and 125th sts) ☎212/427-0253.
Elegant Art Deco Harlem landmark, formerly graced by Billie Holiday, is celebrated for its swanky Zebra Room, whose ceiling is adorned with

zebra skins. Jazz is played on weekends.

Sugar Shack

Map 9, D6. 2611 Frederick Douglass Blvd (at 139th St) ☎212/491-4422.
Just west of Strivers Row, this bar-café comes alive at

HARLEM

night with reggae, blues, comedy and hip hop acts.

The soulfood's also worth the trip.

BROOKLYN

Brooklyn Inn
148 Hoyt St (at Bergen St), Boerum Hill ☏718/625-9741.
Locals – and their dogs – gather at this friendly Boerum Hill favorite with high ceilings and a friendly bar staff. Great place for a daytime buzz or shooting pool in the smoky back room.

Frank's Bar and Grill
660 Fulton St, Fort Greene ☏718/625-9339.
A stone's throw from the Brooklyn Academy of Music, this mellow bar with a classic-to-modern R&B jukebox comes alive at night when DJs spin hip-hop and the party spreads upstairs.

Galapagos
70 N 6th St (between Wythe and Kent aves), Williamsburg ☏718/782-5188.
Gorgeous design – this converted factory features watery pools and candelabras – and avant-garde movies on Sun and Mon nights.

Pete's Candy Store
709 Lorimer St (between the BQE and McCarren Park), Williamsburg ☏718/302-3770.
Once a Mafia joint fronting as a soda parlor, and now a haven of punk rock and seedy, cheap cocktails, *Pete's* retains an underground vibe.

QUEENS

Bohemian Hall and Park

29-19 24th Ave, Astoria

☏718/728-9776.

Old-world Czech Bohemians and twenty-something bohemians mingle at New York's largest beer garden, which features a variety of pilsners. Summer bands range in style from polka to rock to hip-hop.

Café-Bar

32-90 34th Ave, Astoria

☏718/204-5273.

With its plush couches and outdoor seating, the ultra-relaxed *Café-Bar* is the perfect place to kill time before a matinee at the nearby American Museum of the Moving Image.

Live music
and clubs

New York's **music scene** reflects the city's diversity. Traditional and contemporary **jazz** are still in abundance, with the annual JVC and *Knitting Factory's* "What Is Jazz?" festivals bringing top international talent to the city every year. The downtown **avant-garde** scene and its attendant art noise bands – the most famous being Sonic Youth – continue to influence the area's musicians. **Spoken-word** performers, along with the current crop of singer/songwriters, are reviving the Beats' poetry scene. If you travel uptown or to the outer boroughs, you'll find pockets of Brazilian music, West Indian music, reggae and hip-hop, but if you stay downtown, **indie rock** will fill your ears. Techno, hip-hop, and electronica – and every hybrid form thereof, from classical violin played over skrawking German beats on the subway to experiments in mixology at your local bar – are everywhere; dance music has finally taken New York and New York is playing it in every place it can.

Despite what the designers on any avenue would like you to believe, New York is not uptight about appearance. In the most expensive, glitzy **clubs**, however, appearances do matter: acolytes must adhere to the current look, with bouncers guarding the doors against the gauche. But if you just want to dance, there are plenty of more-casual places, especially the city's **gay clubs**, which often offer more creative music and less hassle (see p.300).

The sections that follow provide accounts of the cream of current venues. Remember, though, that the music – and especially the club scenes – change continually. Consult weekly **listings** publications. Excellent freebies include the *Village Voice* (Ⓦwww.villagevoice.com), *New York Press* (Ⓦwww.nypress.com), *Homo Xtra* (Ⓦwww.hx.com) and the monthly club sheet *Flyer* which all contain detailed club, theater and venue listings for the straight and gay scenes; you can find them in corner self-serve newspaper boxes and music stores. Also on the web and on the ball are *Time Out New York* (Ⓦwww.timeoutny.com) and *Citysearch* (Ⓦwww .newyork.citysearch.com)

It may seem a ridiculous and puritanical requirement, but you will undoubtedly be "carded" at the door in New York, so it's imperative to bring your **ID** (driver's license or passport) with you when you go out. Venues and bars do enforce the legal drinking age of 21 and you must be 18 to enter some music venues.

ROCK MUSIC

New York's **rock music** scene is still built on white-boy guitar bands, with three-chord rock the default setting. That said, many foreign acts – especially British bands – travel to New York's shores first when trying to break into America. Frequently you'll have the opportunity to see these groups play in small venues at low admission prices.

In Manhattan, most of the energy is provided by bars and venues located in the East and West Villages. The listings below will point you to the primary spots where you should find something for your ears, no matter what you're looking for.

BIG PERFORMANCE VENUES

Madison Square Garden

Map 6, E4. 7th Ave at W 32nd St ☏212/465-6741.
New York's principal large stage, the Garden hosts not only hockey and basketball but also a good proportion of the stadium rock acts that visit the city. Seating 20,000-plus, the arena is not the most soulful place to see a band, but it may be the only chance that you get.

Radio City Music Hall

Map 7, G7. 1260 6th Ave (at 50th St) ☏212/247-4777.
Not the prime venue it once was; most of the acts that play here now are firmly in the mainstream. The building itself has as great a sense of occasion, though, despite a recent renovation, and Rockette dolls are still sold in the gift shop.

SMALLER VENUES

Apollo Theatre

Map 9, D8. 253 W 125th St (between 7th and 8th aves) ☏212/749-5838 (show info), ☏212/531-5305 (tickets), ☏212/531-5337 (tours), ⊛www.apolloshowtime.com.
Stars are born and legends are still made at the Apollo, where everyone from Billie Holliday to Aretha Franklin and Duke Ellington had their day. Now the just-renovated theater features a cast of black music acts, comedy, and weekly amateur nights (Wed). $13–35.

Arlene Grocery

Map 5, K6. 95 Stanton St (between Ludlow and Orchard sts) ☏212/473-9831.
An intimate, former bodega that hosts nightly free gigs by local, reliably good indie bands – and there's no cover charge during the week.

Frequented by musicians, some talent scouts and open-minded rock fans. Go on Mon nights for the metal and punk karaoke, where you can sing along with a live band. $3 Fri & Sat, $5 Sun.

Beacon Theater
Map 7, C2. 2124 Broadway (between 74th and 75th sts) ☎212/496-7070.
Once the quirky Upper West Side host of off-the-mainstream names, now featuring the more mature artist - from Spinal Tap to Cher. $25–100.

The Bottom Line
Map 5, F4. 15 W 4th St (at Mercer St) ☎212/228-7880.
Not New York's most adventurous venue but one of the better known – where you're most likely to see singer-songwriters. Cabaret setup, with tables crowding out any suggestion of a dance floor. Cover varies, with shows at 7.30pm & 10.30pm. Cash only.

Bowery Ballroom
Map 5, I7. 6 Delancey St (at Bowery) ☎212/533-2111.
A minimum of attitude among staff and clientele, great sound, and even better views has earned this site praise from fans and bands alike. Great bar and solid lineup. Shows $10–20.

Brownies
Map 5, K2. 169 Ave A (between 10th and 11th sts) ☎212/420-8392, ⓦwww.browniesnyc.com.
The place to see major-label one-offs, bands on the cusp of making it big and impressive local talent. Around $7–10.

CBGB (and OMFUG)
Map 5, H5. 315 Bowery (at Bleecker St) ☎212/982-4052.
After 20+ years the black, sticker-covered interior may be the last of its kind in New York, but this legendary punk bastion is not as cutting-edge as it was. Noisy rock bands are the order now, often five or six a night. Shows begin at 7 or 8pm; occasional Sun matinees at 5pm. Prices about $5–10. Less scruffy counterpart next door, *CB's*

ROCK MUSIC

313 Gallery, host folk, acoustic and experimental music seven days a week; $5.

The Cooler

Map 6, C9. 416 W 14th St (between 9th and 10th aves) ☎212/229-0785.
Maybe it's the indigo lighting that lends a *Blue Velvet* feel to this underground bunker – or perhaps it's because the club is a former meat refrigerator. Adventurous indie rock and avant-garde attract a youthful, hip crowd. Mon–Thurs shows begin at 9pm; Fri & Sat shows start at 10pm. free–$12; advance tix from X-Large (see p.263).

Fez

Map 5, G4. 380 Lafayette St (at Great Jones St) ☎212/533-2680.
The mirrored bar and sparkling gold stage curtain suggest a disco fantasy; poetry readings and acoustic performances are high caliber. Around $10.

Hammerstein Ballroom

Map 6, E4. 311 W 34th St (between 8th and 9th aves) ☎212/564-4882.
Refurbished ballroom that hosts a few shows a month, mostly indie rock and electronic music, in a 3600-seat venue. Uptight bouncers limit movement between seating levels and prohibit smoking on the balconies. Cover varies, but upwards of $18.

Irving Plaza

Map 6, K8. 17 Irving Place (between 15th and 16th sts) ☎212/777-6800.
Host to an impressive array of rock, electronic and techno acts. The uproom has wildly divergent acoustics; stand toward the back on the first floor for truest mix of sound. $10–25.

Maxwell's

1039 Washington (at 11th St), Hoboken, New Jersey ☎201/798-0406.
Neighborhood rock club hosting up to a dozen bands a week: some big names and one of the best places to check out the tri-state scene. Admission $6–12.

ROCK MUSIC

Mercury Lounge

Map 5, K5. 217 E Houston St (at Essex St) ⊕212/260-7400. Dark, medium-sized Lower East Side mainstay, which hosts a mix of local, national and international rock acts. It's owned by the same crew as Bowery Ballroom, but generally houses less established bands. Around $7–12.

Roseland Ballroom

Map 7, E7. 239 W 52nd St (between Broadway and 8th Ave) ⊕212/249-0200. A historic ballroom that opened in 1919 and was once frequented by Adele and Fred Astaire, among others. Now a ballroom dancing school that, six times a month, turns into a concert venue, hosting big names and various pop and electronic acts. Take a gander at the shoes and photographs displayed in the entry hall. $10–50.

SOB's (Sounds of Brazil)

Map 5, C6. 204 Varick St (at Houston St) ⊕212/243-4940. Premier place to hear hip-hop, Brazilian, West Indian, Caribbean and world music acts within the confines of Manhattan. Vibrant, with a high quality of music. Two shows nightly, times vary. Admission $10–20 with $10–15 minimum cover at tables.

The Supper Club

Map 7, F8. 240 W 47th St (between Broadway and 8th Ave) ⊕212/921-1940. White linen tablecloths, a large dance floor and upscale lounge jazz/hip-hop groups. Fri and Sat at 8pm, Eric Comstock and the Supper Club's house big-band swing with a vengeance. $25 before 11pm; $15 after.

Village Underground

Map 5, D4. 130 W 3rd St (between Macdougal St and 6th Ave) ⊕212/777-7745, ⊛www .thevillageunderground.com. This no-smoking-yet-smoky wee place is one of the most intimate and innovative spaces around, where you might catch anyone from Guided By Voices to RL Burnside.

ROCK MUSIC

JAZZ

A clutch of new clubs has revived the once-sagging scene, and there still are more than forty locations in Manhattan that present jazz regularly. Look mostly to **Greenwich Village** or **Harlem** for a good place; midtown jazz clubs tend to be slick dinner-dance joints – expensive and over-run by businesspeople looking for culture.

To find out who's playing, check the usual sources, notably the *Voice*, *New York Magazine* and *Hothouse*, a free monthly magazine sometimes available at the venues; or the jazz monthly downbeat. The city's jazz-oriented **radio stations** are also sources of information: two of the best are WBGO (88.5 FM), a 24hr jazz station, and WKCR (89.9 FM), Columbia University's radio station. As a final resort, **Jazzline** (℡212/479-7888) provides recorded information about the week's events.

JAZZ VENUES

55

Map 5, C3. 55 Christopher St (between 6th and 7th aves) ℡212/929-9883.
Really special underground jazz bar; the best of the old guard.

Arthur's Tavern

Map 5, C3. 57 Grove St ℡212/675-6879, ⓦwww.arthurstavernnyc.com.
Small, amiable piano bar with some inspired performers and no cover or minimum. Drinks are pricey.

Birdland

Map 7, E9. 315 W 44th St (8th and 9th aves) ℡212/581-3080, ⓦwww.birdlandjazz.com.
Not the original place where Charlie Parker played, but an established supper club nonetheless. Hosts some big names. Sets nightly at 9pm and 11pm. Music charge of $20–35, with a $10 food/drink minimum and a complimentary drink if you sit at the bar.

The Blue Note
Map 5, D4. 131 W 3rd St (6th Ave) ☏212/475-8592, ⱳwww.bluenote.net.
The famous names here aren't really worth the attendant high prices, cattle-herd atmosphere and minimal legroom. Cover charges vary wildly, from $7 to $65, plus a $5 minimum per person at the tables or a one-drink minimum at the bar. Sets are at 9pm & 11.30pm. On Fri & Sat, the jam sessions after 1am are free if you've seen the previous set, $5 if you haven't.

Café Carlyle
Map 7, I1. The *Carlyle Hotel*, 35 E 76th St (at Madison Ave) ☏212/744-1600.
This intimate place is home to both Bobby Short and Woody Allen, who does the jazz thang here on Mon nights. $30–60 cover, no minimum.

Iridium Jazz Club
Map 7, D4. 44 W 63rd St (at Columbus Ave) ☏212/582-2121.
Contemporary jazz performed seven nights a week in a surrealist decor described as "Dolly meets Disney." The godfather of electric guitar Les Paul plays every Mon. Shows at 8.45pm and 10.45pm, extra Fri & Sat show at 12.15am. Cover $20–35, $10 food and drink minimum, Sun jazz brunch.

Izzy Bar
Map 5, J2. 166 1st Ave (at 10th St) ☏212/228-0444.
Popular with a European crowd, this cavernous hangout is more lounge than bar – but hosts jazz sessions and a variety of other music acts nightly. Admission is $5–10.

Jazz Standard
Map 6, J5. 116 E 27th St ☏212/576-2232, ⱳwww.jazzstandard.com.
A spacious underground room with great sound and even better performers has earned this club high praise and a loyal clientele. Sets Mon–Thurs at 8pm and 10pm, Fri and Sat 8pm, 10.30pm and midnight, Sun

JAZZ

at 7pm and 9pm. Mon $15; Tues–Thurs & Sun $18; Fri & Sat $25; all with $10 minimum.

Joe's Pub

Map 5, G3. 425 Lafayette St ⊤212/539-8777, ⍟www.joespub.org.
Stylishly classic bar in Joe Papp's Public Theater attracts the entertainment crowd. Performances six days a week, ranging from Broadway songbooks to readings from the *New Yorker*'s fiction issues, with the likes of salsa, Indian music and jazz thrown in. Open daily 5pm–4am. $10–25.

Knitting Factory

Map 4, E3. 74 Leonard St (between Church St and Broadway) ⊤212/219-3055, ⍟www.knittingfactory.com.
The refurbished club – two performance spaces, two bars and a microbrewery with eighteen beers on draft – has won the cool kids back, and it's now the place to see avant-garde jazz, experimental acts and big-name rock bands in an intimate setting. $15–20, with shows beginning 8–10pm.

Savoy Lounge

Map 6, D2. 355 W 41st St ⊤212/947-5255, ⍟www.savoylounge.com.
Just behind the Port Authority Bus Terminal, this midtown joint has live jazz and blues nightly, live jams frequented by Broadway pit musicians, super-cheap drinks and an increasingly rare Hammond organ. Sets Sun–Wed at 9pm, 10.30pm and midnight, no cover; jam session Thurs 11.30pm–4am, $5; sets Fri–Sat at 10pm, 11.30pm, 1am. $7.

Smalls

Map 5, C3. 183 W 10th St (at 7th Ave) ⊤212/929-7565, ⍟www.smallsjazz.com.
Tiny West Village club has the best jazz bargain in NY: four to thirteen hours of music for $10, from 10pm to dawn. The weekday program comprises two sets and a late-night jam, by well-knowns and unknowns, the weekends also have an early bird set at 7.30pm. Free juice and non-

JAZZ

alcoholic beverages, or
BYOB.

Smoke

Map 8, B2. 2751 Broadway
(between 105th and 106th St)
Ⓣ212/864-6662,
Ⓦwww.smokejazz.com.
Voted the best club in the
city by *New York* magazine,
this Upper West Side joint is
a real neighborhood treat.
Sets start at 9pm, 11pm and
12.30am, the first two
weekend sets are smoke free,
and there's a retro happy hour
with $3 cocktails Mon–Sun
5-8pm.

Tonic

Map 5, L7. 107 Norfolk St
(between Rivington and
Delancey sts) Ⓣ212/358-7503,
Ⓦwww.tonicnyc.com.
Hip Lower East Side avant-
jazzerie on two levels, with
no cover charge to the lower,
Subtonic lounge. Occasional
movies and Klezmer brunch
on a Sun. Cover varies.

Village Vanguard

Map 5, C2. 178 7th Ave (at
11th St) Ⓣ212/255-4037.
A NYC jazz landmark that
celebrated its sixtieth
anniversary a few years back,
the *Vanguard* supplies a regular
diet of big names.
Mon–Thurs and Sun
admission is $15, with a $10
minimum; Sat–Sun entry is
$20, with a $10 minimum.
Sets are at 9.30pm and
11.30pm, with a 1am set Sat
and Sun.

Zinc Bar

Map 5, E5. 90 W Houston (at
LaGuardia Place) Ⓣ212/477-
8337, Ⓦwww.zincbar.com.
Great jazz venue with strong
drinks and a loyal bunch of
regulars. The blackboard
above the entrance announces
the evening's featured band.
Cover is $5 with a one-drink
minimum. Hosts new talent
and established greats such as
Max Roach, Grant Green
and Astrud Gilberto; also
poetry readings on Sun at
6.30pm and comedy on Tues
at 8pm.

JAZZ

●

FOLK, COUNTRY AND SPOKEN-WORD VENUES

13

Map 5, E1. 35 E 13th St
℡212/979-6677.
Mon night and this cozy bar
is home to "A Little Bit
Louder", a superior evening
of open-mike and poetry
slams. You can dance here,
too – outside in summer – a
rare treat.

Gathering of the tribes

Map 5, N4. 285 E 3rd St
(between Aves C and D)
℡212/674-3778.
This super-cool venue hidden
away in the lowest of the
Lower East Side hosts one of
the city's finest open-mikes
5–7pm on Sun nights. $3.

NuYorican Poet's Café

Map 5, M4. 236 E 3rd St
℡212/505-8183.
This is the godfather of all
slam venues, often featuring
stars of the poetry world who
pop in unannounced.
SlamOpen on Wed and the
Friday Night Slam both cost
$5 and come highly
recommended.

People's Voice Cafe

Map 6, J4. 45 E 33rd St
(between Park and Madison
aves) ℡212/787-3903.
Tucked into the Workmen's
Circle Building, this space
draws those in search of
original music and cultural
acts. $10 cover; seats about
eighty.

Poetry Project

Map 5, I3. St Mark's Church
131 E 10th St (at 2nd Ave)
℡212/674-0910,
ⓦwww.poetryproject.com.
The late Allen Ginsberg, a
Poetry Project protégé, said
"the poetry project burns like
red hot coal in New York's
snow." Make of that what you
will, the thrice-weekly
reading series held here
features some truly, ahem, hot
stuff. Closed July and Aug.

Rodeo Bar

Map 6, K5. 375 3rd Ave (at
27th St) ℡212/683-6500,
ⓦwww.rodeobar.com.
Dust off your spurs, grab your
partner and head down to the

Rodeo for live country tunes   seven days a week. No cover.

NIGHTCLUBS

New York's – especially Manhattan's – **club life** is a rapidly evolving creature. While many of the name DJs remain the same, venues shift around, opening and closing according to finances and fashion. Musically, techno, electronica and house hold sway at the moment, with the emphasis on the deep, vocal style that's always been popular in the city; but reggae, hip-hop, funk, ambient and drum'n'bass all retain interest.

The scene constantly changes, so to ensure that the party is still there, check such listings mags as *Time Out New York*, *Paper Magazine* or *Homo Xtra* – or freebies the *Village Voice* and the *New York Press*. Fliers placed in record and clothing stores in the East Village and SoHo are the best way to find out about the latest clubs and one-off nights. Many fliers also offer substantial discounts.

The best time to go is during the week when crowds are smaller, prices are cheaper, service is better, and clubbers are more savvy. Style can be important, so make an effort and you'll probably get beyond the velvet rope (if there even is one).

13
Map 5, E2. 35 E 13th St, Second Floor ☏212/979-6677. Cute and cozy dance club with an outdoor roof deck and a laid-back, unpretentious clientele. The free Thurs night Eighties night is infinitely more fun than the mediocre $5 weekends.

Centro-Fly
Map 6, H7. 45 W 21st St ☏212/627-7770. If you can stand the attitude, the wait, the rough bouncers and the rope, *Centro-Fly* hosts

NIGHTCLUBS

some of the biggest names in commercial house at the weekends, especially at their Friday night GBH (Great British House) parties ($20, $10 on guestlist ℗212/539-3916). Downstairs in the Pinky things are a little more low-key and sedate. Open till 6am.

Cheetah

Map 6, H7. 12 W 21st St (between 5th and 6th aves) ℗212/206-7770.
A club for lounging around on faux leopard skin in between the occasional dance... much less effort than the sanctimonious *Centro-Fly* down the road.

Frying Pan

Map 6, A7. Pier 63, Chelsea Piers at 23rd St ℗212/439-1147.
This old lightship is one of the coolest club venues in the city – great views, consistently good parties and a relaxed door policy all lend themselves to a damn fine time. $5–15.

Limelight

Map 6, G7. 37 W 20th St (at 6th Ave) ℗212/807-7059.
This is one of the most splendid party spaces in New York: a church designed by Trinity Church-builder Richard Upjohn. A scandalous past has led the club to clean up its ways and it now plays host to more measured monthly events such as Gatecrasher. $30.

Sapphire Lounge

Map 5, J5. 249 Eldridge St (at Houston St) ℗212/777-5153.
Pleasantly sleazy lounge, with a black-lit interior and "arty" films in the back room. Frequented by Lower East Siders. Music of all kinds, from soulful Social Sundays to hip-hop Touch Tuesdays (with half-price drinks till 10pm) and latin and reggae-tinged Infinity on Sat. Open every night, free–$5.

Shine

Map 5, E8. 285 W Broadway (at Canal St) ℗212/941-0900.
Looking every bit what a nightclub should: velvet ropes and angry bouncers outside,

NIGHTCLUBS

high ceilings, plush red curtains and dim lights inside. The place for music industry parties; Thurs nights host Giant Step ($10) while Fri are slamming with the popular Touch parties (guest list ☎212/502-3532). $10–20.

Spa

Map 5, F1. 76 E 13th St ☎212/388-1062.

This funky new space, complete with stage, chill-out room and loads of pretty boys and girls, plays host to hip DJs like Paul Sevigny (brother of Chloe) at their popular Wed night party ($20, free on guest list ☎212/714-5075) and the talented Jackie

Christie and Lady Bunny on Thurs nights ($20).

Tunnel

Map 6, A5. 220 12th Ave (at W 27th St) ☎212/695-4682.

A superclub-style techno and house hall occupying a never-completed subway station, a tad the worse for wear. Check out the Kenny Scharf room with cartoonish decor by the artist and the unisex bathroom with full bar and lounge. The lounge downstairs offers a little sanctuary but watch out for giant crowds of out-of-towners – and the gay college crowd – on the weekends. Open Fri–Sun; $15–30.

The performing arts and film

From Broadway glitter to Lower East Side grunge, the range and variety of the **performing arts** in New York is exactly what you might expect. Broadway, and even Off-Broadway **theater**, is notoriously expensive, but if you know where to look, there are a variety of ways to get tickets cheaper, and on the Off-Off-Broadway fringe you can see a play for little more than the price of a movie ticket. As for **dance**, **music** and **opera**, the big mainstream events are extremely expensive, but smaller ones are often equally as interesting and far cheaper. New York gets the first run of most American **films** (and many foreign ones before they reach Europe) and has a very healthy arthouse and revival scene.

Listings for the arts can be found in a number of places. The most useful sources are the clear and comprehensive listings in *Time Out New York*, the free *Village Voice* (especially the pull-out "Voice Choices" section), or the also-free *New York Press*, all especially useful for things downtown and vaguely "alternative." For tonier events try the "Cue" section in the weekly *New York Magazine*, the

"Goings On About Town" section of the *New Yorker*, or Friday's "Weekend" or Sunday's "Arts and Leisure" sections of the *New York Times*. Specific Broadway listings can be found in the free *Official Broadway Theater Guide*, available at theater and hotel lobbies or at the New York Convention and Visitors' Bureau (see p.9).

THEATER

Theater venues are referred to as **Broadway**, **Off-Broadway**, or **Off-Off-Broadway**, classifications that represent a descending order of ticket price, production polish, elegance and comfort (but don't necessarily have much to do with location) and an ascending order of innovation, experimentation and theater for the sake of art rather than cash. In the past few years, Peter Brook's *Hamlet* and an adaptation of Mel Brooks' movie *The Producers* have taken the city by storm, while lively, imaginative musicals like *The Lion King*, *Kiss Me Kate*, *Rent*, *Chicago* and *Annie Get Your Gun* continue to draw crowds and acclaim.

Off-Broadway, while less glitzy, is the best place to discover new talent and adventurous new American drama and musicals like the Blue Man Group's recent sensation *Tubes*. It's Off-Broadway where you'll find social and political drama, satire, ethnic plays and repertory. Lower operating costs also mean that Off-Broadway often serves as a forum to try out what sometimes ends up as a big Broadway production.

Off-Off-Broadway is New York's fringe: shows range from shoestring productions of the classics to outrageous performance art; likewise, prices (cheap to free) and quality (execrable to electrifying) can vary.

TICKETS

Tickets for Broadway shows can cost as much as $75 for orchestra seats (sometimes even $100 for the hottest show in town) and as little as $15 for day-of-performance rush tickets for some of the longer-running shows. Off-Broadway's best seats are cheaper than those on Broadway, averaging $25–55. Off-Off Broadway, however, tickets should rarely set you back more than $15 at most.

Line up at the **TKTS booth** (☎212/768-1818, ⓦwww.tdf.org), where you can obtain cut-rate tickets on the day of performance (up to half off plus a $2.50 service charge) for many Broadway and Off-Broadway shows (though seldom for the more recently opened popular shows). The booth, located at Duffy Square, where Broadway and Seventh Avenue meet between 45th and 47th streets, has long lines and is open Mon–Sat 3–8pm, 10am–2pm for Wed and Sat matinees, and 11am–7pm for all Sun performances.

Look for **twofer discount coupons** in the New York Convention and Visitors' Bureau and many shops, banks, restaurants and hotel lobbies. These entitle two people to a hefty discount and, unlike TKTS, it's possible to book ahead, though don't expect to find coupons for the latest shows. The Hit Show Club, 630 9th Ave at 44th Street (☎212/581-4211) also provides discount vouchers up to fifty percent off that you present at the box office.

Same-day standing-room tickets are also available for some sold-out shows for $10–20. Check listings magazines for availability.

If you're prepared to pay full price you can, of course, go directly to the theater, or call one of the following ticket sales agencies. **Tele-Charge** (☎212/239-6200 or 1-800/432-7250 outside NY) and **Ticketmaster** (☎212/307-4100 or 1-800/755-4000 outside NY) sell tickets over the phone to Broadway shows, but note that no show is represented by both these agencies. **Tickets Central** (☎212/279-4200) sells tickets to many Off-Broadway theaters 1–8pm daily. You can also buy theater tickets at individual theater websites or at ⓦwww.ticketmaster.com and ⓦwww.telecharge.com.

ON AND OFF-BROADWAY

Astor Place Theater

Map 5, H3. 434 Lafayette St ☎212/254-4370.
Since 1992, the theater has been the home of the comically absurd but very popular performance artists The Blue Man Group (ⓦwww.blueman.com).

Brooklyn Academy of Music

30 Lafayette Ave, Brooklyn ☎718/636-4100, ⓦwww.bam.org.
BAM regularly presents theater on its three stages. The academy has imported a number of stunning productions directed by Ingmar Bergman in recent years and played host to Peter Brooks' wonderful *Hamlet*. Every autumn the annual Next Wave festival is the city's most exciting showcase for large-scale performance art by the likes of Robert Wilson, Robert LePage, Laurie Anderson and Pina Bausch.

Daryl Roth Theatre

Map 6, J9. 20 Union Square E (at 15th St) ☎212/239-6200.
Site of the rambunctious, airborne frat-party of a show that is *De La Guarda*. Wear old clothes and be prepared to be hoisted in the air by swooping performance artistes.

The Joseph Papp Public Theater

Map 5, H3. 425 Lafayette St ☎212/239-6200, ⓦwww.publictheater.org.
This major Off-Broadway venue produces serious and challenging theater from new, mostly American, playwrights

ON AND OFF-BROADWAY

year-round, and is the major presenter of Shakespeare productions in the city. In the summer the Public runs the free Shakespeare Festival at the open-air Delacorte Theater in Central Park (℡212/861–8277).

Manhattan Theater Club

Map 7, F6. 131 W 55th St (between 6th and 7th aves) ℡212/581-1212, ⓦwww.mtc-nyc.org.

Major midtown venue for serious new theater, many of whose productions eventually transfer to Broadway. See them here first.

New Amsterdam Theater

Map 6, F1. 214 W 42nd St (between 7th and 8th aves) ℡212/307-4100.

Disney's recently renovated Times Square palace is home to Julie Taymor's Tony award-winning extravaganza *The Lion King*.

St James Theatre

Map 7, F8. 246 W 44th St ℡212/239-6200.

The Producers, NYC's most popular musical, has its run at this large Broadway theater.

Shubert Theater

Map 7, F9. 225 W 44th St (between 7th and 8th aves) ℡212/239-6200.

Fred Astaire and Katherine Hepburn are just two of the stars to have graced the Shubert's stage. These days, it's home to the well-known musical *Chicago*.

Studio 54

Map 7, E7. 524 W 54th St (between Broadway and 8th ave) ℡212/239-6200, ⓦwww.cabaret-54.com.

The disco legend has been recently transformed into the perfect setting for the Tony award-winning revival of *Cabaret*.

OFF-OFF-BROADWAY AND PERFORMANCE ART SPACES

Bouwerie Lane Theater

Map 5, H5. 330 Bowery (at Bond St) ℡212/677-0060.

Home of the Jean Cocteau Repertory, which produces plays by Genet, Sophocles,

Shaw, Strindberg, Sartre, Wilde, Williams, etc.

Dixon Place

Map 6, M6. 309 E 26th St (between 1st and 2nd aves) ☎212/532-1546, ⊛www.dixonplace.org. Popular small venue dedicated to experimental theater, dance, readings and the like. On the first Wed of the month, Dixon Place has an "Open Performance Night," where the first ten people to sign up can present ten minutes of anything goes.

Expanded Arts

Map 5, K7. 113 Ludlow St (below Delancey) ☎212/358-5096. Lower East Side performance venue that also produces the summer-long "Shakespeare in the Park(ing Lot)" series of free performances at the Municipal Parking Lot at Broome and Ludlow sts.

La Mama E.T.C.

Map 5, H4. 74A E 4th St (between the Bowery and 2nd Ave) ☎212/475-7710, ⊛www.lamama.org.

The mother of all Off-Off-theaters and venue for some of the most exciting theater, performance and dance seen in the city for more than 30 years.

New York Theater Workshop

Map 5, H4. 79 E 4th St (between Bowery and 2nd Ave) ☎212/460-5475, ⊛www.nytw.org. Innovative and respected space that seems to choose cult hit shows – it was the original host of the hugely successful *Rent*.

Ontological-Hysteric Theater at St. Mark's Church

Map 5, I2. 131 E 10th St (at 2nd Ave) ☎212/533-4650, ⊛www.ontological.com. Produces some of the best radical theater in the city; especially famous for the work of independent theater legend Richard Foreman.

Performing Garage

Map 5, E8. 33 Wooster St ☎212/966-3651, ⊛www.thewoostergroup.org.

OFF-OFF-BROADWAY AND PERFORMANCE ART SPACES

The well-respected experimental Wooster Group (whose most famous member is Willem Dafoe) perform regularly in this SoHo space. Tickets are gold dust but worth every effort.

P.S. 122

Map 5, J3. 150 1st Ave (at 9th St) ☎212/477-5288, ⓌWww.ps122.org.
A converted school in the East Village that is a perennially popular venue for a jam-packed schedule of radical performance art, dance and one-person shows.

Theater for the New City

Map 5, J2 . 155 1st Ave (at 10th St) ☎212/254-1109.
Known for following the development of new playwrights and integrating dance, music and poetry with drama. TNC also performs outdoors for free at a variety of venues throughout the summer and hosts the Lower East Side Festival of the Arts at the end of May.

LITERARY EVENTS AND READINGS

92nd St Y Unterberg Poetry Center

Map 8, J6. 1395 Lexington Ave ☎212/415-5500, ⓌWwww.92ndsty.org.
Quite simply, the definitive place to hear all your Booker, Pulitzer and Nobel Prize–winning favorites, as well as many other exciting new talents.

Symphony Space

Map 8, B5. 2537 Broadway (at 95th St) ☎212/864-5400, ⓌWwww.symphonyspace.org.
The highly acclaimed Selected Shorts series, in which actors read the short fiction of a variety of authors, packs the Symphony Space theater and can be heard across the country on the radio.

DANCE

As with theater, the range of **dance** offered in the city is vast. New York has five major ballet companies, dozens of modern troupes and untold thousands of soloists, and you would have to be very particular indeed in your tastes not to find something of interest. Events are listed in broadly the same periodicals and websites as music and theater – though you might also want to pick up *Dance Magazine* or check out ⓦwww.danceline.com. The following is a list of some of the major dance venues in the city, though a lot of the smaller, more esoteric companies and solo performers also perform at many of the spaces like the Kitchen and P.S.122, which are listed above under "Off-Off Broadway and performance art spaces."

Brooklyn Academy of Music

30 Lafayette St (between Flatbush Ave and Fulton St), Brooklyn ⓣ718/636-4100, ⓦwww.bam.org.

One of the busiest and most daring dance producers in New York. In the autumn, BAM's Next Wave festival showcases the hottest international attractions in avant-garde dance and music; in winter visiting artists appear, and each spring BAM hosts the annual DanceAfrica Festival, America's largest showcase for African and African-American dance and culture, now in its twentieth year.

City Center

Map 7, F6. 131 W 55th St (between 6th and 7th aves) ⓣ212/581-1212 or 581-7907, ⓦwww.citycenter.org.

This large, midtown venue hosts some of the most important troupes in modern dance, such as the Merce Cunningham Dance Company, the Paul Taylor Dance Company, the Alvin Ailey American Dance Theater, the Joffrey Ballet and the Dance Theater of Harlem.

DANCE

Cunningham Studio

55 Bethune St (at Washington St) ☎212/691-9751 ext 30. The home of the Merce Cunningham Dance Company in the far west reaches of the Village stages performances once a week by emerging modern choreographers.

Dance Theater Workshop's Bessie Schönberg Theater

Map 5, F8. 219 W 19th St (between 7th and 8th aves) ☎212/924-0077, ⓦwww.dtw.org. DTW boasts more than 175 performances from nearly 70 artists and companies each season. On the second floor of a former warehouse, the theater has an unintimidating, relaxed atmosphere and ticket prices are very reasonable.

Danspace Project

Map 5, I2. St Mark's-Church-in-the-Bowery, 131 E 10th St (at 2nd Ave) ☎212/674-8194, ⓦwww.danspaceproject.org. Experimental contemporary dance, with a season running from Sept to June in one of the more beautiful performance spaces.

The Joyce Theater

Map 6, E8. 175 8th Ave (at 19th St) ☎212/242-0800, ⓦwww.joyce.org. The Joyce hosts short seasons by a wide variety of acclaimed dance troupes such as Pilobolus, the Parsons Dance Company and Donald Byrd/The Group. In a space in SoHo at 155 Mercer St (between Prince and Houston sts) ☎212/431-9233, the Joyce hosts a three-week concert series of collaborating choreographers each spring.

Juilliard Dance Workshop

Map 7, D4. Juilliard Theater, 155 W 65th St (at Broadway) ☎212/799-5000. The dance division of the Juilliard School often gives free workshop performances, and each spring six students work with six composers to present a "Composers and Choreographers" concert.

Lincoln Center's Fountain Plaza

Map 7, D4. 65th St (at Columbus Ave) ☎212/875-5766, ⓦwww.lincolncenter.org. Open-air summer venue for the enormously popular offering, "Midsummer Night Swing," where you can learn a different dance en masse each night (everything from polka to rockabilly) and watch a performance all for $12. Tickets go on sale at 5.45pm on the night.

Metropolitan Opera House

Map 7, D4. 65th St (at Columbus Ave), Lincoln Center ☎212/362-6000, ⓦwww.metopera.org.

Home of the renowned American Ballet Theater, which performs at the Opera House from early May into July. Prices for ballet at the Met range from $275 for the best seats at special performances to $12–16 for standing-room tickets, which go on sale the morning of the performance.

New York State Theater

Map 7, D4. 65th St (at Columbus Ave), Lincoln Center ☎212/870-5570, ⓦwww.lincolncenter.org. Lincoln Center's major ballet venue is home to the revered New York City Ballet, which performs for a nine-week season each spring.

CLASSICAL MUSIC AND OPERA

New Yorkers take **serious music** seriously. Long lines form for anything popular, many concerts sell out, and summer evenings can see a quarter of a million people turning up in Central Park for free performances by the New York Philharmonic. The range of what's available is wide – but it's big names at big venues that pull in the crowds.

OPERA VENUES

Amato Opera Theater

Map 5, H5. 319 Bowery (at
2nd St) ⓣ212/228-8200,
ⓦwww.amato.org.
This Bowery venue presents
an ambitious and varied
repertory of classics
performed by up-and-coming
young singers and
conductors. Performances at
weekends only, closed in the
summer.

Juilliard School

Map 7, D4. 60 Lincoln Center
Plaza (at Broadway and 65th St)
ⓣ212/799-5000,
ⓦwww.juilliard.edu.
Right next door to the Met,
Julliard students often
perform under the control of
a famous conductor, usually
for low ticket prices.

Metropolitan Opera House

Map 7, D4. Columbus Ave (at
64th St), Lincoln Center
ⓣ212/362-6000,
ⓦwww.metopera.org.
New York's premier opera
venue is home to the

Metropolitan Opera
Company from Sept to late
April. Tickets are expensive
and can be quite difficult to
obtain, though 175 standing-
room tickets for $12–16 go
on sale every Sat morning at
10am (the line has been
known to form at dawn).

The New York State Theater

Map 7, D4. at 64th St, Lincoln
Center ⓣ212/870-5570.
Playing David to the Met's
Goliath, the City Opera's
wide and adventurous
program varies wildly in
quality – sometimes
startlingly innovative,
occasionally mediocre, but
seats go for less than half the
Met's prices.

CONCERT HALLS

The Alice Tully Hall

Map 7, D4. at 64th St, Lincoln
Center ⓣ212/721-6500
A smaller venue for chamber
orchestras, string quartets and
instrumentalists. Prices similar
to those in Avery Fisher.

FREE SUMMER CONCERTS

In the light of high concert ticket prices, it's welcoming that so many events in the city, especially in summer, are free. The SummerStage Festival (☎212/360-2777, ⓦwww.Summer Stage.org) in Central Park puts on an impressive range of free concerts of all kinds of music throughout the summer (see p.116). On occasional Wednesday nights the New York Grand Opera performs Verdi operas at SummerStage. Central Park is also one of the many open-air venues for the New York Philharmonic's Concerts in the Park series (☎212/875-5709, ⓦwww.nyphilharmonic.org) of concerts and fireworks displays that turns up all over the city and the outer boroughs in July, and the similar Met in the Parks series (☎212/362-6000, ⓦwww.metopera.org) in June and July. All summer, Lincoln Center Out-of-Doors (☎212/875-5108, ⓦwww.lincolncenter .org) hosts a varied selection of free performances of music and dance on the plaza.

The Avery Fisher Hall
Map 7, D4. at 64th St, Lincoln Center ☎212/875-5030, ⓦwww.Lincolncenter.org. Home of the New York Philharmonic, and temporary one to visiting orchestras and soloists. Ticket prices for the Philharmonic are in the range of $12–50. An often fascinating bargain are the NYP open rehearsals at 9.45am on concert days, which cost just $14. Avery Fisher also hosts the very popular annual Mostly Mozart Festival (☎212/875-5103) in Aug.

Bargemusic
Fulton Ferry Landing, Brooklyn ☎718/624-4061 or ☎624-2803, ⓦwww.bargemusic.org. Chamber music in a wonderful river setting below the Brooklyn Bridge on Thurs and Fri at 7.30pm, and Sun at 4pm. Tickets are $30, $25 for senior citizens, $15 for students.

CONCERT HALLS

Brooklyn Academy of Music

30 Lafayette Ave (near Flatbush Ave), Brooklyn ☎718/636-4100, ⍟www.bam.org.
See "Dance," p.283.

Carnegie Hall

Map 7, F6. 154 W 57th St (at 7th Ave) ☎212/247-7800, ⍟www.carnegiehall.org.
The greatest names from all schools of music performed here in the past, from Tchaikovsky and Toscanini to Gershwin and Billie Holiday. Labeled "one of the finest orchestral showplaces on the planet" by Alex Ross in the *New Yorker*.

Merkin Concert Hall

Map 7, D3. 129 W 67th St (between Broadway and Amsterdam Ave) ☎212/501-3330, ⍟www.merkinconcerthall.org.
In the Elaine Kaufman Cultural Center, this intimate and adventurous venue is a great place to hear music of any kind. Plays host to the New York Guitar Festival in Sept.

CABARET AND COMEDY

Comedy clubs and **cabaret spots** are rife in New York; the list below represents the best-known venues in town, but as ever, check *Time Out New York* and *Village Voice* for the fullest and most up-to-date listings.

Caroline's on Broadway

Map 7, F8. 1626 Broadway (at 49th St) ☎212/757-4100.
Having moved to Times Square from the Seaport, *Caroline's* still books some of the best stand-up acts in town. $12–15 cover Sun–Thurs, $17–21.50 Fri and Sat. Two-drink minimum. Also has a restaurant, *Comedy Nation*, upstairs.

Chicago City Limits Theater

Map 7, K5. 1105 1st Ave (at 61st St) ☎212/888-5233.
Improvization theater playing one show nightly, two on

weekends. Closed Tues. Admission is $20, $10 on Mon. New York's oldest improv club.

Nightly shows, three on weekends. Weekdays $7 cover, Fri and Sat $12. Two-drink minimum.

Stand Up New York

Map 7, C1. 236 W 78th St (at Broadway) ☎212/595-0850, ⓦwww.standupny.com. Upper West Side all-ages forum for established comics, many of whom have appeared on Leno, Letterman and the like. Hosts the Toyota Comedy festival in June.

Surf Reality

Map 5, J6. 172 Allen St (between Stanton and Rivington sts) ☎212/673-4182, ⓦwww.surfreality.org. The Sun night open-mikes here are some of the most raucous – and amusing – in town. $3–10 cover.

FILM

New York is a **movie-lover's dream**. New state-of-the-art movie theaters are popping up all over the city, with more than a hundred new screens being added. Most will be in multiscreen complexes with all the charm of large air-ports but with the advantages of superb sound, luxurious seating and perfect stadium-seating sightlines, as in the megaplexes at Union Square and Kips Bay.

For **listings** your best bets are the weekly *Village Voice* or the *New York Press* (both free), *Time Out New York*, or the daily papers on Fridays, when reviews come out. Beware that listings in papers are not *always* entirely accurate, but you can phone ☎212/777-FILM or visit the website ⓦwww.moviefone.com for accurate showtimes and com-puterized film selections. Ticket prices have risen to as high as $10.50, and there are no reduced matinee prices in Manhattan, nor cheap evenings.

FILM

The city also supports a number of major **film festivals** (see also Chapter 31), the biggest being the **New York Film Festival**, which runs for two weeks from the end of September, at Alice Tully Hall (Lincoln Center).

If you don't mind the heat and would rather watch your movies outside, Bryant Park (6th Ave and 42nd St ℡212/512-5700, ⓦwww.bryantpark.org) hosts free, outdoor screenings of old Hollywood favorites on Monday nights at sunset throughout the summer.

REVIVALS

The American Museum of the Moving Image
35th Ave (at 36th St), Astoria, Queens ℡718/784-0077, ⓦwww.ammi.org.
Showing films only on weekends during the day, AMMI (see p.159) is well worth a trip out to Queens either for the films – serious director retrospectives, silent films and a good emphasis on cinematographers – or for the cinema museum itself.

Anthology Film Archives
Map 5, I5. 32 2nd Ave (at 2nd St) ℡212/505-5181, ⓦwww.anthologyfilmarchives.org.
The bastion of experimental filmmaking where programs of mind-bending abstraction, East Village grunge flicks, auteur retrospectives and the year-round Essential Cinema series rub shoulders.

Cinema Classics
Map 5, J2. 332 E 11th St ℡212/677-6309, ⓦwww.cinemaclassics.com.
It's a grungy, sit-on-folding-chairs affair, but the film selections are excellent, the café's sofas and cakes divine and all tickets are $5.50. They also have an esoteric collection of cult videos for sale.

Film Forum
Map 5, C6. 209 W Houston St (between 6th and 7th aves)

Ⓣ212/727-8110,
Ⓦwww.filmforum.com.
The cozy three-screen Film Forum has an eccentric but famously popular program of new independent movies, documentaries and foreign films on two screens, and a repertory program in Film Forum 2 specializing in silent comedy, camp classics and cult directors.

Ocularis

70 N 6th St (between Wythe and Kent sts), Williamsburg, Brooklyn Ⓣ718/388-8713, Ⓦwww.billburg.com/ocularis. This small space housed inside the *Galapagos* bar is transformed into an independent cinema on Sun nights, screening rarely seen cult classics, foreign gems and pioneering work by new directors.

Walter Reade Theater

Map 7, D4. 165 W 65th St (between Broadway and Amsterdam Ave) Ⓣ212/496-3809, Ⓦwww.filmlinc.com. Simply the best place in town to see great films. Opened in 1991, this beautiful modern theater with perfect sightlines, a huge screen and impeccable sound elevates the art of cinema to the position it deserves within Lincoln Center. The emphasis is on foreign cinema and the great auteurs.

FILM

Gay and lesbian New York

There are few places in America – indeed in the world – where **gay culture** thrives as it does in New York. A glance at the pages of the *Village Voice*, where gay theater, gossip and politics share space with more mainstream goings-on, gives a quick inkling.

Socially, lesbians and gay men are fairly visible, and while it's not recommended that you and your partner hold hands in public before checking out the territory, there are neighborhoods in the city where you'll find yourself in a comfortable majority. A strong presence lingers in the vicinity of **Christopher Street** in the West Village, but it's in **Chelsea** that gay socializing is most out and open. The other haven is Brooklyn's Park Slope, though perhaps more for women than for men.

GAY MEDIA

The following are a selection of outlets with up-to-date listings and insider information on the gay and lesbian scene.

The Advocate Ⓦwww.advocate.com. National gay and lesbian newsmagazine.

HX Magazine Ⓦwww.hx.com. Vital homosexual listings mag.

Metrosource Magazine Ⓦwwwmetrosource.com. National gay and lesbian lifestyle magazine with a local directory of gay-friendly professionals and businesses.

Out Magazine Ⓦwww.out.com. A lifestyle magazine covering everything from politics to health.

LESBIAN AND GAY RESOURCES

GENERAL HELP AND ADVICE

Association of the Bar of the City of New York – Committee on Lesbian & Gay Rights
42 W 44th St, NY 10036
Ⓣ212/382-6600.
The committee recommends legal policies for employers and law schools, and addresses general policy issues regarding lesbian and gay rights.

Bisexual Information and Counseling Services, Inc.
599 West End Ave, Suite 1A, NY 10024 Ⓣ212/595-8002, Ⓦwww.bisexualcounseling.org. Offers help on health and relationship issues; general and professional discussion groups.

Empire State Pride Agenda
647 Hudson St, NY 10014
Ⓣ212/627-0305,
Ⓦwww.espany.org.

Political organization lobbies legislature and governor, helps elect gay-supportive candidates through financial/campaign assistance, organizes constituent pressure, educates public about lesbians/gay life.

Gay and Lesbian National Hotline

☎1-888/THE-GLNH or 212/989-0999, ⓦwww.glnh.org (Mon–Fri 6–10pm, Sat noon–5pm). Information, help and referrals.

Gay Yellow Pages

PO Box 533, Village Station, NY 10014-0533 ☎212/674-0120, ⓦwww.gayellowpages.com. Annual directory of gay/lesbian businesses and resources.

GLAAD-NY (Gay and Lesbian Alliance Against Defamation)

150 W 26th St at 7th Ave, Suite 503 ☎212/807-1700, ⓦwww.glaad.org. Monitors the portrayal of gays, lesbians and bisexuals in the media, and organizes caucuses and discussion groups on media topics. Volunteers and visitors welcome.

Lambda Legal Defense and Education Fund

120 Wall St, 15th floor, NY 10005 ☎212/809-8585, ⓦwww.lambdalegal.org. Active against discrimination affecting people with AIDS and the lesbian, gay, bisexual and transgender community; publications, speakers and newsletter.

The Lesbian, Gay, Bisexual & Transgender Community Services Center

208 W 13th St, NY 10014 (west of 7th Ave) ☎212/620-7310, ⓦwww.gaycenter.org. The Center's free paper, *Center Voice*, is mailed to more than 55,000 households, which should give you an idea of how it's grown since it opened in 1983. The Center also sponsors workshops, dances, movie nights, youth services and lots more.

EXCLUSIVELY LESBIAN ORGANIZATIONS

Astraea

116 E 16th, 7th floor, NY 10003, #520 (between Park Ave S and Irving Place) ☏212/529-8021, ⓦwww.astraea.org.
National lesbian foundation offering financial support, education and networking to lesbian organizations and projects.

Center for Anti-Violence Education/Brooklyn Women's Martial Arts

421 5th Ave, 2nd floor, Brooklyn, NY 11215 ☏718/788-1775, ⓦwww.cae-bkln.org.
Self-defense and martial arts classes integrate a political understanding of violence; not-for-profit, feminist and anti-racist.

Social Activities for Lesbians (SAL)

PO Box 2270, Church Street Station ☏212/330-6582.
A social group that organizes dinners, parties, cultural excursions, video nights and the like. Call for details and calendar.

AIDS/HIV-RELATED ORGANIZATIONS

ACT UP (AIDS Coalition to Unleash Power)

332 Bleecker St, Suite G5, NY 10014 ☏212/966-4873, ⓦwww.actupny.org.
The first and most prolific of the direct action groups, ACT UP advocates group empowerment and action, advocating that silence will only equal death. Meets Mon, 7.30pm, at the Center, 208 W 13th St.

AIDS Hotline

☏212/447-8200.
Information, counseling and referrals available seven days a week, 9am–9pm.

AIDS Treatment Data Network (The Network)

611 Broadway, Room 613, NY 10012 ☏212/260-8868 or toll-free 1-800-734-7104, ⓦwww.aidsinfonyc.org/network.
Not-for-profit community-based organization provides

information on treatment, counseling and referral services to people with HIV/AIDS.

Gay Men's Health Crisis (GMHC)

119 W 24th St (between 6th and 7th aves) ☎212/807-6664, Ⓦwww.gmhc.org.

Despite the name, this organization – the oldest and largest not-for-profit AIDS

organization in the world – provides information and referrals to everyone.

HIV/AIDS Legal Service Project

153 Waverly Place, NY 10014 ☎212/243-1313.

Free childcare, discrimination, housing and health planning services for people with AIDS/HIV.

ACCOMMODATION

The following places are friendly to gays and lesbians and convenient for the scene. For price codes, see p.177.

Chelsea Mews Guest House

Map 6, D9. 344 W 15th St, NY 10011 (between 8th and 9th aves) ☎212/255-9174.

All-male gay guesthouse. Local calls are included. ❷–❸

Chelsea Pines Inn

Map 6, D9. 317 W 14th St (between 8th and 9th aves) ☎212/929-1023, Ⓦwww.chelseapinesinn.com.

Well-priced hotel, whose guests are mostly gay, housed in an old brownstone on the

Greenwich Village/Chelsea border that offers clean, comfortable, attractively furnished rooms. Best to book in advance. ❶–❹; three-night minimum stay at weekends.

Chelsea Savoy Hotel

Map 6, F6. 204 W 24th St (at 7th Ave) ☎212/929-9353, Ⓦwww.chelseasavoynyc.com.

This relative newcomer, housed in a new building, makes up for a lack of charm with clean and modern amenities in every room. ❷

Colonial House Inn

Map 6, D7. 318 W 22nd St, NY 10011 (between 8th and 9th aves) ☎212/243-9669, ⓦwww.colonialhouseinn.com. Economical, twenty-room bed-and-breakfast in the heart of Chelsea. Also welcomes straight guests. Boasts a clothing-optional roofdeck. ❶, with fifteen percent off in Jan and Feb.

Incentra Village House

Map 5, A1. 32 8th Ave (between 12th and Jane sts) ☎212/206-0007. Twelve-room townhouse, some rooms with kitchenette. Three-night minimum stay at weekends. Also welcomes straight guests. ❷

BARS

Gay men's **bars** cover the spectrum: from relaxed, mainstream cafés to some hard-hitting clubs full of glamour and attitude. Most of the more established places are in Greenwich Village and Chelsea, and along Avenue A in the East Village. For women, Park Slope in Brooklyn edges out the East Village and Hudson Street in the West as the center of happenings. Things tend to get raunchier further west as you reach the bars and cruisers of the wild West Side Highway and the Meatpacking District, both of which are pretty hardcore.

MAINLY FOR MEN

The Bar

Map 5, I4. 68 2nd Ave (at E 4th St) ☎212/674-9714. A longstanding neighborhood hideaway with a pool table in the East Village. Fairly relaxed on weeknights, cruisier at the weekend.

Barracuda

Map 6, F7. 275 W 22nd St (between 7th and 8th aves) ☎212/645-8613.

BARS

A favorite spot in New York's gay scene, and as laid-back as you'll find in Chelsea. Two-for-one happy hour from 4–9pm during the week, crazy drag shows and pick-up lines and a hideaway lounge out back.

Brandy's Piano Bar

Map 8, K8. 235 E 84th St (between 2nd and 3rd aves) ☏212/744-4949.
Handsome uptown cabaret/piano bar with a crazy mixed and generally mature clientele. Definitely worth a visit.

The Cock

Map 5, K2. 188 Ave A (at 12th St) ☏212/777-6724.
With amateur "talent" contests and strip karaoke to kill for, it's dirty, sleazy and a social hodgepodge – and a whole lot of fun.

The Dugout

Map 5, A5. 185 Christopher St (at Weehawken St) ☏212/242-9113.
Right by the river, this friendly West Village hangout with TV, pool table and video games might be the closest you'll find to a gay sports bar.

Dusk Lounge

Map 6, G6. 147 W 24th St (between 6th and 7th aves) ☏212/924-4490.
A place to chill out and unwind, this Chelsea stalwart is perfect on a weekday afternoon.

Julius

Map 5, C3. 159 W 10th St (at Waverly Place) ☏212/929-9672.
As the oldest gay bar in the city, this quaint, wooden affair deserves at least one drink.

The Monster

Map 5, C3. 80 Grove St (at Waverly Place) ☏212/924-3558.
Large, campy bar with drag cabaret, piano and downstairs dance floor. Very popular, especially with tourists, yet has a strong neighborhood feel.

Phoenix

Map 5, J1. 447 E 13th St (between 1st Ave and Ave A) ☏212/477-9979.
This relaxed East Village

favorite is much loved by the so-not-scene-they're-scene boys and guys who really just want a drink.

Rawhide

Map 6, E7. 212 8th Ave (at 21st St) ☎212/242-9332. Hell-bent for leather, Chelsea's Rough Rider Room opens at 8am for those who have beer for breakfast (and closes fairly late too).

Stonewall

Map 5, C3. 53 Christopher St (between Waverly Place and 7th Ave S) ☎212/463-0950. Yes, that *Stonewall*, site of the seminal 1969 riot, mostly refurbished and flying the pride flag like they own it – which, one supposes, they do.

Wonder Bar

Map 5, K3. 505 E 6th St (between aves A and B) ☎212/777-9105. Cramped, festive and lesbian-friendly, this is a truly wonderful and unpretentious find for the thinking boy. Still mainly for the men, though.

MAINLY FOR WOMEN

Ginger's

363 5th Ave, Park Slope, Brooklyn ☎718/788-0924. Relative newcomer that's dark and atmospheric, with a great happy hour.

Henrietta Hudson

Map 5, B5. 438 Hudson St (between Morton and Barrow sts) ☎212/924-3347. Laid-back in the afternoon but brimming by night, especially on weekends. Lounging, pool and dancing areas are all separated and guys are welcome too.

Julie's

Map 7, J6. 204 E 58th St (between 2nd and 3rd aves) ☎212/688-1294. Fairly sedate and couply throughout the week, except for Thurs nights when the single girls come out to play. One of your few choices around midtown or uptown.

Marie's Crisis

Map 5, C3. 59 Grove St ☎212/243-9323.

BARS

●

Well-known cabaret/piano bar popular with tourists and locals alike. Features old-time singing sessions on Fri and Sat nights.

Meow Mix

Map 5, L5. 269 E Houston St (at Suffolk St) ☎212/254-0688. One of the city's hottest girl venues. Bands or performances most nights, for which men are welcome if they behave themselves.

The Rising

186 5th Ave (at Sackett St), Park Slope, Brooklyn ☎718/789-6340.
A relaxed neighborhood favorite, this laid-back brunch spot has live music on Wed, Fri and Sun and a DJ on Sat nights.

Rubyfruit Bar & Grill

Map 5, A4. 531 Hudson St (at 10th St) ☎212/929-3343.
A cozy, friendly place for grown-up dykes, *Rubyfruit* is all about couches, cheap drinks and good company.

CLUBS

Gay and lesbian **clubs** in New York can be some of the most outrageous in the world, while many of the city's non-denominational nightspots have a very open-door policy (as regards sexuality) and often host weekly gay parties. Again, check out the *Village Voice* (ⓦwww.villagevoice .com) and *HX* (ⓦwww.hx.com) for the latest in homosexual hip.

J's Hangout

Map 6, E9. 675 Hudson St (at 14th St) ☎212/242-9292.
Very cruisey late-night spot with very dark rooms and a "buff" Sat night. Open nightly from midnight.

La Nueva Escuelita

Map 6, E2. 301 W 39th St (at 8th Ave) ☎212/631-0588.
Exclusive and elusive, this is also one of the city's very best gay clubs. It's all about kitsch, dress-up, salsa and drag and

(wo)men. Expect to wait in line for a while.

Free during the week, $5 at the weekend.

The Monster

Map 5, C3. 80 Grove St (at Sheridan Square) ☏212/924-3558.

Every night here brings something different, from Latin grooves to retro hits and a Sun afternoon tea dance (free before 8pm, $3 after).

The Web

Map 7, H6. 40 E 58th St ☏212/978-9988.

A predominantly Asian crowd congregates here for theme-party nights and drag competitions ($5–10), as well as Wed night bingo and karaoke Sun (free).

CLUBS

●

Parades and festivals

Major cultural holidays are celebrated with **parades and festivals**. The city takes these, especially the parades, very seriously. Almost every large ethnic group in the city holds an annual get-together, often using Fifth Avenue as the main drag. The events are often political or religious in origin, though now are just as much an excuse for music, food and dance.

Whatever your flavor, chances are your stay will coincide with at least one such celebration. For more details and exact dates, phone ☎1-800/NYC-VISIT, or go to ⓦwww.nycvisit.com. Also, look at listings in *New York* magazine's "CUE" section, the *New Yorker* magazine's "Goings on About Town," the *Village Voice*'s "Cheap Thrills," or the weekly "Obsessive guide to impulsive entertainment," in *Time Out New York* magazine.

JANUARY

Chinese New Year and Parade
First full moon between Jan 21 and Feb 19
A noisy, colorful occasion celebrated from noon to sunset around Mott St. Though dragons still dance in the street, firecrackers no longer chase away evil spirits because former Mayor Giuliani banned them for most events. The chances of getting a meal anywhere in Chinatown at this time are slim; ☎212/431-9740.

Winter Antiques Show
Mid-Jan
This is the foremost American antiques show in the country, at the Seventh Regiment Armory, Park Ave and 67th St ☎212/777-5218.

FEBRUARY

Twenty-four-Hour Marriage Marathon
Valentine's Day
Get hitched or watch while more than fifty couples take the plunge 110 stories and 1377ft above Manhattan on the Observation Deck of the Empire State Building ☎212/323-2340.

Empire State Building Run Up Foot Race
Mid-Feb
Sponsored by the New York Road Runners Club, contenders race up the 1575 steps of this New York City landmark ☎212/423-2229, ⓦwww.nyrrc.org.

MARCH

St Patrick's Day Parade
March 17
Celebrating an impromptu march through the streets by Irish militiamen on St Patrick's Day in 1762, this has

become a draw for every Irish band and organization in the US and Ireland. Usually starting just before noon, it heads up 5th Ave between 44th and 86th sts ⓣ212/484-1222.

Greek Independence Day Parade
Late March
Not as long or as boozy as St Pat's, more a patriotic nod to the old country from floats of pseudo-classically dressed Hellenes. When Independence Day falls in the Orthodox Lent, the parade is shifted to April or May. It usually kicks off from 62nd St and 5th Ave to 79th St ⓣ718/204-6500.

The Circus Animal Walk
Late March to early April
At midnight the animals from Ringling Brothers' Barnum & Bailey Circus march from their point of arrival to Madison Square Garden prior to opening of circus; ⓣ212/465-6741 for tickets or 212/302-1700 for information.

APRIL

Easter Parade
Easter Sun
From Central Park down to Rockefeller Center on 50th St, New Yorkers dress up in outrageous Easter bonnets. 10am–5pm. There's also an Eggstravaganza, a children's festival including an egg-rolling contest in Central Park, on the Great Lawn.

New Directors, New Films
Early April
Lincoln Center and MoMA have presented this popular two-week film festival for more than 25 years, showcasing films of overlooked or emerging filmmakers ⓣ212/875-5638, ⓦwww.filmlinc.com.

APRIL

MAY

Ukrainian Festival
Mid-May
This extravaganza fills a weekend on E 7th St between 2nd and 3rd aves with marvelous Ukrainian costumes, folk music and dance, plus authentic foods. At the Ukrainian Museum (12th St and 2nd Ave) there's a special exhibition of *pysanky* – traditional hand-painted eggs ⊤212/674-1615.

Martin Luther King Jr Parade
Mid-May
Celebrating Dr King's contribution to civil rights, the parade covers 5th Ave from 66th to 86th sts. It also pays tribute to African-Americans who have served in the US military ⊤212/374-5176.

Ninth Avenue International Food Festival
Mid-May
The festival closes down 9th Ave between 37th and 57th sts for the weekend and offers tantalizing food, delicious scents, colorful crafts and great deals ⊤212/484-1222.

Fleet Week
End of May
The annual welcome of sailors from the US, Canada, Mexico the UK, among others, held at the Intrepid Sea-Air-Space Museum; activities and events ⊤212/245-0072.

JUNE

Museum Mile Festival
First Tues evening
On 5th Ave from 82nd St to 105th St. Museums, including the Museum of the City of New York, Jewish Museum, Guggenheim, the Met and others are open free 6–9pm ⊤212/606-2296, Ⓦwww.museummile.org.

Puerto Rican Day Parade
Second Sun

The largest of several Puerto Rican celebrations in the city, seven hours of bands and baton-twirling from 44th to 86th sts on 5th Ave, then east to 3rd Ave ⓣ718/401-0404, ⓦwww.nationalpuerto ricanparade.org.

Lower East Side Jewish Spring Festival
Check the *Jewish Weekly* for date and location

Kosher foods, Yiddish and Hebrew folk singing and guided tours of the Jewish Lower East Side.

Mermaid Parade
First Sat after June 21

At this hilarious event, participants dress like mermaids and King Neptune and saunter down the Coney Island boardwalk, after which everyone throws fruit into the sea. If you're around – don't miss it ⓣ718/392-1267, ⓦwww.coneyislandusa.com.

Lesbian and Gay Pride Week
Late June

The world's biggest Pride event kicks off with a rally and ends with a parade, street fair and dance ⓣ212/807-7433, ⓦwww.nycpride.org.

Washington Square Music Festival
Late June to early July

A series of free Tues night classical, jazz and big-band concerts at this outdoor venue ⓣ212/431-1088.

JULY

Independence Day
July 4

The fireworks from Macy's, South Street Seaport and the display over the East River are visible all over Manhattan, but the best place to view them is either from the Seaport, Battery Park, the Esplanade at Brooklyn Heights or from atop almost any building at about 9pm

℡212/484-1222 or 560-4060.

New York City Tap Festival
Mid-July
The weeklong festival features hundreds of tap dancers who perform and give workshops ℡646/230-9564, Ⓦwww.nyctapfestival.com.

AUGUST

Harlem Month
Culminates with Harlem Day on the third Sun
The monthlong celebration of African, Caribbean and Latin culture includes a children's festival, a dance show, a fashion parade, talent contest and other festivities, such as the Black Film Festival and the Taste of Harlem ℡212/862-7200.

Dance Theater of Harlem Street Festival
Usually the second week
A variety of dance performances plus events for children, on 152nd St between Amsterdam and Convent aves ℡212/690-2800.

New York International Fringe Festival
Usually mid-Aug
Cutting-edge performance art, theater, dance, puppetry, etc. at many different venues on the Lower East Side ℡212-420-8877, Ⓦwww.fringeny.com.

SEPTEMBER

West Indian-American Day Parade and Carnival
Labor Day
Brooklyn's largest parade, modeled after the carnivals of Trinidad and Tobago, features

music, food and dance.
☎718/774-8807 or
212/484-1222.

Broadway on Broadway
Sun after Labor Day
Free performances feature
songs by casts of virtually
every Broadway musical,
culminating in a shower of
confetti; held in Times
Square ☎212/768-1560 or
563-BWAY.

Festival of the Feast of San Gennaro
Ten days in mid-Sept
Boisterous event in honor of
the patron saint of Naples,
held along Mulberry St. The
saint's statue is carried

through the streets with
donations of dollar bills
pinned to his cloak
☎212/764-6330.

African-American Day Parade
Late Sept
Runs from 111th St and
Adam Clayton Powell Blvd to
142nd St, then east toward
5th Ave, Harlem
☎212/862-7200.

New York Film Festival
Two weeks late Sept to mid-Oct
One of the world's leading
film festivals unreels at
Lincoln Center ☎212/875-
5610, Ⓦwww.filmlinc.com/
nyff/nyff.

OCTOBER

Columbus Day Parade
On or around Oct 12
One of the city's largest
binges pays tribute to the
city's Italian heritage and
commemorates the day
America was put on the map;
5th Ave from 44th to 79th sts
☎212/249-2360.

DUMBO Art Under the Bridge Festival
Mid-Oct
More than 700 emerging and
professional artists show their
work in 250 open galleries.
The Parade of Concept
(robots, remote-controlled
vehicles and floats) kicks off

OCTOBER

the show in the neighborhood of DUMBO (Down Under the Manhattan Bridge Overpass) – in Brooklyn between the Manhattan and Brooklyn bridges ☎718/624-3772, Ⓦwww.dumboartscenter.org.

Greenwich Village Halloween Parade
Oct 31
In the 7pm procession on 6th Ave from Spring to 23rd sts you'll see spectacular costumes, wigs and make-up. The music is great and the spirit is wild and gay. Get there early for a good viewing spot ☎212/475-3333 ext 4044, Ⓦwww.halloween-nyc.com.

NOVEMBER

Veteran's Day Parade
Nov 11
The United War Veterans sponsor this annual event on 5th Ave from 39th to 23rd sts ☎212/693-1475.

Fall Antiques Show
Mid-Nov
Foremost American antiques show in the country, at the Seventh Regiment Armory, Park Ave and 67th St ☎212/777-5218.

Macy's Thanksgiving Day Parade
Thanksgiving Day
New York's most televised parade, with floats, dozens of marching bands from around the country, the Rockettes, and Santa Claus's first appearance of the season. More than two million spectators watch it from 77th St down Central Park W to Columbus Circle, then down Broadway to Herald Square, 9am–noon ☎212/494-4495, Ⓦwww.macysparade.com.

NOVEMBER

●

DECEMBER

Rockefeller Center Christmas Tree Lighting
Early Dec
The lighting of the tree begins the festivities ☎212/632-3975.

Chanukah Celebrations
Usually in mid-Dec
During the eight nights of this holiday, usually in mid-Dec, a menorah-lighting ceremony takes place at Brooklyn's Grand Army Plaza ☎718/778-6000.

Holiday Windows
Beginning Dec 1
The windows on 5th Ave, especially those of Lord & Taylor and Saks Fifth Avenue, are well worth waiting on their long lines for.

New Year's Eve in Times Square
Dec 31
Some 200,000-plus revelers party in the cold streets ☎212/768-1560, ⓦwww.timessquarebid.org. There are also fireworks at the South Street Seaport, Central Park and Brooklyn's Prospect Park. More family-oriented, alcohol-free First Nights with dancing, music and food take place throughout the city ☎212/818-1777.

Shops and markets

New York's **shops** cater to every possible taste, in any combination and in many cases at any time of the day or night. As such, they're a great reason for visiting the city, even if the invasion of chains, like Barnes & Noble, Filene's Basement and even the world's largest K-Mart have caused some worry. Nevertheless, many of the oddest and oldest stores remain, and nothing beats discovering a quirky, independent shop that may specialize only in vintage cufflinks or rubber stamps.

Remember that an 8.25 percent **sales tax** will be added to your bill; this is bypassed sometimes when paying cash in a market or discount store. Finally, wherever you're shopping, be careful. Manhattan's crowded, frenzied stores are ripe territory for pickpockets and bag-snatchers.

ANTIQUES

New York is the premier **antique** source in the country, excellent for browsing, with museum-quality pieces available (typically costing a fortune) as well as lots of interesting, fairly priced stuff at the junkier end of the market. Prime locations are the East and West Villages, SoHo, Chelsea, Lower Broadway and the Upper East Side.

Chameleon

Map 5, G7. 231 Lafayette St
(between Spring and Prince sts)
☎212/343-9197.
Interesting collection of
antique lighting fixtures
dating from the nineteenth
century to the 1960s. Many
from New York residences.

Chelsea Antiques Building

Map 6, G6. 110 W 25th St
(between 6th and 7th aves)
☎212/929-0909.
Better quality, better
condition, and higher prices
than above listings. 150
dealers on twelve floors offer
exceptional estate treasures
and collectibles. Open
Mon–Fri 10am–6pm,
Sat–Sun 8.30am–6pm.

The Showplace

Map 6, H6. 40 W 25th St
(between 6th Ave and
Broadway) ☎212/741-8520.
Indoor market of more than
100 dealers of antiques and
collectibles plus an espresso
bar. Mon–Fri 9am–6pm, Sat
& Sun 8.30am–5.30pm.

BOOKS

Book lovers bemoan the steady disappearance of New
York's independent bookstores, and attribute their loss to
the phenomenon of Barnes & Noble superstores, but there's
still no shortage of places to find **books**, no matter how
esoteric your tastes may be.

SUPERSTORES AND CHAINS

- - - - - - - - - - - - - - - - - - - -

Barnes & Noble

Map 5, G3. 4 Astor Place (at
Broadway and Lafayette)
☎212/420-1322; **Map 6, I3.**
385 5th Ave (at 36th St)
☎212/779-7677; **Map 6, G7.**
675 6th Ave (at W 22nd St)
☎212/727-1227; **Map 7, H8.**
600 5th Ave (at W 48th St)
☎212/765-0592; **Map 7, J8.**
750 3rd Ave (at 47th St)
☎212/697-2251; **Map 8, B8.**
2289 Broadway (at W 82nd St)
☎212/362-8835; **Map 8, K7.**

240 E 86th St (at 2nd Ave)
☎212/794-1962; **Map 8, J7.**
1280 Lexington (at E 86th St)
☎212/423-9900; **Map 7, D4.**
1972 Broadway (across from
Lincoln Center) ☎212/595-
6859; and **Map 6, J8.** 33 E
17th St (Union Square)
☎212/253-0810.
Major US chain, many of its
stores with attendant *Starbucks*
cafés. Presentations by
authors take place about five
evenings a week.

Borders Books and Music

Map 7, I6. 461 Park Ave (at
57th St) ☎212/980-6785; **Map
6, L4.** 550 2nd Ave (at 32nd St)
☎212/685-3938.
This Ann Arbor–based chain
rivals Barnes & Noble for
selection, though not
saturation.

GENERAL INTEREST AND NEW BOOKS

St Mark's Bookshop
Map 5, H3. 31 3rd Ave
(between 8th and 9th sts)
☎212/260-7853.
Wonderfully eclectic selection
of new titles from mainstream
to way alternative.

Shakespeare & Co
Map 7, J3. 939 Lexington (at
69th St) ☎212/570-0201; **Map
5, G4.** 716 Broadway and
Washington Place
☎212/529-1330; **Map 6, K7.**
137 E 23rd St ☎212/570-0201;
and **Map 4, E8.** 1 Whitehall St
☎212/742-7025.
New and used books, paper
and hardcover, with some
great fiction and psychology
selections. There's also a
branch in Brooklyn, at the
Brooklyn Academy of Music.

Three Lives & Co
Map 5, C3. 154 W 10th St and
Waverly Place ☎212/741-2069.
Excellent literary bookstore
that has an especially good
array of books by and for
women, as well as general
titles. There's an excellent
reading series in the fall.

SECONDHAND BOOKS

Argosy Bookstore 1
Map 7, I5. 16 E 59th St

BOOKS

(between Lexington and Park aves) ☎212/753-4455. Unbeatable for rare books, it also sells clearance books and titles of all kinds, though the shop's reputation means you may find mainstream works cheaper elsewhere.

Strand Bookstore

Map 5, G2. 828 Broadway (at 12th St) ☎212/473-1452. With about eight miles of books and a stock of 2.5 million+, this is the largest book operation in the city – and one of the few survivors in an area once rife with secondhand bookstores.

TRAVEL AND OTHER SPECIALTY BOOKSTORES

The Complete Traveler

Map 6, I3. 199 Madison Ave (at 35th St) ☎212/685-9007. Manhattan's premier travel bookshop, excellently stocked, new and secondhand – including a huge collection of Baedekers.

Oscar Wilde Memorial Bookshop

Map 5, C3. 15 Christopher St (between Gay St and Greenwich Ave) ☎212/255-8097, ⓦwww.oscarwildebooks.com. Aptly situated gay and lesbian bookstore – probably the first in the city – with rare book collection, signed and first editions and framed signed letters from famous authors.

CLOTHES, FASHION AND ACCESSORIES

If you are prepared to search the city with sufficient dedication you can find just about anything, but it's the **designer clothes** and the snob values that go with them that predominate. **Secondhand clothes**, of the "vintage" or "antique" variety, have caught on of late. If you're looking for things to complete your look, plenty of **shoe** stores are available, especially around W 8th Street; and there's no shortage of **make-up** emporia as well.

CHAIN STORES

Ann Taylor
Map 7, H8. 575 5th Ave (at 47th St; flagship store) ☎212/922-3621.
Mid-priced business and elegant casual clothing for women. More than ten branches throughout the city.

Benetton
Map 7, H8. 597 5th Ave (at 48th St) ☎212/317-2501.
Italian chain offering youthful, contemporary, casual, bright-colored clothing for women, men and children.

Brooks Brothers
Map 7, I9. 346 Madison Ave (at 44th St) ☎212/682-8800.
Something of an institution in New York, this flaghsip store, founded in 1915, offers classic conservative style, selling tweeds and quietly striped shirts and ties.

Burberry's
Map 7, H6. 9 E 57th St (between 5th and Madison aves) ☎212/371-5010.
Classic plaids and tweeds, with a distinctly British feel to the conservative design.

Diesel
Map 7, J5. 770 Lexington (at 60th St) ☎212/308-0055.
One of five US stores that sell this Italian-designed label. Funky, some vintage-inspired clubwear, lots of denim. The two floors include a café.

Eileen Fisher
Map 6, I8. 103 5th Ave (between 17th and 18th sts) ☎212/924-4777.
This is the largest of their five NY shops full of loose and elegantly casual clothes for women. Their outlet is on 9th St between 1st and 2nd aves ☎212/529-5715.

Gap
Map 6, G3. 60 W 34th St and Herald Square (flagship store)

⊤212/643-8960.

Branches are on every other corner of the city; check the phone book for locations. Circular sale racks in the back of many stores offer terrific reductions.

DESIGNER STORES

Anna Sui
Map 5, F6. 113 Greene St (between Prince and Spring sts) ⊤212/941-8406.

Bagutta
Map 5, E7. 402 West Broadway (at Spring St) ⊤212/925-5216.
A confluence of top designers including Helmut Lang, Prada, Gaultier, Plein Sud, Dolce & Gabbana.

Beau Brummel
Map 5, E6. 421 West Broadway (between Prince and Spring sts) ⊤212/219-2666.

DKNY
Map 7, I5. 655 Madison Ave (at 60th St) ⊤212/223-3569.

Dolce & Gabbana
Map 7, I3. 825 Madison Ave (between 68th and 69th sts).

Emporio Armani
Map 6, I8. 110 5th Ave (at 16th St); and **Map 7, I6.** 601 Madison Ave (between 57th and 58th sts).

Gianni Versace
Map 7, H7. 647 5th Ave (between 51st and 52nd sts) ⊤212/317-0224, and **Map 7, I4** 815 Madison Ave (at 68th St) ⊤212/744-6868.

Giorgio Armani
Map 7, I4. 760 Madison Ave (at 65th St) ⊤212/988-9191.

Gucci
Map 7, H7. 685 5th Ave (at 54th St) ⊤212/826-2600.

Helmut Lang
Map 5, F7. 80 Greene St (at Spring St) ⊤212/925-7214.

Hermes
Map 7, H6. 11 E 57th St between 5th and Madison aves) ⊤212/751-3181.

Pleats Please

Map 5, E6. 128 Wooster St (at Prince) ☎212/226-3600.

FUNKY, TRENDY, HIP
- - - - - - - - - - - - - - - - - - - -

Canal Jean Co

Map 5, F7. 504 Broadway (between Spring and Broome sts) ☎212/226-1130.
Enormous warehousey store sporting a prodigious array of jeans, jackets, T-shirts, dresses, hats and more, new and secondhand. Young, fun and reasonably cheap.

Diesel StyleLab

Map 5, E7. 416 West Broadway (at Spring St) ☎212/343-3863.
The ultrahip top-shelf branch of this Italian chain has taken New York by storm.

New York Firefighter's Friend

Map 5, G7. 263 Lafayette (between Spring and Broome sts) ☎212/226-3142.
Get those NY Fire Dept tees and trucks here; an NYPD section is next door.

Old Japan

Map 5, A3. 382 Bleecker St (at Perry St) ☎212/633-0922.
Gorgeous, authentic Japanese clothes and trinkets, with a fantastic selection of antique kimonos.

X-Large

Map 5, G6. 267 Lafayette (between Prince and Spring sts) ☎212/334-4480.
Check out the Mini line for women, X-Large for men. Cutting edge streetwear for B-boys and gals. Sonic Youth's Kim Gordon and the Beastie Boys' Mike D are part owners.

VINTAGE/ SECONDHAND
- - - - - - - - - - - - - - - - - - - -

Allan & Suzi

Map 8, C9. 416 Amsterdam Ave (at 80th St) ☎212/724-7445.
Beautiful far-out fashion from the last several decades. Claims to have singlehandedly restarted the platform shoe craze.

CLOTHES, FASHION AND ACCESSORIES

●

Darrow Vintage

Map 6, H8. 7 W 19th St (between 5th and 6th aves) ☏212/255-1550.

Designer and never-worn vintage, with a friendly and helpful staff. Popular with top models.

The Fan Club

Map 6, H8. 22 W 19th St (between 5th and 6th aves) ☏212/929-3349.

An amazing selection of vintage clothes, many from movies, TV and theater, with a good supply of Marilyn Monroe frocks usually on display in the front window. The store benefits three AIDS charities.

Love Saves the Day

Map 5, I3. 119 2nd Ave (at 7th St) ☏212/228-3802.

Cheap vintage as well as classic lunchboxes and other kitschy nostalgia items, including valuable Kiss and Star Wars dolls.

Screaming Mimi's

Map 5, G4. 382 Lafayette St (between 4th St and Great Jones) ☏212/677-6464.

One of the most established vintage stores in Manhattan. Vintage clothes (including lingerie), bags, shoes and housewares at reasonable prices.

Tokio 7

Map 5, J3. 64 E 7th St (between 1st and 2nd aves) ☏212/353-8443.

Attractive secondhand and vintage designer consignment items – a little pricier than most, but a good selection.

THRIFT STORES

- - - - - - - - - - - - - - - - - - - -

Housing Works Thrift Shop

Map 6, G8. 143 W 17th St (between 6th and 7th aves) ☏212/366-0820.

Upscale thrift shop where you can find secondhand designer wear in very good condition. All proceeds benefit Housing Works, an AIDS social service organization.

DISCOUNT CLOTHING

Dave's Army & Navy Store
Map 6, G8. 581 6th Ave (between 16th and 17th sts) ☏212/989-6444.
The best place to buy jeans in Manhattan. Helpful assistants, no blaring music, and brands other than just Levi's.

Loehmann's
Map 6, F8. 101 7th Ave (between 16th and 17th sts) ☏212/352-0856.
New York's best-known department store for designer clothes at knockdown prices. No refunds and no exchanges, but there are individual dressing rooms.

SHOES AND OTHER ACCESSORIES

Kate Spade
Map 5, F7. 454 Broome St (at Mercer St) ☏212/274-1991.

SAMPLE SALES

At the beginning of each season, designers and manufacturers' showrooms are full of leftover merchandise that is removed via these informal sales. You'll always save at least fifty percent off the retail price, though you may not be able to try on the clothes and you can never return them. The best times for sample sales are spring and fall. Short of waiting for advertisement fliers to be stuffed into your hands while walking through the garment district, the following sources are helpful.

Daily Candy The website to find out about coveted designs at bargain rates before the city's fashionistas commence their stampede. ⊛www.dailycandy.com.

Nice Price 493 Columbus Ave (at 84th St) ☏212/362-1020. Pick up a printed card at the store or call their sample sale hotline ☏212/947-8748.

CLOTHES, FASHION AND ACCESSORIES

All the rage, these boxy fabric bags with the little logo-label are a generic assertion of "Manhattan chic."

Kenneth Cole

Map 7, D1. 353 Columbus Ave (at 77th St) ☎212/873-2061. Classic and contemporary shoes, beautiful bags, excellent full-grain leather. Call for more locations.

Mary Quant Colour Concept Shop

Map 7, I7. 520 Madison Ave (at 53rd St) ☎212/980-7577. Mod make-up in every conceivable shade, all with the so-cool 1960s' flower motif.

Otto Tootsi Plohound

Map 6, I7. 137 5th Ave (at 20th St) ☎212/460-8650 and 38 E 57th St (near Park Ave) ☎212/231-3199.
If you want to run with a trendy crowd, these shoes will help. Very current designs.

Robert Marc

Map 7, I6. 575 Madison Ave (between 56th and 57th sts) ☎212/319-2000 and four other

locations.
Exclusive New York distributor of designer frames like Lunor and Kirei Titan; also sells Retrospecs, restored antique eyewear from the 1890s to the 1940s. Very expensive and very hot.

Sephora

Map 7, H7. 636 5th Ave (at 51st St) ☎212/245-1633. Breathtaking "warehouse" of perfumes, make-up and body-care products. You have to see (or smell) it to believe it.

Steve Madden

Map 8, J7. 150 E 86th St (between Lexington and 3rd aves) ☎212/426-0538; **Map 5, G6.** 540 Broadway (at Prince St) ☎212/343-1800; **Map 8, B7.** 2315 Broadway (near 86th St) ☎212/799-4221 and **Map 6, G3.** 41 W 34th St (at 6th Ave) ☎212/736-3283.
Very popular copies of up-to-the-minute styles, well-loved for their ability to take on New York's "shoe-killing" streets.

DEPARTMENT STORES AND MALLS

DEPARTMENT STORES

Barney's

Map 7, I5. 600 Madison Ave (at 61st St) ⓣ212/826-8900. Mon–Fri 10am–8pm, Sat 10am–7pm.

Though a proper department store, Barney's actually concentrates on clothes, particularly men's, with the emphasis on high-flying, up-to-the-minute designer garments and women's wear.

Bergdorf Goodman

Map 7, H6. 754 5th Ave (at 57th St) ⓣ212/753-7300. Mon–Fri 10am–8pm, Sat 10am–7pm, Sun 11am–6pm. Come if only to ogle the windows, which approach high art with their rhinestone-encrusted diaphanous dress displays. Everything about Bergdorf's speaks of its attempt to be New York City's most elegant and wealth-oriented

department store. The men's store is across 5th Ave.

Bloomingdale's

Map 7, J5. 1000 3rd Ave (at 59th St) ⓣ212/705-2000. Mon–Fri 10am–8.30pm, Sat 10am–7pm, Sun 11am–7pm. It has the atmosphere of a large, bustling bazaar, packed with concessionaires offering perfumes and designer clothes.

Henri Bendel

Map 7, H6. 712 5th Ave (between 55th and 56th sts) ⓣ212/247-1100. Mon–Wed, Fri & Sat 10am–7pm, Thurs 10am–8pm, Sun noon–6pm. This store, more gentle in its approach than the biggies – its refinement thanks in part to its classy reuse of the Coty perfume building, with windows by Rene Lalique – has a name for exclusivity and top modern designers.

Lord & Taylor

Map 6, I2. 424 5th Ave (at 39th St) ⓣ212/391-3344. Mon, Tues

& Sat 10am–7pm, Wed & Fri 10am–8.30pm, Thurs 9am–8.30pm, Sun 11am–7pm.

The most venerable of the New York specialty stores, in business since 1826 and to some extent the most pleasant, has a more traditional feel than Macy's or Bloomingdale's. Still good for classic designer fashions, petites, winter coats, household goods and accessories and the more basic items.

Macy's

Map 6, G3. 151 W 34th St (on Broadway at Herald Square) ☎212/695-4400 or 1-800-289-6229. Mon–Sat 9am–9pm, Sun 11am–7pm.

Quite simply, the largest department store in the world with two buildings, two million square feet of floor space and ten floors (four for women's garments alone). Unfortunately, most merchandise is of mediocre quality, although real fashion is steadily returning.

Saks 5th Avenue

Map 7, H8. 611 5th Ave (at 50th St) ☎212/753-4000. Sun–Wed, Fri & Sat 10am–6.30pm, Thurs 10am–8pm.

The name is virtually synonymous with style, and, although Saks has retained its name for quality, it has also updated itself to carry the merchandise of all the big designers. The first floor is lovely when decorated with sparkling white branches at Christmas time.

Takashimaya

Map 7, H6. 693 5th Ave (between 54th and 55th sts) ☎212/350-0100. Mon–Sat 10am–8pm, Sun noon–5pm.

This beautiful Japanese department store offers a scaled-down assortment of expensive merchandise, simply displayed, and exquisitely wrapped purchases. The café, *The Tea Box*, on the lower level, has an assortment of teapots and loose tea.

SHOPPING MALLS

South Street Seaport

Map 4, H6. 12 Fulton St
℡212/732-7678. Mon–Sat
10am–9pm, Sun 11am–8pm.
The barn-like building and its
historic surroundings of ships,
docks and old warehouses are
fascinating and fun, the river
views from the deck are
lovely, and The Sharper
Image stocks some terrifying
and ingenious toys for adults.

Trump Tower

Map 7, H6. 725 5th Ave
(between 56th and 57th sts)
℡212/832-2000. Mon–Sat
10am–6pm, Sun noon–5pm.
Donald Trump's retail
triumph was constructed in
his own image. This gaudy
caterer to the wealthy offers a
range of exclusive boutiques
set around a deep, marbled
atrium with a several-story
goldtone waterfall – a tourist
attraction in itself.

THE DIAMOND DISTRICT

The strip of 47th Street between Fifth and Sixth avenues is
known as the Diamond District. Crammed into this one block
are more than 100 shops: combined they sell more jewelry
than any other block in the world. The industry has traditionally
been run by Hassidic Jews, and you'll run into plenty of black-
garbed men with *payess* (sidelocks) here.

Some good starting points are Andrew Cohen, Inc (579 5th
Ave, 15th floor), for diamonds; Myron Toback (25 W 47th St), a
trusted dealer of silver findings; and Bracie Company Inc (608
5th Ave, suite 806), a friendly business specializing in antique
and estate jewelry. Once you buy, there's AA Pearls & Gems
(10 W 47th St), the industry's choice for pearl and gem string-
ing; and, if you want to get your gems graded, the
Gemological Institute of America (580 5th Ave, 2nd floor).

DEPARTMENT STORES AND MALLS

FOOD AND DRINK

Food – the buying as much as the consuming of it – is a New York obsession. Though you can find a deli on pretty much any corner, it's in the gourmet markets and specialty shops – cheese, bread, smoked fish, what have you – that the city really shines.

GOURMET MARKETS

Around the Clock Center, Chelsea Market

Map 6, D9. 75 9th Ave (between 15th and 16th sts) ☎212/243-6005.

A complex of eighteen former industrial buildings, among them the late nineteenth-century Nabisco Cookie Factory.

Balducci's

Map 5, D2. 424 6th Ave (between 9th and 10th sts) ☎212/673-2600.

The longtime rival of the Upper West Side's Zabar's, this is a family-run store that's no less appetizing – though some say it's slightly pricier.

Dean and Deluca

Map 5, G6. 560 Broadway (between Prince and Spring sts) ☎212/226-6800.

One of the original big neighborhood food emporia. Very chic, very SoHo and not at all cheap. There's also a café on Prince St.

Fairway

Map 7, C2. 2127 Broadway (between 74th and 75th sts) ☎212/595-1888.

Long-established Upper West Side grocery store that for many locals is the better-value alternative to Zabar's. They have their own farm on Long Island, so the produce is always fresh, and their range in some items is enormous. Fantastic organic selection upstairs.

Russ & Daughters

Map 5, J5. 179 E Houston St (between Allen and Orchard sts) ☎212/475-4880.

Technically, this store is

known as an "appetizing" – the original Manhattan gourmet shop, set up about 1900 to sate the appetites of homesick immigrant Jews, selling smoked fish, caviar, pickled vegetables, cheese and bagels. This is one of the oldest.

Zabar's
Map 8, B9. 2245 Broadway (between 80th and 81st sts) ☏212/787-2000.
The apotheosis of New York food-fever, Zabar's is still the city's most eminent foodstore. Choose from an astonishing variety of cheeses, cooked meats and salads, fresh baked bread and croissants, excellent bagels, and cooked dishes to go. Not to be missed.

CHEESE AND DAIRY
- - - - - - - - - - - - - - - - - - - -

Alleva Latticini
Map 5, H8. 188 Grand St (at Mulberry St) ☏212/226-7990. Oldest Italian cheesery in America; also a grocer. Makes own smoked mozzarella and ricotta.

Joe's Dairy
Map 5, D6. 156 Sullivan St (between Houston and Prince sts) ☏212/677-8780.
Family store considered New York's best bet for fresh mozzarella in several varieties.

Murray's Cheese Shop
Map 5, C4. 257 Bleecker St (between 6th and 7th aves) ☏212/243-3289.
A variety of more than 300 fresh cheeses and excellent fresh panini sandwiches, all served by knowledgeable staff. Free tastings on Sat afternoons.

FISH AND SEAFOOD
- - - - - - - - - - - - - - - - - - - -

Barney Greengrass
Map 8, C7. 541 Amsterdam Ave (between 86th and 87th sts) ☏212/724-4707.
"The Sturgeon King" – an Upper West Side smoked-fish brunch institution since 1908 that also sells brunch-makings to go.

Citarella
Map 7, C2. 2135 Broadway (at 75th St) ☏212/874-0383.

FOOD AND DRINK

GREENMARKETS

Several days each week, long before sunrise, hundreds of farmers from Long Island, the Hudson Valley and parts of Pennsylvania and New Jersey set out in trucks transporting their fresh-picked bounty to New York City, where they are joined by bakers, cheesemakers and others at greenmarkets. Usually you'll find apple cider, jams and preserves, flowers and plants, maple syrup, fresh meat and fish, pretzels, cakes and breads, herbs, honey – just about anything and everything produced in the rural regions around the city – not to mention occasional live worm composts and baby dairy goats.

Call ☏212/477-3220 for the greenmarket nearest you, or try a location below:

Bowling Green Map 4, E7. at Broadway and Battery Place Thurs 8am–5pm, year-round.

City Hall Map 4, E4. Chambers and Centre sts Tues & Fri 8am–3pm, year-round.

Washington Market Map 4, C3. Park at Greenwich and Reade sts Wed 8am–3pm, year-round.

Federal Plaza Map 4, E6. Broadway and Thomas sts Fri 8am–4pm, year-round. Lafayette St Map 5, G7. at Spring St Thurs 8am–5pm, July–Oct.

Tompkins Square Map 5, K3. 7th St and Ave A Sun 10am–5pm, year-round.

St Mark's Church Map 5, I2. E 10th St and 2nd Ave Tues 8am–7pm, June–Dec.

Abingdon Square Map 6, E9. W 12th St and 8th Ave Sat 8am–3pm, May–Dec.

Union Square Map 6, J8. at E 17th St Broadway Mon, Wed, Fri & Sat 8am–6pm, year-round.

I.S. 44 Map 7, D1. W 77th St and Columbus Ave Sun 10am–5pm, Fri 8am–2pm, year-round.

FOOD AND DRINK

The largest and most varied fish and seafood source in the city, now with gourmet baked goods, cheese, coffee, meat, and prepared food.

Petrossian

Map 7, F6. 182 W 58th St (at 7th Ave) ☎212/245-2214.
This celebrated shop imports only the finest Russian caviar, alongside a range of other gourmet products – smoked salmon and other fish mainly – as well as pricey implements to eat it all with.

HEALTH FOOD, VEGETARIAN AND SPICE SHOPS

Aphrodisia

Map 5, C4. 264 Bleecker St (between 6th and 7th aves) ☎212/989-6440.
For herbs, spices and seasoning oils only, this place is hard to beat.

Healthy Pleasures

Map 5, F2. 93 University Place (between 11th and 12th sts) ☎212/353-3663; **Map 5, E7.** 489 Broome St (between West Broadway and Wooster St) ☎212/431-7434; and **Map 8, B6.** 2493 Broadway (between 92nd and 93rd sts).
These giant stores have juice bars, incredible salad-bar selections and all manner of healthy delights. The bottom floor of the Broadway branch is entirely kosher.

Kalustyan's

Map 6, K5. 123 Lexington Ave (between 28th and 29th sts) ☎212/685-3451.
The best of the groceries in the tiny Little India district of Manhattan. Good spice selection.

TEA AND COFFEE

Empire Coffee and Tea Co

Map 6, D2. 568 9th Ave (between 41st and 42nd sts) ☎212/268-1220.
This store for the serious addict has been fueling New York's caffeine habits since 1908.

FOOD AND DRINK

●

Porto Rico Importing Company

Map 5, D5. 201 Bleecker St (between 6th Ave and MacDougal St) ☎212/477-5421; **Map 5, I3.** 40 1/2 St Mark's Place (off 2nd Ave); and **Map 5, E6.** 107 Thompson St (between Prince and Spring sts).

Best for coffee, and local rumor has it that the house blends are as good as many of the more expensive coffees. The Thompson St branch has a smaller selection and is primarily a café.

LIQUOR STORES

Prices for all kinds of **liquor** are controlled in New York State and vary little from one shop to another. We've listed a few that have an especially good selection or tend to be a touch less expensive. A state law forbids the sale of hard liquor and wine on Sundays; supermarkets may sell beer, but not wine or spirits.

Astor Wines and Spirits

Map 5, G3. 12 Astor Place (at Lafayette St) ☎212/674-7500. Manhattan's best selection and some of the city's most competitive prices. Good kosher and organic wine section.

Chelsea Wine Vault

Map 6, D9. 75 9th Ave (in Chelsea Market) ☎212/462-4244.

These incredibly knowledgeable folk will sell, store and even teach you about wine.

Warehouse Wines and Spirits

Map 5, G3. 735 Broadway (between 8th and Waverly Place) ☎212/982-7770. The top place to get a buzz for your buck, with a wide selection and frequent reductions on popular lines.

MUSIC

While the top music megastores in New York are the British chain HMV, Tower Records and the Virgin Megastore, specialty pop music stores are clustered in the East and West villages.

CHAINS

HMV

Map 7, C2. 2081 Broadway (at 72nd St) ☎212/721-5900. Also **Map 8, J7.** 1280 Lexington Ave (at 86th St) ☎212/348-0800; **Map 6, G3.** 57 W 34th (at 6th Ave) ☎212/629-0900; and **Map 7, H8.** 565 5th Ave (at 46th St) ☎212/681-6700. The most pleasant and most fun of the megastores.

J&R Music World

Map 4, E5. 23 Park Row (between Beekman and Anne sts) ☎212/238-9000. A large downtown store with a decent selection and good prices.

Virgin Megastore

Map 7, F9. 1540 Broadway (at 45th St) ☎212/921-1020; and **Map 6, J9.** 52 E 14th St (Union Square) ☎212/598-4666.

SPECIAL INTEREST AND SECONDHAND

Fat Beats

Map 5, D3. 406 6th Ave, 2nd floor (between 8th and 9th sts) ☎212/673-3883. The name says it all. It's *the* source for hip-hop on vinyl in New York City.

Footlight Records

Map 5, G2. 113 E 12th St (between 3rd and 4th aves) ☎212/533-1572. The place for show music, film soundtracks and jazz. Everything from Broadway to Big Band, Sinatra to Merman. A must for record collectors.

Vinyl Mania

Map 5, C5. 60 Carmine St (between Bleecker St and 7th Ave) ☎212/924-7223. This is where DJs come for

MUSIC

●

the newest, rarest releases, especially of dance music. Hard-to-find imports too, as well as homemade dance tapes.

SPORTING GOODS

The **sporting goods** scene is dominated by chains such as Foot Locker, The Athlete's Foot, Sports Authority and Modell's, though there are a few other options – "theme park" sports clothes stores, as well as stores tightly focused on one sport. Use them for merchandise as well as a wealth of information about that sport in NY.

SUPERSTORES

Niketown

Map 7, H6. 6 E 57th St (between 5th and Madison aves) ☏212/891-6453.
You can enter this sneaker temple through Trump Tower, literally hearing crowds cheer as you pass through the door. Every thirty minutes, a screen descends the full five stories of the store and shows Nike commercials.

Reebok Store

Map 7, D3. 160 Columbus Ave (between 67th and 68th sts) ☏212/595-1480.

Not as dazzling as Niketown, but it does show ads on two big screens, houses the Reebok Sports Club and features European Reebok lines not found anywhere else in the States.

SPECIALTY STORES

Bicycle Habitat

Map 5, G6. 244 Lafayette St (between Spring and Prince sts) ☏212/431-3315.
This unassuming store is frequented by bike messengers. Buy a bike here, and they'll service your brakes forever.

SPORTING GOODS

Mason's Tennis Mart
Map 7, H7. 56 E 53rd St
☎212/755-5805.

New York's last remaining
tennis specialty store – they
let you try out all racquets.

Commercial galleries

There are roughly 500 **art galleries** in the city, and even if you have no intention of buying, many of these galleries are well worth seeing. Most galleries are found in five main areas: in the 60s and 70s on the Upper East Side for antiques and the occasional (minor) Old Master; 57th Street between Sixth and Park avenues for big, established modern and contemporary names; SoHo for established but hip artists; Chelsea for trendy and up-and-comers; and TriBeCa for more experimental displays.

Opening times are roughly Tues–Sat 10am–6pm, but many galleries have truncated summer hours and are closed during August. The best time to gallery-hop is on weekday afternoons; the absolute worst time is on Saturday.

One of the best ways to see the top galleries is with Art Tours of Manhattan (see p.14), which runs informed (if pricey) guided tours. Also, pick up a copy of the *Gallery Guide* – available upon request in the larger galleries – for listings of current shows and each gallery's specialty. The weekly *Time Out New York* offers broad listings of the major commercial galleries. Listed below are some of the more interesting options in Manhattan.

SOHO AND TRIBECA
----

123 Watts
Map 4, B1. 123 Watts St (between Greenwich and Hudson) ☎212/219-1482. Trendy gallery known for its photography, along with other forms of contemporary art; has shown work by Robert Mapplethorpe, Arturo Cuenca and Bruno Ulmer.

John Gibson
Map 5, G6. 568 Broadway (at Prince St), Suite 101 ☎212/925-1192. Avant-garde and old school American painting, sculpture and prints, with an emphasis on conceptual art and abstract works.

Lehmann Maupin
Map 5, F8. 39 Greene St (between Canal and Grand sts) ☎212/965-0753. Shows a range of established international and American

contemporary artists working in a wide range of media.

Louis Meisel
Map 5, E6. 141 Prince St (at West Broadway) ☎212/677-1340. Specializes in Photorealism – past shows have included Richard Estes and Chuck Close – as well as Abstract Illusionism.

CHELSEA

Annina Nosei
Map 6, B7. 530 W 22nd, 2nd floor (between 10th and 11th aves) ☎212/741-8695. Global works, especially contemporary pieces by emerging Latin American and Middle Eastern artists. Mon–Fri 11am–6pm.

Barbara Gladstone Gallery
Map 6, B6. 515 W 24th St (between 10th and 11th aves) ☎212/206-9300.

SOHO AND TRIBECA ●

Paintings, sculpture and photography by hot contemporary artists such as Matthew Barney and Rosemarie Trockel.

Gagosian Gallery

Map 6, B6. W 24th St (between 10th and 11th aves) ☎212/228-2828.
This stalwart of the New York scene, owned by an ex-LA poster salesman, features modern and contemporary art.

Matthew Marks Gallery

Map 6, B7. 522 W 22nd St (between 10th and 11th aves) ☎212/243-0200.
The centerpiece of Chelsea's art scene, it shows the work of such well-known minimalist and abstract artists as Cy Twombly, Ellsworth Kelly and Lucien Freud. See also the branch at 523 W 24th St.

Pat Hearn

Map 6, B7. 530 W 22nd St (between 10th and 11th aves) ☎212/727-7366.
This longtime venue was an influential presence in its former SoHo location, and continues to specialize in abstract and conceptual artists, and risky exhibits.

Paula Cooper

Map 6, B7. 534 W 21st St (between 10th and 11th aves) ☎212/255-1105.
Another influential gallery that shows a wide range of contemporary painting, sculpture, drawings, prints and photographs, particularly minimalist and abstract works.

Robert Miller

Map 6, B6. 524 W 26th St (between 10th and 11th aves) ☎212/366-4774.
Exceptional shows of twentieth-century art, including paintings by David Hockney and Lee Krasner, and photographs by artists sich as Diane Artus and Robert Mapplethorpe.

Sonnabend

Map 6, B7. 536 W 22nd St (between 10th and 11th aves) ☎212/627-1018.
A top gallery featuring painting, photography and video from contemporary

American and European artists, including Robert Morris and Gilbert and George.

MIDTOWN AND UPPER EAST SIDE

Knoedler & Co.

Map 7, H3. 19 E 70th St (between 5th and Madison aves) ☎212/794-0550.
Highly renowned gallery specializing in abstract and Pop artists and post-war and contemporary art with a focus on the New York School. Shows some of the best-known names in twentieth-century art, including Stella, Rauschenberg and Fonseca.

Leo Castelli

Map 7, H1. 59 E 79th St ☎212/249-4470.
One of the original dealer-collectors, Castelli was instrumental in aiding the careers of Rauschenberg and Warhol, and offers big contemporary names at big prices.

Marlborough/ Marlborough Graphics

Map 7, H6. 40 W 57th St ☎212/541-4900.
Internationally renowned galleries show the cream of modern and contemporary artists and graphic designers, including Francis Bacon, R.B. Kitaj and others.

Mary Boone

Map 7, H6. 745 5th Ave, 4th floor (between 57th and 58th sts) ☎212/752-2929.
Specializes in installations, paintings and works by up-and-coming European and American artists. A top gallery, now with an interesting Chelsea addition (**Map 6, B6.** 541 W 24th St between 10th and 11th aves ☎212/752-2929).

PaceWildenstein

Map 7, H6. 32 E 57th St ☎212/421-3292.
This celebrated gallery has carried works by most of the great modern American and European artists; from Picasso to Rothko. A SoHo satellite located at 142 Greene St

MIDTOWN AND UPPER EAST SIDE

(Ⓣ212/431-9224) specializes in edgier works and large installations.

SPACES

The galleries below provide a forum for the kind of risky and non-commercially viable art that many other galleries – reliant on trying to get art into the hands of buyers – may not be able to afford to show.

Artists Space Map 5, F8. 38 Greene St, 3rd floor (between Canal and Grand sts) Ⓣ212/226-3970. One of the most respected alternative spaces, with frequently changing theme-based exhibits, film screenings, and the like.

Clocktower Map 4, E3. 346 Broadway (between Worth and Leonard sts) Ⓣ212/233-1096. Temporary exhibitions, and an annual studio program run by PS1, in which artists work in the studio space within the clock tower. Visitors are allowed to wander around and talk to the artists about their work. Go just to see the incredible views of downtown.

DIA Center for the Arts Map 6, B7. 548 W 22nd St Ⓣ212/989-5566, Ⓦwww.diacenter.org. The pre-eminent Alternative Art Foundation's largest gallery space shows year-long exhibitions of work by artists such as Joseph Beuys, Dan Graham, Robert Ryman and Kids of Survival.

PS 1 Contemporary Arts Center 22–25 Jackson Ave (46th St, Long Island City, Queens). Ⓣ718/784-2084, Ⓦwww.ps1.org. $2 suggested donation. Based in an old schoolhouse, this is the place for avant-garde and experimental new art.

Sports and outdoor activities

New York is one of the most avid **sports** cities in America. TV stations cover most regular-season games and all postseason games in the big four American team sports – **baseball**, **football**, **basketball** and **ice hockey**. Some tickets can be hard to find, some impossible and most don't come that cheap. Bars – specifically **sports bars** – are a good alternative to actually being there.

Many **participatory activities** in the city are free or affordable. You can **swim** either at the local pools or the borough beaches, usually for a small fee; **jog**, still one of the city's main obsessions; or have your fill of spaces to **bike** or **rollerblade**.

Tickets for most events can be booked through Ticketmaster (☏212/307-7171), though it's cheaper – and of course riskier for popular events – to try to pick up tickets on the night of the event. You can also get advance tickets direct from the stadium box office.

BASEBALL

From April to October, **New York Yankees** and the **New York Mets** play 162 games (81 home games each; playoffs run through Oct), giving you plenty of excuses to head out for a sunny day at the ballpark, not to mention the fact that baseball games, of all spectator sports, are by far the least expensive.

The Yankees (lovingly called the Bronx Bombers) are the most successful baseball franchise in history, with the most World Series titles (26 through the year 2000). If you get to the game early, you can visit Monument Park, where all their greats are memorialized. The Mets have been on a roller-coaster ride ever since the lovably inept team of 1962 matured into the 1969 World Series champions, and then took a nose dive from their second World Series win in 1986 to the "worst team money can buy" in the early 1990 – and are back on the upswing.

Shea Stadium

126th St (at Roosevelt Ave), Queens; box office Mon–Fri 9am–6pm, Sat, Sun & holidays 9am–5pm; tickets $12–33; ☎718/507-8499, ⓦwww.mets.com. Subway #7 to Willets Point.

Yankee Stadium

161st St and River Ave, the Bronx; box office Mon–Sat 9am–5pm, Sun 10am–4pm; tickets $8–65; ☎718/293-6000, ⓦwww.yankees.com. Subway #C, #D or #4 to 161st St Station.

BASKETBALL

The National Basketball Association's regular season begins in November and runs through the end of April. The two professional teams in the New York area are the **New York Knicks**, who play at Madison Square Garden, and the **New Jersey Nets**, whose venue is the Continental Airlines

Arena at the Meadowlands Sports Complex in New Jersey. The **New York Liberty** of the Women's National Basketball Association also play their games at Madison Square Garden during the summer.

The Knicks have a loyal following that counts such celebrities as Spike Lee, Woody Allen, Sarah Jessica Parker and a contingent of Baldwin brothers. It is hard to get tickets to see them play, even during down years. Long playing in the long shadow of the Knicks, the Nets have emerged as one of the more exciting teams in the NBA, and if you are willing to make the pilgrimage to New Jersey, you should find it fairly easy to get tickets.

Madison Square Garden

Map 6, E4. 7th Ave (between 31st and 33rd sts); tickets $10–60; ⓣ212/465-6741. Subway #1, #2, #3, #9, #A, #C and #E to 34th St Penn Station.

Continental Airlines Arena

Meadowlands Sports Complex off routes 3, 17, and Turnpike exit 16W, East Rutherford, New Jersey; box office 9am–6pm, Sat 10am–6pm, Sun noon–5pm; tickets $30–75; ⓣ1-800/7NJ-NETS, ⓦwww.nba.com/nets.

BICYCLING

There are 100 miles of **cycle paths** in New York; those in Central Park, Riverside Park and the East River Promenade are among the nicest. Transportation Alternatives (115 W 30th St ⓣ212/629-8080, ⓦwww.transalt.org), while concentrating on the environmental aspects, lobbies for funding for bike-related projects, like ramps for bridge access, free bike racks, and additional car-free hours in Central Park. They also sponsor the Century Bike Tour in September (a 35-, 50-, 75-, or 100-mile ride through the boroughs), and have some good maps.

Bicycle Habitat
Map 5, G3. 244 Lafayette St
☎212/431-3315.
Known for an excellent repair service, they also offer rentals for $25 a day (plus a deposit equal to the value of the bike) or $7.50 an hour, with a two-hour minimum. You can also have a tune-up (priced at $75 and up). The very knowledgeable staff here helps cyclists of all levels of expertise.

Five Borough Bike Club
☎212/932-2300 ext 115 for membership details.
This club organizes rides throughout the year, including the Montauk Century, a hundred-mile ride from New York to Montauk, Long Island.

BOWLING

Bowlmor Lanes
Map 5, F2. 110 University Place (between 12th and 13th sts) ☎212/255-8188.
Long-established and large bowling alley with a bar and shop. Open Mon & Fri 10am–4am, Tues & Wed 10am–1am, Thurs 10am–2am, Sat 11am–4am, Sun 11am–1am. $6 per game per person before 5pm, $7 after 5pm. $4 shoe-rent.

Leisure Time Bowling
Map 6, E1. 2nd floor of Port Authority, 625 8th Ave, near 40th St ☎212/268-6909.
The nicest place in the city to bowl. $5 per game per person ($6 after 5pm), plus $3.50 shoe-rent.

FOOTBALL

The **National Football League** (NFL) season stretches from September until the Super Bowl, typically played on the fourth Sunday in January. Although tickets are sold out for both local teams, the **Giants** and **Jets**, well in advance,

CHELSEA PIERS

The **Chelsea Piers** complex, entered at W 23rd St and the Hudson River covers six blocks (☎212/336-6666), and is comprised of four completely renovated piers, on which all manner of activity takes place.

The Sports Center at Pier 60 features a quarter-mile running track, the largest rock-climbing wall in the northeast, three basketball/volleyball courts, a boxing ring, a 24-yard swimming pool and whirlpool, indoor sand-volleyball courts, exercise studios offering more than 100 classes weekly, a cardiovascular weight-training room, a sundeck right on the Hudson River and spa services. Day-passes are available for $50. Mon–Fri 6am–11pm, Sat & Sun 8am–9pm. ☎212/336-6000.

The Roller Rinks are on Pier 62. They are outdoors and open year-round, weather permitting. Daily session starts at noon, exact times vary. $6.50; children under 12 $5.50. Rentals available. ☎212/336-6200.

The Sky Rink is on Pier 61. Ice-skate year-round on this indoor rink. Daily sessions start at noon, exact times vary. $11.50; children under 12 $8; seniors $7.50. Rentals $5. ☎212/336-6100.

if you're willing to pay the price you can buy tickets outside the stadium before the game (from scalpers). Both play at Giants Stadium in East Rutherford, New Jersey.

With a twenty-year waiting list for season tickets, the Giants, who have won four NFL and two Super Bowls in 1987 and 1991, have a devoted following. Since 1984, the Jets have been subtenants of the Giants at Giant Stadium. While they have not had the historical success of the Giants, they are generally as competitive.

FOOTBALL

Giants Stadium

The Meadowlands Sports Complex off routes 3, 17, and Turnpike exit 16W, East Rutherford, New Jersey; box office Mon–Fri 9am–6pm, Sat 10am–6pm, Sun noon–5pm; tickets $45 and $50; ☎201/935-3900. Regular buses are available from Port Authority Bus Terminal on 42nd St and 8th Ave.

GYMS, POOLS AND BATHS

You can join one of several newly renovated city **recreation centers** for $25 per year (ages 18–54) or $10 (kids 13–17 and seniors). All have gym facilities and most have an indoor and/or outdoor pool. Call ☎212/447-2020 or look in the Manhattan Blue Pages (within the *White Pages*) under NY City Parks; centers are listed under "Recreation" and "Swimming Pools."

John Jay Pool

Map 7, M1. 77th and Cherokee Place ☎212/794-6566.

Above the FDR Drive, this six-lane, fifty-yard pool is surrounded by playgrounds and park benches. Although it opened in 1940, it is in remarkably great condition. Free to anyone; bring a padlock.

Sutton Gymnastics and Fitness Center

Map 5, H3. 20 Cooper Square ☎212/533-9390.

One of the few gyms in New York where you need not be a member to use the facilities. Classes for around $25, generally only in summer. Call for hours and class schedule.

Tenth Street Turkish Baths

Map 5, I2. 268 E 10th St; Mon, Tues, Thurs & Fri 11am–10pm, Wed 9am–10pm, Sat–Sun 7.30am–10pm; men only Sun opening until 2pm; women only Wed opening until 2pm; coed otherwise; ☎212/473-8806 or 674-9250.

An ancient place, something

of a neighborhood landmark and still going, with steam baths, sauna and an ice-cold pool, as well as massage and a restaurant. Free lockers, locks, shorts, towel, robe and slippers. Admission $22, extra for massage, etc.

HORSE RACING

Aqueduct, in Howard Beach, Queens, has thoroughbred racing from October to May. To get there by subway, take the #A train to the Aqueduct station. **Belmont**, in Elmont, Long Island, is home to the Belmont Stakes (June), one of the three races in which three-year-olds compete for the Triple Crown. Belmont thoroughbred racing is open May–July and September–October. Take the #E or #F subway train to 169th St and then the #16 bus to the track, or take the Long Island Railroad to the Belmont Race Track stop. For both Belmont and Aqueduct, call ☏718/641-4700. Admission at both tracks ranges from $1 to $4 depending on where you park and sit. Valet parking costs $5 at Aqueduct and $6 at Belmont.

ICE HOCKEY

The two New York National Hockey League teams are the **Rangers**, who play at Madison Square Garden (see listing, p.339), and the **Islanders**, whose venue is the Nassau Coliseum on Long Island. The **New Jersey Devils** play at the Continental Airlines Arena (see listing, p.339). The regular season lasts throughout the winter and into early spring, when the playoffs take place. Prices for games range $14–85.

The Rangers ended a 54-year drought in 1994, when they won the Stanley Cup. Since then they have not had as much success, but are always competitive. The Islanders, New York's "other" hockey team, are undergoing a resurgence after years of mediocrity. The Devils won the Stanley Cup in 2000, and the 2001 campaign saw them battle (and ultimately lose to) the Colorado Avalanche in the finals.

Nassau Coliseum
1255 Hempstead Turnpike, Uniondale, New York; box office daily 10.45am–5.45pm; tickets $14–85; ☎516/794-9300. Take the Long Island Railroad to Hempstead, then bus #N70, #N71 or #N72 from Hempstead bus terminal, one block away.

ICE-SKATING

In winter, the freezing weather makes for good **ice skating**. In milder weather, roller skating is popular, on the paths in Central Park and specifically near the northwest corner of the Sheep Meadow, in Riverside Park and in many smaller open spaces.

Rockefeller Center Ice Rink
Map 7, H8. Between 49th and 50th sts, off 5th Ave
☎212/332-7654.
Without doubt the slickest place to skate, though you may have to wait in line and

CENTRAL PARK

Central Park is an obvious focus for recreation. from croquet and chess to soccer and swimming. Joggers, in-line skaters, walkers and cyclists have the roads to themselves on weekdays 10am–3pm & 7–10pm and all day on weekends. In addition, boaters can head to the Loeb Boathouse (☎212/517-2233; $10/hr), which hires out rowboats in warm weather months. To find out what is going on where and when, try the Arsenal, at 830 5th Ave at 64th Street, and pick up the **Green Pages**, which tell you about every activity, from archery to wild-food walks. For more on Central Park, see Chapter 18.

ICE-SKATING

it's pricier than anywhere else. Call for hours and prices.

Sky Rink

Map 6, A8. Chelsea Piers
℡212/336-6100.
(See box p.34)

Wollman Rink

Map 7, G5. 62nd St, Central Park ℡212/396-1010.
Lovely rink, where you can skate to the marvelous, inspiring backdrop of the lower Central Park skyline – incredibly impressive at night. Call for hours and prices.

IN-LINE SKATING

You'll see commuters to freestylists on **in-line skates** – also known as **rollerblades** – in New York. For the best place, go to the skate circle near Naumberg Bandshell in Central Park at 72nd Street. World-class bladers maneuver between cones with all kinds of fancy footwork just inside Central Park's *Tavern on the Green* entrance, near W 68th Street. Other than Central Park, the best place to skate is Battery Park.

Blades

Map 4, D4. 128 Chambers St (between West Broadway and Church St) ℡212/964-1944;
Map 7, D2. 120 W 72nd St (between Columbus and Broadway) ℡212/787-3911;
Map 8, J7. 160 E 86th St (between Lexington and 3rd aves) ℡212/996-1644.
Rents skates out for $20 for 24 hours.

JOGGING

Jogging is still very much the number one fitness pursuit in the city. A favorite circuit in the park is 1.57 miles around the reservoir; just make sure you jog in a counter-clockwise direction. For company, contact the New York Road Runners Club, 9 E 89th St (℡212/860–2280,

Ⓦwww.nyrrc.org) to get their schedule for Central Park and elsewhere. The East River Promenade, Riverside Park and almost any other stretch of open space long enough to get up speed are also well jogged.

POOL

Along with bars and nightclubs, a good option for an evening in Manhattan is to play **pool**, not in dingy halls but in gleaming bars where yuppies mix with the regulars.

The Billiard Club
Map 6, F8. 220 W 19th St
(between 7th and 8th aves)
Ⓣ212/206-7665.
A pool club with a nice, vaguely European atmosphere and a small bar serving beer, liquor and soft drinks.

Chelsea Billiards
Map 6, H7. 54 W 21st St
(between 5th and 6th aves)
Ⓣ212/989-0096.
A casual place with both snooker and pool tables. Bar serves beer and soft drinks.

SOCCER

The **New York/New Jersey Metrostars**, who play at Giants Stadium (see p.342), are the metropolitan area's Major League Soccer representatives; tickets are typically available and range $15–30. The season takes place from May until September.

TENNIS

The **US Open Championships**, held each September at the National Tennis Center, in Flushing Meadows–Corona Park, in Queens, is the top US tennis event of the year.

Tickets go on sale the first week or two of June at the Tennis Center's box office (☎718/760-6200), open Mon–Fri 9am–5pm and Sat 10am–4pm. To book by phone, call Ticketmaster (☎866/673-6849). Promenade level at the stadium costs $22–69 (better seats can cost several hundred dollars), and seats are more expensive at night and closer to the finals. Tickets for the big matches are incredibly hard to get.

If you'd like to **play**, there are courts public and private all round the city, but getting on can be difficult; the former are all controlled through the City Parks department, and require a $50 permit (☎212/360-8133). The nicest such courts are probably at Central Park, but they are also the most crowded; try Riverside Park (see p.139) instead. Otherwise, rates at places like Sutton East Tennis Club, York Ave and 59th Street (☎212/751-3452) and Midtown Tennis Club, 341 8th Ave (☎212/989-8572), can run anywhere from $30 to $90 per hour, depending on the season and time of day.

TENNIS

●

Kids' New York

New York can be a wonderful city to visit with **children**. Obvious attractions include museums, skyscrapers and ferry rides, as well as the simple pleasures of just walking the streets, seeing the street entertainers and taking in the shopping scene. Free events, especially common in the summer, range from puppet shows and nature programs in the city's parks to storytelling hours at local libraries and bookstores. In addition, many museums and theaters have specific children's programs.

For a further **listing** of what is available when you're in town, see Friday's *Daily News* or *New York Times*, and "Activities for Children" in the weekly *New York* magazine, as well as *Time Out* and the *Village Voice*. An excellent automated directory of family-oriented current events all around the city is available through the New York Convention and Visitors Bureau, 810 7th Ave (between 52nd and 53rd sts), NY 10019 ☎212/484-1222 (Mon–Fri 8.30am–6pm, Sat & Sun 9am–5pm; ⓦwww.nycvisit.com).

MUSEUMS

One could spend an entire holiday just checking out the city's many museums, which almost always contain something of interest for the kids; the following is a brief overview of the ones that should evoke more than just the usual enthusiasm. See the appropriate chapters for more details on these and other museums.

American Museum of Natural History and the Rose Center for Earth and Space

Map 8, E9. Central Park W at 79th St. Sun–Thurs 10am–5.45pm, Fri & Sat 10am–8.45pm; $10, students $7.50, children $6; IMAX films, the Hayden Planetarium and certain special exhibits cost extra; ☎212/769-5100, Ⓦwww.amnh.org

The planetarium is sure to sate most kids intergalactic desires, and the dinosaurs are also a sure-fire attraction.

Children's Museum of the Arts

Map 5, G8. 182 Lafayette St (between Broome and Grand sts). Wed noon–7pm, Thurs–Sun noon–5pm; $5, under 1 free; ☎212/274-0986.

Art gallery of works by or for children. Children are encouraged to look at different types of art and then create their own, with paints,

clay, plaster of Paris and any other simple medium.

Children's Museum of Manhattan

Map 8, C8. 212 W 83rd St (between Broadway and Amsterdam Ave). Tues–Sun 10am–5pm; $6, under 1 free; ☎212/721-1234, Ⓦwww.cmom.org.

A terrific participatory museum, with exhibit space over five floors; not to be missed is "Seuss!" – a whimsical area with decor inspired by the Dr. Seuss books, where kids can (literally) cook up some green eggs and ham. For ages 1–12, and highly recommended.

Fire Museum

Map 5, C7. 278 Spring St (between Hudson and Varick sts). Tues–Sun 10am–4pm; $4, students $2, under 12 $1; ☎212/691-1303.

More popular than ever now, this unspectacular but pleasing homage to New

MUSEUMS

York City's firefighters, and indeed firepeople everywhere, has fire engines from yesteryear, helmets, dog-eared photos and a host of other motley objects.

Intrepid Sea-Air-Space Museum

Map 7, A8. W 46th St and 12th Ave at Pier 86. April–Sept Mon–Fri 10am–5pm, Sat–Sun 10am–7pm; Oct –March Tues–Sun 10am–5pm, last admission 1 hour prior to closing; $12, children 12–17 $9, children 6–11 $6, children 3–5 $2, under 2 free; ☎212/245-0072, ⓦwww.intrepidmuseum.org. The world's fastest spy plane, a guided missile submarine, and other modern and vintage air and sea craft are all here; not recommended for kids under five years.

Museum of the City of New York

Map 8, H3. 1220 5th Ave (103rd St). Wed–Sat 10am–5pm, Sun noon–5pm, Tues 10am–2pm for pre-registered tour groups only; suggested donation $7, students $4, families $12; ☎212/534-1672, ⓦwww.mcny.org. The New York Toy Stories is a super way to bring young ones back to simpler times, before video games, when wooden toys, rubber balls, and board games were just about the only options in the late 1800s. For girls (and grownups) there is a worthwhile and surprising group of dollhouses.

National Museum of the American Indian (Smithsonian Institution)

Map 4, E8. 1 Bowling Green (at Battery Park). Daily 10am–5pm, Thurs until 8pm; free; ☎212/514-3700, ⓦwww.si.edu/nmai. Kids will enjoy looking at the ancient dolls and feathered headdresses and the replicas of a reservation home and schoolroom. Programs often include theater troupes, performance artists, dancers and films.

CENTRAL PARK

Year-round, Central Park provides sure-fire entertainment for children. In the summer it becomes one giant playground, with activities ranging from storytelling to rollerblading to rowboating. The following are merely a few of the highlights – for much more detailed information on these and other sights, see Chapter 18, "Central Park."

The Carousel 64th St mid-park. For just $1, children can take a spin on the country's largest hand-carved horses.

Central Park Wildlife Conservation Center (Zoo), 5th Ave at 64th St. A small but enjoyable zoo, with sea lions, polar bears, monkeys and the Tisch Children's zoo.

Hans Christian Andersen statue 72nd St on the East Side (next to the Boat Pond). A forty-or-so-year tradition of storytelling sessions; Wed & Sat 11am–noon, June to Sept.

Loeb Boathouse 72nd St mid-park. Rent a rowboat on the Central Park lake and enjoy the views or take a gondola ride in the evening. Bike rentals available too.

Wollman Rink 62nd St mid-park ☏212/396-1010. Roller/inline skating during the summer and ice-skating during the winter. Skate rental and instruction available.

SIGHTS AND ENTERTAINMENT

Bronx Zoo (formally, the International Wildlife Conservation Park)
Bronx River Parkway at Fordham Rd. March–Oct Mon–Fri 10am–5pm, Sat & Sun 10am–5.30pm; Nov–Feb daily 10am–4.30pm; $9, kids $5, free on Weds, rides and some exhibits are an additional charge; ☏718/367-1010, ⓦwww.wcs.org.

The largest urban zoo in America has more than 4000 species of animals, reptiles and birds on display, many in huge simulated natural habitats. A children's section allows kids to climb around on large exhibits, including a giant spider web, and pet some of the tamer animals.

New York Aquarium

W 8th St and Surf Ave, Coney Island, Brooklyn (Mon–Fri 10am–5pm, Sat & Sun 10am–5.30pm; $9.75; ℡718/265-FISH).

The aquarium is largely a series of darkened halls containing creatures from the deep, but open-air shows of whales and dolphins are held several times daily, as are the shark, sea otter and walrus feedings. Call for daily show/program info.

Skyride

Map 6, H4. 350 5th Ave (at 34th St) in the Empire State Building. Daily 10am–10pm; $13.50, 4–12 $10.50; combination ticket to Skyride and observatory $17 and $10; ℡212/279-9777.

The Skyride, in the Empire State Building, is a big-screen thrill ride through the most well-known sights in the city, complete with tilting seats and surround sound. Bring a strong stomach; it may be too much for small children.

SHOPS: TOYS, BOOKS AND CLOTHES

Books of Wonder

Map 6, H8. 16 W 18th St (between 5th and 6th aves) ℡212/989-3270.

Excellent kids' bookstore, with a great story-hour on Sun at 11.45am, and author appearances Sat in the spring and fall.

F.A.O. Schwarz

Map 7, H6. 767 5th Ave (at 58th St) ℡212/644-9400.

Showpiece of a nationwide chain sporting three huge floors of everything a child could want. Fans of Barbie will want to check out the Barbie store, in the back of F.A.O. Schwarz, with its own Madison Ave entrance.

Penny Whistle Toys

Map 8, I6. 1283 Madison Ave (at 91st St) ℡212/369-3868; also 448 Columbus Ave (at 81st St) ℡212/873-9090.
Wonderful shop selling a fun, imaginative range of toys that deliberately eschews guns and war accessories, including replicas of old-fashioned toys rarely seen these days. Highly recommended.

Red Caboose

Map 7, H9. 23 W 45th St (between 5th and 6th aves); lower level – follow the flashing railroad sign in back of lobby ℡212/575-0155.
A unique shop specializing in models, particularly trains and train sets.

Tannen's Magic Studio

Map 6, H6. 24 W 25th St (between Broadway and 6th Ave) ℡212/929-4500.
Kids will never forget a visit to the largest magic shop in the world, with nearly 8000 props and magic sets. The staff consists of magicians who perform free shows throughout the day.

THEATER, PUPPET SHOWS, CIRCUSES AND OTHERS

The following is a highly selective roundup of miscellaneous activities, particularly cultural ones that might be of interest to young children.

Barnum & Bailey Circus

Map 6, E4. Madison Square Garden ℡212/465-6741.
This large touring circus is usually in New York between the end of March and the beginning of May.

Big Apple Circus

Map 7, D4. Lincoln Center ℡212/546-2656.
Small circus that performs in a tent in Damrosch Park next to the Met, from late Oct to early Jan. Tickets $10–45.

New Victory Theater
Map 6, F1. 209 W 42nd St
ⓣ646/223-3020.
There is always a rich mix of affordable theater, music, dance, storytelling, film and puppetry, in addition to pre-performance workshops and post-performance participation. Everything about this theater is child-oriented, including the duration of performances (60–90 minutes). Closed during the summer.

Thirteenth Street Repertory Company
Map 5, D1. 50 W 13th St (between 5th and 6th aves) ⓣ212/675-6677. Sat & Sun 1pm and 3pm, year-round; $7. Forty-five-minute original musicals – such as "Rumplewho?" – specifically created for "little humans." Reservations needed, as these are very popular shows.

Directory

Airlines Toll-free phone numbers of foreign airlines include: Air India ☎1-800/223-7776; Air New Zealand ☎1-800/262-1234; British Airways ☎1-800/247-9297; El Al ☎1-800/223-6700; Japan Air Lines ☎1-800/525-3663; Korean Airlines ☎1-800/438-5000; Kuwait Airways ☎1-800/458-9248; Qantas Airways ☎1-800/227-4500; Virgin Atlantic Airways ☎1-800/862-8621.

Consulates Australia, 150 E 42nd St (☎212/351-6500); Canada, 1251 6th Ave at 50th St (☎212/596-1628); Denmark, 1 Dag Hammarskjöld Plaza (☎212/223-4545); France, 934 5th Ave (☎212/606-3600); Germany, 871 UN Plaza (☎212/610-9700); Ireland, 345 Park Ave at 51st St (☎212/319-2555); Italy, 690 Park Ave (☎212/737-9100); Netherlands, 1 Rockefeller Plaza (entrance at 14 W 49th St between 5th and 6th aves) (☎212/246-1429); New Zealand, 780 3rd Ave (☎212/832-4038); Spain, 150 E 58th St (☎212/355-4080); Sweden, 1 Dag Hammarskjöld Plaza (☎212/583-2550); UK, 845 3rd Ave between 51st and 52nd sts (☎212/745-0200).

Electric Current 110V AC with two-pronged plugs. Unless they're dual voltage, all British appliances will need a voltage converter as well as a plug adapter. Be warned, some converters may not be able to handle certain high-wattage items, especially those with heated elements.

Emergencies For Police, Fire or Ambulance dial ⓣ911.

ID Carry some at all times, as there are any number of occasions on which you may be asked to show it. Two pieces of ID are preferable and one should have a photo – passport and credit card are the best bets.

Laundry Hotels do it but charge a lot. You're much better off going to an ordinary laundromat or dry cleaner, both of which you'll find plenty of in the *Yellow Pages*.

Left Luggage The most likely place to dump your stuff is Grand Central Station (42nd St and Park Ave ⓣ212/340-2555), where the luggage/lost and found department is by Track 100, on the lower level, open Mon–Fri 7am–11pm, Sat & Sun 10am–11pm, and charges $2 per item per calendar day. Photo ID required.

Lost Property Things lost on buses or on the subway: NYC Transit Authority, at the 34th St/8th Ave Station at the north end on the lower level subway mezzanine (Mon–Wed & Fri 8am–noon, Thurs 11am–6.30pm ⓣ212/712-4500). Things lost on Amtrak: Penn Station (Mon–Fri 7.30am–4pm ⓣ212/630-7389). Things lost in a cab: Taxi & Limousine Commission Lost Property Information Dept, 40 Rector St between Washington St and the West Side Highway (Mon–Fri 9am–5pm except national holidays ⓣ212/302-8294).

Noticeboards For contacts, casual work, articles for sale, etc, it's hard to beat the noticeboard just inside the doorway of the *Village Voice* office at 36 Cooper Square (just south of the Astor Place subway stop). Otherwise there are numerous noticeboards up at Columbia University, in the Loeb Student Center of NYU on Washington Square, and in the groovier coffee shops, health food stores and restaurants in the East Village.

Public Holidays You'll find all banks, most offices, some stores and certain museums closed on the following days: January 1; Martin Luther King's Birthday (third Mon in Jan); Presidents' Day (third Mon in Feb); Memorial Day (last Mon in May); Independence Day (July 4 or, if it falls on a weekend, the following Mon); Labor Day (first Mon in Sept); Columbus Day (second Mon in Oct); Veterans Day (Nov 11); Thanksgiving (the third or last Thurs in Nov); Christmas Day (Dec 25). Also, New York's numerous parades mean that on certain days – St Patrick's Day, Gay Pride Day, Easter Sunday and Columbus Day, to name a few – much of 5th Ave is closed to traffic altogether.

Tax Within New York City you'll pay an 8.25 percent sales tax on top of marked prices on just about everything but the very barest of essentials, a measure brought in to help alleviate the city's 1975 economic crisis, and one that stuck.

Terminals and Transit Information Grand Central Terminal, 42nd St and Park Ave (Metro-North commuter trains ☎212/532-4900); Pennsylvania Station, 33rd St and 8th Ave (Amtrak ☎1-800/USA-RAIL or 212/582-6875); New Jersey Transit (☎973/762-5100); Long Island Railroad (LIRR ☎718/217-5477); PATH trains (☎1-800/234-7284); Port Authority Bus Terminal, 41st St and 8th Ave, and George Washington Bridge Bus Terminal, W 178th St (between Broadway and Fort Washington) both ☎212/564-8484; Greyhound (☎1-800/231-2222); Peter Pan Trailways (☎1-800/343-9999); Bonanza (☎1-800/556-3815).

Time Three hours ahead of West Coast North America, five hours behind Britain and Ireland, fourteen to sixteen hours behind East Coast Australia (variations for Daylight Savings Time), sixteen to eighteen hours behind New Zealand (variations for Daylight Savings Time).

Tipping Expected everywhere a service is performed; in restaurants, easiest just to double the tax.

TAX–TIPPING

CONTEXTS

A brief history of New York City

Early days and colonial rule

Before the arrival of European explorers, Native Americans populated the area now encompassing New York City. In 1524, 32 years after Christopher Columbus had sailed to the New World, **Giovanni da Verrazano**, an Italian in the service of the French King Francis I, arrived in New York Harbor. In 1609 **Henry Hudson**, an Englishman employed by the Dutch East India Company, landed at Manhattan and sailed his ship upriver as far as Albany. The Dutch established a trading post at the most northerly point Hudson had reached, Fort Nassau. In 1624, four years after the Pilgrim Fathers had sailed to Massachusetts, thirty families left Holland to become New York's first European settlers.

Most sailed up to Fort Nassau, but a handful – eight families in all – staying behind on what is now Governors Island, which they called Nut Island because of the many walnut trees there. Slowly the community grew as more settlers arrived, and the little island became crowded; the decision was made to move to the limitless spaces across the water, and the settlement of **Manhattan**, taken from the Algonquin Indian word *Manna-Hata* meaning "Island of the Hills," began.

The Dutch gave their new outpost the name **New Amsterdam** though following British conquest of the island in 1664 the settlement took its new name from its owner the Duke of York – **New York**.

Revolution

By the 1750s the city had reached a population of 16,000, spread roughly as far north as Chambers Street. As the new community grew more confident, it realized that it could exist independently of the government in Britain. In a way, New York's role during the **War of Independence** was not critical, for all the battles fought in and around the city were generally won by the British, who ultimately lost the war. **George Washington**, who had held the American army together by sheer willpower, celebrated in New York riding in triumphal procession down Canal Street and saying farewell to his officers at **Fraunces Tavern**, a building that still stands at the end of Pearl Street. On April 30, 1789, Washington took the oath of president at the site of the **Federal Hall National Memorial** on Wall Street. The federal government was transferred to the District of Columbia one year later.

Immigration and civil war

The opening of the **Erie Canal** in 1825 allowed New York to expand massively as a port. The Great Lakes were suddenly opened to New York, and with them the rest of the country; goods manufactured in the city could be sent easily and cheaply to the American heartland. It was because of this transportation network, and the mass of **cheap labour** that flooded in throughout the nineteenth and early twentieth centuries, that New York – and to an extent the nation – became wealthy. The first waves of **immigrants**, mainly **German** and **Irish**, began to arrive in the mid-nineteenth century, the latter forced out by the potato famine of 1846, the former by the failed revolutions of 1848–49. The city could not handle people arriving in such great numbers and epidemics of yellow fever and cholera were common, exacerbated by poor water supplies, unsanitary conditions and the poverty of most of the newcomers. Despite this, in the 1880s large-scale **Italian** immigration began, while at the same time refugees from **Eastern Europe** started to arrive – many of them Jewish. The two communities shared a home on the **Lower East Side**, which became one of the worst slum areas of its day. On the eve of the Civil War (1861–65) the majority of New York's 750,000 population were immigrants; in 1890 one in four of the city's inhabitants was Irish.

When the **Civil War** broke out, caused by growing differences between the northern and southern states, notably on the issues of slavery and trade. New York sided with the Union (North) against the Confederates (South), but none of the actual hand-to-hand fighting that ravaged the rest of the country took place near the city itself. It did, however, form a focus for much of the radical thinking behind the war, particularly with **Abraham Lincoln**'s influential "Might makes Right" speech from the **Cooper Union Building** in 1860. In 1863 a **conscription law** was passed that allowed the rich to buy themselves out of military service. Not surprisingly this was deeply unpopular, and New Yorkers rioted, burning buildings and looting shops: more than a thousand people were killed in these **Draft Riots**.

IMMIGRATION AND CIVIL WAR

The late nineteenth century

The end of the Civil War saw much of the country devastated but New York intact, and it was fairly predictable that the city would soon become the wealthiest and most influential in the nation. New York was also the greatest business, commercial and manufacturing center in the country. **Cornelius Vanderbilt** controlled a vast shipping and railroad empire, and **J.P. Morgan**, the banking and investment wizard, was instrumental in organizing financial mergers that led to the formation of the prototypical corporate business.

The latter part of the nineteenth century was in many ways the city's golden age: **elevated railways** sprung up to transport people quickly and cheaply around the city; **Thomas Edison** lit the streets with his new electric light bulb, powered by the first electricity plant on Pearl Street; and in 1883, to the wonderment of New Yorkers, the **Brooklyn Bridge** was completed, linking Brooklyn and Manhattan. Brooklyn, Staten Island, Queens and the part of Westchester known as the Bronx, along with Manhattan, were officially **incorporated** into New York City in 1898. All this commercial expansion stimulated the city's cultural growth; **Walt Whitman** eulogized the city in his poetry, while **Henry James** recorded its manners and mores in such novels as *Washington Square*.

Turn-of-the-nineteenth-century development

At the same time, the emigration of Europe's impoverished peoples continued unabated, and in 1884 new immigrants from Asia settled in what became known as **Chinatown**; Jewish and other European immigrants continued to arrive, and in 1898 the population of New York amounted to more than three million, making it the largest city in the world. Twelve years earlier the **Statue of Liberty** was completed, holding a symbolic torch to guide the huddled masses; now pressure grew to limit immigration, but still people flooded in. **Ellis Island**, the depot that processed arrivals, was handling two thousand people a day, leading to a total of ten million by 1929, when laws were passed to curtail immigration. The first two decades of the century saw a further wave of immigration. In that period one-third of all the Jews in Eastern Europe arrived in New York, and upwards of 1.5 million of them settled in New York City, primarily in the Lower East Side.

The war years and the Depression: 1914–45

With America's entry into World War I in 1917, New York benefited from wartime trade and commerce. Perhaps surprisingly, there was little conflict between the various European communities crammed into the city. Although Germans comprised roughly one-fifth of the city's population, there were few of the attacks on their lives or property that occurred elsewhere in the country.

The postwar years saw one law and one character dominating the New York scene: the law was **Prohibition**, passed in 1920 (and not repealed until 1933) in an attempt to sober up the nation; the character was **Jimmy Walker**, elected mayor in 1925. Walker led a far from sober lifestyle, "No civilized man," he said, "goes to bed the same day he wakes up," and it was during his flamboyant career that the Jazz Age came to the city. In speakeasies all over town the bootleg liquor flowed and writers as diverse as Damon Runyon, F. Scott Fitzgerald, and Ernest Hemingway portrayed the excitement of the times and musicians such as George Gershwin and Benny Goodman packed nightclubs with their new sound.

With the **Wall Street** crash of 1929 the party came to an abrupt end. Yet during the Depression three of New York's most opulent – and most beautiful – skyscrapers were built: the **Chrysler Building** in 1930, the **Empire State** in 1931 and in 1932 **Rockefeller Center** – all very impressive, but of little immediate help to those in the other depressed parts of the city.

The country's entry into World War II in 1941 had little direct impact on New York City: lights were blacked out at night in case of bomb attacks, two hundred Japanese were interned on Ellis Island and guards were placed at the entrances to bridges and tunnels. But, more importantly, the **Manhattan Project**, which took place behind the scenes at Columbia University, succeeded in splitting the uranium atom, thereby creating the first atomic weapon.

The postwar years

Following racial tensions in the 1950s there was a general exodus of the white middle classes out of New York – the **Great White Flight** as the media labeled it. Between 1950 and 1970 more than a million families left the city. Things went from bad to worse during the 1960s with **race riots** uptown in Harlem and in Brooklyn's Bedford-Stuyvesant neighborhood. The **World's Fair** of 1964 was a white elephant to boost the city's international profile, but on the streets the call for civil liberties for blacks and protest against US involvement in Vietnam (1964–75) were as strong as any in the rest of the country.

Manhattan reached **crisis point** in 1975. By now the city was spending more than it received in taxes – billions of dollars more. Essential services, long shaky due to underfunding, were ready to collapse. Tourism, caused by cheap transatlantic airfares, and a new mayor, **Edward I. Koch** helped save the city. Despite the fact that New York was no longer facing bankruptcy, it was still suffering from the massive nationwide recession, and the city turned to its nightlife for relief. Starting in the mid-1970s, singles bars sprang up all over the city, gay bars proliferated in the Village, and Disco was King. **Studio 54** was an internationally known hotspot, and drugs and illicit sex were the main events off the dance floor.

In the 1980s the real estate and stock markets boomed and another era of Big Money was ushered in; fortunes were made and lost overnight and big Wall Street names, most notably **Michael Milken**, were thrown in jail for insider trading. A spate of building gave the city yet more fabulous architecture, notably **Battery Park City** downtown, and master builder **Donald Trump** provided glitzy housing for the super-wealthy.

In 1989, Koch lost the Democratic nomination for the mayoral elections to David Dinkins, the first African-American mayor of New York, yet the stock market crash in 1987 had started yet another downturn. By the end of the 1980s New York was slipping hard and fast into a **massive recession**: in 1989 the city's budget deficit ran at $500 million; and one in four New Yorkers was officially classed as poor – a figure unequaled since the Depression. In the 1993 mayoral elections, Dinkins narrowly lost to the brash prosecutor **Rudolph Giuliani**. New York, traditionally a firmly Democratic city, wanted a change and with Giuliani – the city's first Republican mayor in 28 years – it got it.

The Giuliani years

Though it may have been coincidental, **Giuliani's first term** helped usher in a dramatic upswing in New York's prosperity. A *New York Times* article described 1995 as "the best year in recent memory for New York City." Even the pope came to town and called New York "the capital of the world." The city's reputation flourished, with remarkable decreases in crime statistics and a revitalized economy that helped spur the tourism industry to some of its best years ever. Such successes helped the mayor withstand a bitter fight over rent control in 1997 as well as continued concern over serious overcrowding in the public school system and cutbacks in health and welfare programs. Giuliani won re-election in 1997 in a landslide.

The early years of his **second term** were characterized by the continued growth of the city's economy, and more civic improvements, such as the "cleaning up" of previously crime-ridden neighborhoods like Times Square, the renovation of Grand Central Station and the building of new hotels and office buildings. All these developments greatly boosted tourism and thus the city's coffers, but they also raised protests that the mayor would do anything to attract national chains to the city, often at the expense of local business and local workers.

Several high-profile incidents, such as the Abner Louima torture case involving shocking allegations of police brutality, led to charges of disregard for minority rights. With reports on racial profiling somewhat backing this up, Giuliani's popularity, once amazingly high in this heavily Democratic city, dwindled significantly – though it was soon to be resuscitated in a big way.

September 11, 2001, and beyond

Nothing could have prepared New York – or indeed the world – for the morning of **September 11, 2001**, when terrorists took over four hijacked planes, crashing two of them into the Twin Towers of the World Trade Center, a third plane into the Pentagon in Washington, DC, and a fourth in a field south of Pittsburgh, PA. New York was hit hardest: within hours, each tower had collapsed, and the fallout and debris resulted in the destruction of a number of nearby buildings. Around 3000 people were killed in the attack, while smoking rubble piled several stories high. The signature skyline was no more.

Beyond the staggering number of lives lost, the billions in assets wiped out, the wreckage of subway lines and so on, there were other holes to deal with: entire firefighting crews, and quite a few at or near the top of the ranks in the fire and police departments died in the collapse. New Yorkers – and many from around the world – rallied to the rescue effort under the compassionate yet firm leadership of Giuliani. Suddenly, few wanted to see him go, though he was precluded by law for running for a third term in the elections (whose primaries, ironically, had been scheduled for September 11th).

The man who did eventually take control, new Republican mayor **Michael Bloomberg** (an ex-Democrat to boot), has a yeoman's task ahead. Rebuilding the city will take a long while; restoring shaken faith and economic fortune will take more than just time – and it's not as if the city's other problems have gone away, just taken a back seat and been put in slightly different perspective. Still, if any city is resilient enough to weather the damage and bounce back, clearly it's New York.

SEPTEMBER 11, 2001, AND BEYOND

Books

S ince the number of books about or set in New York is so vast, what follows is necessarily selective – use it as a launchpad for further sleuthing. Publishers are given in the order British/American if they are different for each country; where a book is published only in one country, it is designated UK or US; o/p indicates a book out of print, UP indicates University Press.

Essays, poetry and impressions

Phillip Lopate (ed) *Writing New York* (Library of America, US). A massive literary anthology taking in both fiction and non-fiction writings on the city, and with selections from everyone from Washington Irving to Tom Wolfe.

Frederico Garcia Lorca *Poet in New York* (Penguin/Grove Weidenfeld, o/p). The Andalucian poet and dramatist spent nine months in the city

around the time of the Wall Street Crash. This collection of over thirty poems reveals his feelings on the brutality, loneliness, greed, corruption, racism and mistreatment of the poor.

Joseph Mitchell *Up in the Old Hotel* (Random House, US). Mitchell's collected essays (he calls them stories), all of which appeared in the *New Yorker*, are works of a sober if manipulative genius. Mitchell depicts characters and situations with a reporter's precision and near-perfect style – he is the definitive chronicler of NYC street life.

Jan Morris *Manhattan '45* (Penguin/Oxford UP). Morris's best piece of writing on Manhattan, reconstructing New York as it greeted returning GIs in 1945. Effortlessly written, fascinatingly anecdotal, marvelously warm about the city. See also *The Great Port* (Oxford UP).

History, politics and society

Herbert Asbury *The Gangs of New York* (Thunder's Mouth Press, US). First published in 1928, this fascinating account of the seamier side of New York is essential reading. Full of historical detail, anecdotes and character sketches of crooks, the book describes New York mischief in all its incarnations and locales.

Edwin G. Burrows and Mike Wallace *Gotham: A History of New York City to 1898* (Oxford UP). Enormous and encyclopedic in its detail, this is a serious history of the development of New York, with chapters on everything from its role in the Revolution to reform movements to its racial make-up in the 1820s.

Robert A. Caro *The Power Broker: Robert Moses and the Fall of New York* (Random House, US). Despite its imposing length, this brilliant and searing critique of New York City's most powerful twentieth-century figure is one of the most important books ever written about the city and its environs. Caro's book brings to light the megalomania and manipulation responsible for the creation of the nation's largest urban infrastructure.

Kenneth T. Jackson (ed) *The Encyclopedia of New York* (Yale UP). Massive, engrossing and utterly comprehensive guide to just about everything in the city. Much dry detail, but packed with incidental wonders.

Luc Sante *Low Life: Lures and Snares of Old New York* (Vintage, US). This chronicle of the seamy side between 1840 and 1919 is a pioneering work. Full of outrageous details usually left out of conventional history, it reconstructs the day-to-day life of the urban poor, criminals and prostitutes with a shocking clarity. Sante's prose is poetic and nuanced, his evocations of the seedier neighborhoods, their dives and pleasure-palaces, quite vivid.

Art, architecture and photography

H. Klotz (ed) *New York Architecture 1970–1990* (Prestel/Rizzoli). Extremely well-illustrated account of the shift from modernism to postmodernism and beyond.

Jacob Riis *How the Other Half Lives* (Dover/Hill & Wang). Republished photojournalism reporting on life in the Lower East Side at the end of the nineteenth century. Its original publication awakened many to the plight of New York's poor.

Stern, Gilmartin, Mellins; Stern, Gilmartin, Massengale; Stern, Mellins, Fishman *New York 1900; 1930; 1960* (Rizzoli, US). These three exhaustive tomes, subtitled "Metropolitan Architecture and Urbanism,"

contain all you'd ever want or need to know about architecture and the organization of the city. The facts are dazzling and numbing, the photos nostalgia-inducing.

N. White and E. Willensky (eds) *AIA Guide to New York* (Macmillan/Harcourt Brace). Perhaps even more than the above, the definitive contemporary guide to the city's architecture, far more interesting than it sounds, and useful as an on-site reference.

Gerard R. Wolfe *New York: A Guide to the Metropolis* (McGraw-Hill, US). Set up as a walking tour, this is a little more academic – and less opinionated – than others, but it does include some good stuff on the outer boroughs. Also informed historical background.

Fiction

Martin Amis *Money* (Penguin/Viking Penguin). Following the wayward movements of degenerate film director John Self between London and New York, a weirdly scatological novel that's a striking evocation of 1980s excess.

James Baldwin *Another Country* (Penguin/ Vintage). Baldwin's best-known novel, tracking the feverish search for meaningful relationships among a group of 1960s New York bohemians. The so-called liberated era in the city has never been more vividly documented – nor its knee-jerk racism.

Truman Capote *Breakfast at Tiffany's* (Penguin/Random House). Far sadder and racier than the movie, this novel is a rhapsody to New York in the early 1940s, tracking the dissolute youthful residents of an uptown apartment building and their movements about town.

Chester Himes *The Crazy Kill* (Canongate Pub Ltd). Himes wrote violent, fast-moving and funny thrillers set in Harlem; this and *Cotton Goes to Harlem* are among the best.

Henry James *Washington Square* (Penguin/Viking Penguin). Skillful and engrossing examination of the mores and strict social expectations of New York genteel society in the late nineteenth century.

Joyce Johnson *Minor Characters* (Penguin). Women were never a prominent feature of the Beat generation; its literature examined a male world through strictly male eyes. This book, written by the woman who lived for a short time with Jack Kerouac, redresses the balance superbly; there's no better novel on the Beats in New York.

Jay McInerney *Bright Lights, Big City* (Flamingo/Vintage). A trendy, "voice of a generation" book when it came out in the 1980s, it follows a struggling New York writer in his job as a fact-checker at an literary magazine, and from one cocaine-sozzled nightclub to another. Amusing now, as it vividly captures the times.

Henry Miller *Crazy Cock* (HarperCollins/Grove Weidenfeld, o/p). Semiautobiographical work of love, sex and angst in Greenwich Village in the 1920s. The more easily available trilogy of *Sexus*, *Plexus* and *Nexus* (HarperCollins/Grove) and the

FICTION

famous *Tropics* duo (*...of Cancer*, *...of Capricorn*) contain generous slices of 1920s Manhattan sandwiched between the bohemian life in 1930s Paris.

Dorothy Parker *Complete Stories* (Penguin). Parker's stories are, at times, surprisingly moving. She depicts New York in all its glories, excesses and pretensions with perfect, searing wit. "The Lovely Leave" and "The Game," which focus, as many of the stories do, on the lives of women, are especially worthwhile.

Damon Runyon *First to Last* and *On Broadway* (Penguin); also *Guys and Dolls* (River City). Collections of short stories drawn from the chatter of *Lindy's Bar* on Broadway and since made into the successful musical *Guys 'n' Dolls*.

J.D. Salinger *The Catcher in the Rye* (Penguin/Bantam). Salinger's gripping novel of adolescence, following Holden Caulfield's sardonic journey of discovery through the streets of New York. A classic.

● **Hubert Selby Jr.** *Last Exit to Brooklyn* (Paladin/Grove Weidenfeld). When first published in Britain in 1966 this novel was tried on charges of obscenity and even now it's a disturbing read, evoking the sex, the immorality, the drugs and the violence of downtown Brooklyn in the 1960s with fearsome clarity. An important book, but to use the words of David Shepherd at the obscenity trial, you will not be unscathed.

Betty Smith *A Tree Grows in Brooklyn* (Pan/HarperCollins). Something of a classic, and rightly so, in which a courageous Irish girl learns about family, life and sex against a vivid prewar Brooklyn backdrop. Totally absorbing.

Edith Wharton *Old New York* (Virago/Scribners). A collection of short novels on the manners and mores of New York in the mid-nineteenth century, written with Jamesian clarity and precision. Virago/Scribner also publish her *Hudson River Bracketed* and *The Mother's Recompense*, both of which center around the lives of women in nineteenth-century New York.

New York in film

With its still-dashing skyline and its rugged facades, its mean streets and its swanky avenues New York is probably the most filmed city on earth, or at least the one most instantly recognizable from the movies. It would be fruitless to enumerate them all; we've just given a small sampling below of films that best capture the city's atmosphere, its pulse and its style and, if nothing else, give you a pretty good idea of what you're going to get before you get there.

Thirteen great New York movies

Annie Hall (Woody Allen, 1977). Oscar-winning autobiographical comic romance, which flits from reminiscences of Alvy Singer's childhood living beneath the Coney Island rollercoaster, to life and love in uptown Manhattan, is a valentine both to then-lover and co-star Diane Keaton if not to the city. Simultaneously clever, bourgeois and very winning. All of Allen's movies are New York-centric; also don't miss **Manhattan** (1979), which with its Gershwin soundtrack and stunning black-and-white photography is probably the greatest eulogy to the city ever made.

Breakfast at Tiffany's (Blake Edwards, 1961). This most charming and cherished of New York movie romances stars

Audrey Hepburn as party girl Holly Golightly flitting through the glittering playground of the Upper East Side. Hepburn and George Peppard run up and down each other's fire-escapes and skip down Fifth Avenue taking in the New York Public Library and that jewelry store.

Do the Right Thing (Spike Lee, 1989). Set over 24 hours on the hottest day of the year in Brooklyn's Bed-Stuyvesant section – a day on which the melting pot is reaching boiling point – Spike Lee's colorful, stylish film moves from comedy to tragedy to compose an epic tale of New York.

The French Connection (William Friedkin, 1971). Plenty of heady Brooklyn atmosphere in this sensational Oscar-winning cop thriller starring Gene Hackman, whose classic car-and-subway chase takes place under the Bensonhurst Elevated Railroad.

The Godfather Part II (Francis Ford Coppola, 1974). Flashing back to the early life of Vito Corleone, Coppola's great sequel re-created the Italian immigrant experience at the turn of the century, portraying Corleone quarantined at Ellis Island and growing up tough on the meticulously re-created streets of Little Italy.

Midnight Cowboy (John Schlesinger, 1969) The odd love story between Jon Voight's bumpkin hustler and Dustin Hoffman's touching urban creep Ratso Rizzo plays out against both the seediest and swankiest of New York locations.

On the Town (Gene Kelly, Stanley Donen, 1949). Three sailors get 24-hours' shore leave in NYC and fight over whether to do the sights or chase the girls. This exhilarating, landmark musical with Gene Kelly, Frank Sinatra, and Ann Miller flashing her gams in the American Museum of Natural History was the first to take the musical out of the studios and onto the streets.

On the Waterfront (Elia Kazan, 1954). Few images of New York are as indelible as Marlon Brando's rooftop pigeon coop at dawn and those misty views of New York Harbor (actually

TWELVE GREAT NEW YORK MOVIES

shot just over the river in Hoboken), in this unforgettable story of long-suffering long-shoremen and union racketeering.

Rosemary's Baby (Roman Polanski, 1968). Mia Farrow and John Cassavettes move into their dream New York apartment in the Dakota Building (72nd and Central Park West) and think their problems stop with nosy neighbors and thin walls until Farrow gets pregnant and hell, literally, breaks loose. Arguably the most terrifying film ever set in the city.

The Sweet Smell of Success (Alexander Mackendrick, 1957). Broadway as a nest of vipers. Gossip columnist Burt Lancaster and sleazy press agent Tony Curtis eat each other's tails in this jazzy, cynical study of showbiz corruption. Shot on location, and mostly at night, in steely black and white, Times Square and the Great White Way never looked so alluring.

Taxi Driver (Martin Scorsese, 1976). A long night's journey into day by the great chronicler of the dark side of the city – and New York's greatest filmmaker. Scorsese's New York is hallucinatorily seductive and thoroughly repellent in this superbly unsettling study of obsessive outsider Travis Bickle (Robert De Niro).

West Side Story (Robert Wise, Jerome Robbins, 1961). Sex, singing and Shakespeare in a hyper-cinematic Oscar-winning musical (via Broadway) about rival street gangs. Lincoln Center now stands where the Sharks and the Jets once rumbled and interracial romance ended in tragedy.

TWELVE GREAT NEW YORK MOVIES

Index

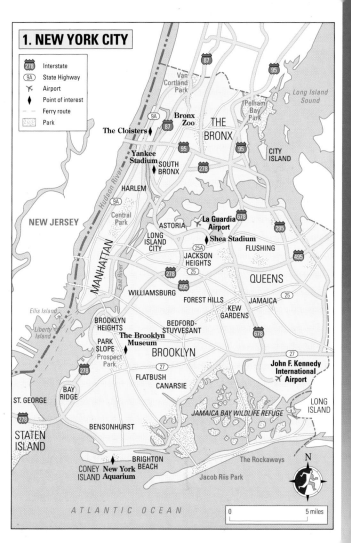

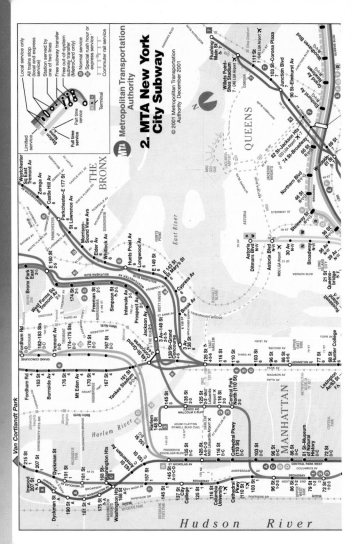

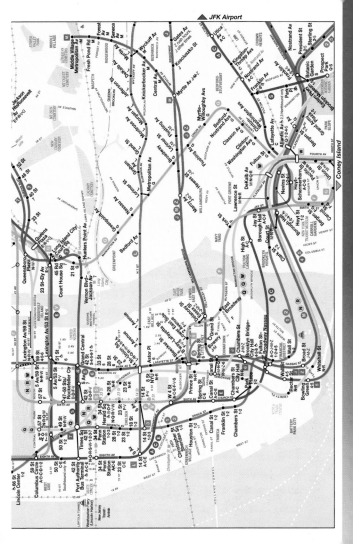

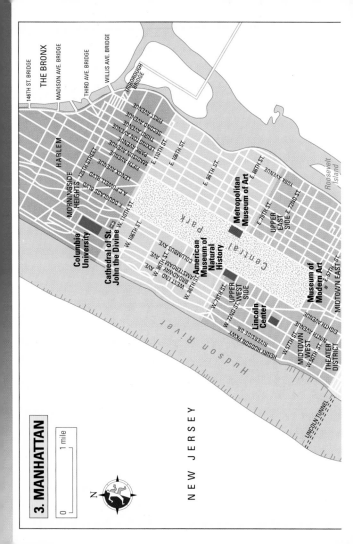

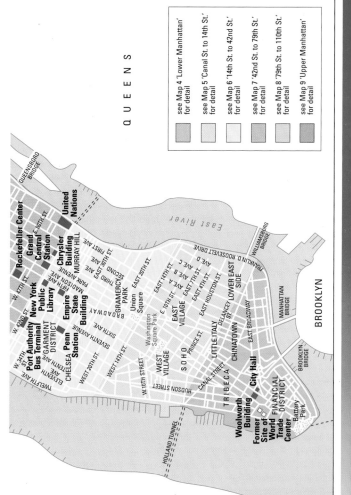

QUEENS

see Map 4 'Lower Manhattan' for detail

see Map 5 'Canal St. to 14th St.' for detail

see Map 6 '14th St. to 42nd St.' for detail

see Map 7 '42nd St. to 79th St.' for detail

see Map 8 '79th St. to 110th St.' for detail

see Map 9 'Upper Manhattan' for detail

QUEENSBORO BRIDGE

United Nations

Rockefeller Center

E 50TH ST.

Grand Central Station

Chrysler Building

W 47TH ST.

New York Public Library

MADISON AVE

PARK AVENUE

FIFTH AVE

MURRAY HILL

FIRST AVE

East River

W 42ND ST.

Port Authority Bus Terminal

Empire State Building

SECOND AVE

THIRD AVE

GARMENT DISTRICT

Penn Station

GRAMERCY PARK

W 34TH ST.

CHELSEA

SEVENTH AVE

Union Square

SIXTH AVE

BROADWAY

EAST 20TH ST.

WEST 20TH ST.

E 10TH ST.

AVE A

AVE B

AVE C

AVE D

WEST 14TH ST.

EAST 14TH ST.

ELEVENTH AVENUE

TWELFTH AVE

TENTH AVENUE

NINTH AVENUE

Washington Square Park

EAST VILLAGE

EAST 7TH ST.

WILLIAMSBURG BRIDGE

W 10TH STREET

WEST VILLAGE

SOHO

PRINCE ST.

EAST HOUSTON ST.

LOWER EAST SIDE

FRANKLIN D. ROOSEVELT DRIVE

HUDSON STREET

CANAL STREET

LITTLE ITALY

DELANCEY ST.

EAST BROADWAY

MANHATTAN BRIDGE

HOLLAND TUNNEL

TRIBECA

CHINATOWN

Woolworth Building

City Hall

BROOKLYN BRIDGE

Former Site of World Trade Center

FINANCIAL DISTRICT

Battery Park

BROOKLYN

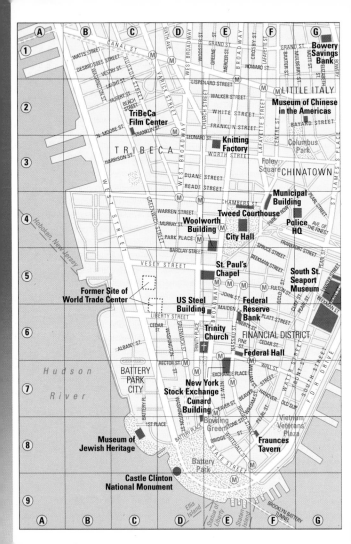

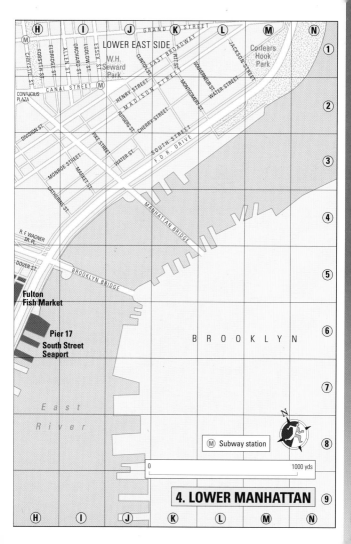

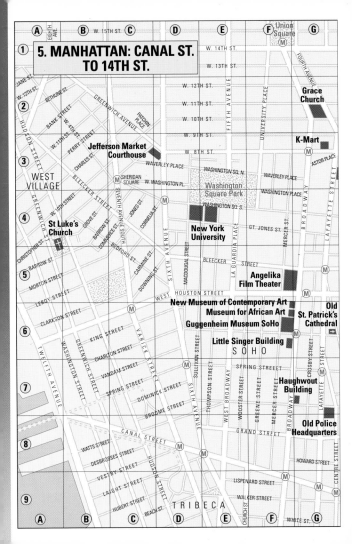

5. MANHATTAN: CANAL ST. TO 14TH ST.

EIGHTH AVE

W. 15TH ST.

W. 14TH ST.

W. 13TH ST.

Union Square

FOURTH AVENUE

JANE ST.

W. 12TH ST.

BETHUNE ST.

BANK STREET

W. 12TH ST.

W. 11TH ST.

GREENWICH AVENUE

PATCHIN PLACE

FIFTH AVENUE

UNIVERSITY PLACE

Grace Church

HUDSON STREET

W. 4TH ST.

W. 11TH ST.

PERRY STREET

W. 10TH ST.

W. 9TH ST.

W. 8TH ST.

Jefferson Market Courthouse

CHARLES ST.

WAVERLEY PLACE

WASHINGTON SQ. N.

K-Mart

ASTOR PLACE

WEST VILLAGE

BLEECKER STREET

SHERIDAN SQUARE

W. WASHINGTON PL.

WAVERLEY PLACE

WASHINGTON PLACE

Washington Square Park

GREENWICH STREET

W. 10TH STREET

GROVE ST.

SEVENTH AVENUE SOUTH

JONES ST.

CORNELIA ST.

WASHINGTON SQ. S.

New York University

LAFAYETTE STREET

St Luke's Church

BARROW ST.

BEDFORD ST.

CARMINE ST.

SIXTH AVENUE

MACDOUGAL STREET

GT. JONES ST.

MERCER ST.

BROADWAY

MORTON STREET

DOMINICK ST.

BLEECKER STREET

LA GUARDIA STREET

LEROY STREET

DOWNING ST.

WEST HOUSTON STREET

Angelika Film Theater

CLARKSON STREET

New Museum of Contemporary Art
Museum for African Art
Guggenheim Museum SoHo

Old St. Patrick's Cathedral

KING STREET

VARICK STREET

GREENWICH STREET

Little Singer Building

SOHO

CHARLTON STREET

SULLIVAN STREET

SPRING STREET

CROSBY STREET

TWELFTH AVENUE

WASHINGTON STREET

VANDAM STREET

THOMPSON STREET

WEST BROADWAY

WOOSTER STREET

GREENE STREET

MERCER STREET

Haughwout Building

SPRING STREET

DOMINICK STREET

BROADWAY

LAFAYETTE STREET

BROOME STREET

Old Police Headquarters

CANAL STREET

GRAND STREET

WATTS STREET

HUDSON STREET

DESBROSSES STREET

VESTRY STREET

HOWARD STREET

LAIGHT STREET

LISPENARD STREET

CENTRE STREET

HUBERT STREET

BEACH ST.

TRIBECA

WALKER STREET

WHITE ST.

CHURCH STREET

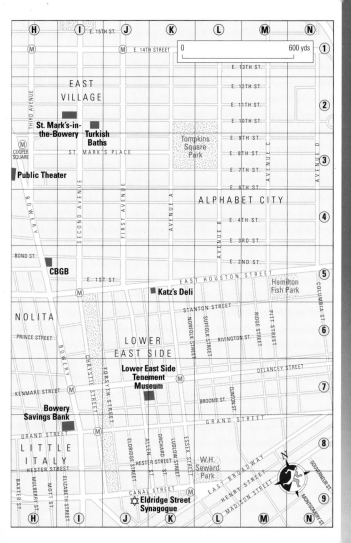

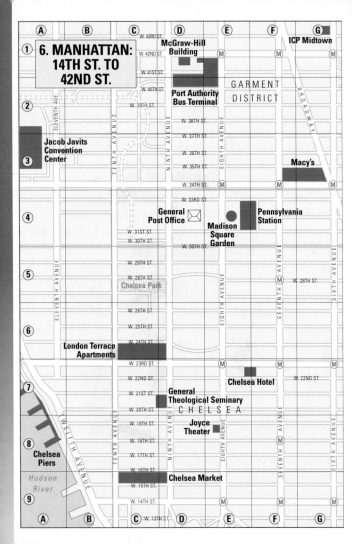

6. MANHATTAN: 14TH ST. TO 42ND ST.

ICP Midtown

McGraw-Hill Building

W. 43RD ST.

W. 42ND ST.

W. 41ST ST.

W. 40TH ST.

Port Authority Bus Terminal

GARMENT

DISTRICT

BROADWAY

W. 39TH ST.

W. 38TH ST.

W. 37TH ST.

Jacob Javits Convention Center

W. 36TH ST.

W. 35TH ST.

Macy's

W. 34TH ST.

ELEVENTH AVENUE

TENTH AVENUE

NINTH AVENUE

EIGHTH AVENUE

W. 33RD ST.

General Post Office

Madison Square Garden

Pennsylvania Station

W. 31ST ST.

W. 30TH ST.

W. 30TH ST.

W. 29TH ST.

W. 28TH ST.

Chelsea Park

W. 28TH ST.

SEVENTH AVENUE

SIXTH AVENUE

W. 26TH ST.

W. 25TH ST.

ELEVENTH AVENUE

London Terrace Apartments

W. 24TH ST.

W. 23RD ST.

W. 22ND ST.

Chelsea Hotel

W. 22ND ST.

General Theological Seminary

W. 21ST ST.

W. 20TH ST.

CHELSEA

Joyce Theater

W. 19TH ST.

EIGHTH AVENUE

SEVENTH AVENUE

SIXTH AVENUE

W. 18TH ST.

Chelsea Piers

TWELFTH AVENUE

TENTH AVENUE

NINTH AVENUE

W. 17TH ST.

W. 16TH ST.

Chelsea Market

W. 15TH ST.

Hudson River

W. 14TH ST.

W. 13TH ST.